A PRACTICAL APPROACH

TO

COMPUTING

A PRACTICAL APPROACH

TO

COMPUTING

W. Y. ARMS
J. E. BAKER
R. M. PENGELLY

Faculty of Mathematics, The Open University

John Wiley & Sons

CHICHESTER . NEW YORK . BRISBANE . TORONTO

Copyright © 1976, by John Wiley & Sons Ltd.

Reprinted with corrections December 1979

Library of Congress Cataloging in Publication Data:

Arms, W. Y.
A practical approach to computing.

'A Wiley–Interscience publication.'
1. Electronic digital computers—Programming. I. Baker, J. E.,
joint author. II. Pengelly, R. M., joint author. III. Title.
QA76.6.A73   001.6'42   75–15787

ISBN 0 471 03324 3 (Cloth)
ISBN 0 471 99736 6 (Pbk)

Filmset by Technical Filmsetters Europe Limited, Manchester.
and
Printed at the Pitman Press, Bath.

PREFACE

Courses in computer science do not always go hand in hand with the needs of practical computing. This situation has come about partly as a result of computer science wishing to establish itself as an academic discipline and therefore stressing the theory of algorithms and programming techniques, and partly because the traditional links between computing and mathematics departments have often led to an over emphasis on numerical methods and a neglect of data handling. This is doubly unfortunate since the ideas behind data handling, file processing and system software are both elegant and straightforward, but these ideas are often buried in so much technical detail that many commercial programmers are unaware of the essentially simple concepts behind the methods with which they work.

This book is an introduction to these latter ideas. Since inevitably we have had to be selective in the topics discussed, we have been guided by the wish that this book should look at practical computing from the programmer's point of view. For example, we do not discuss the logic of electronic circuit design, since we feel that it is unimportant to a programmer, but we have included a thorough treatment of file handling, a topic which is fundamental to many fields of computing, but often sadly neglected in computing courses. The book can be divided into three main sections.

(i)   Techniques that can be used when all the data in a problem can be held in the computer's store (Chapters 1 to 6).
(ii) Methods for handling large amounts of data that require the use of backing store (Chapters 7 to 10).
(iii) An introduction to the software that makes efficient use of a computer possible (Chapters 11 to 14).

Programming as such is not included, but throughout the book we assume that the reader has had at least some experience of drawing flow charts and writing programs in a high level language. Our approach is to illustrate general points by particular examples. Even when tackling complex types of software we have always tried to draw a flow chart of a simple example. Computing is a practical subject and we hope that readers who have access to a computer will take the opportunity to write programs from many of the flow charts.

Although few programmers ever need to write programs in a low level language, a full understanding of many topics requires a more detailed knowledge of computing than can be achieved by programming entirely in a high level language. In particular after programming in a language such as FORTRAN it is difficult to know what ideas are common to any programming language and which are peculiarities of the particular language used. For this reason we include a short description of a typical machine code and how instructions operate on data in the computer store. This not only leads naturally into our discussion of data structures and file handling, but also allows a much fuller treatment of peripheral operation, supervisors and compiling than would be possible otherwise.

Contents

SOFTWARE

ACKNOWLEDGEMENTS

Much of the material in this book is derived from the Open University course, *An Algorithmic Approach to Computing*. During its first year of presentation the course was taken by more than one thousand students which naturally gave us a great deal of information about the material and the methods of presenting it. In this second attempt we have followed much the same approach as before but the material has been completely rewritten; large sections have been deleted, new sections added and many chapters totally restructured. Our thanks are due to the Open University both for allowing us to use copyright material originally produced for the course and also for providing us with much clerical assistance in preparing the manuscript of this book. Three other members of the original course team must also be named, Jim Burrows who provided much of the initial momentum, Paul Hare for many elegant computer programs (in particular a simulator for the machine code described in Chapters 2 and 6, and the ACE compiler described in Chapter 14) and Peter Enge who devised many of the exercises. We are also grateful to Sophie Baker for the photographs.

NOTATION

We use the following notation for our flow charts.

Input

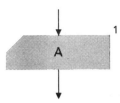

We use a box shaped like a punched card. The figure shows an instruction to input a value into a location called A.

Output

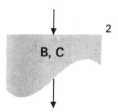

The shape of this box represents the paper (torn across the bottom) that emerges from a line printer. This figure shows an instruction to print the values of B and C.

Assignment

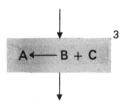

Assignment instructions to change the current values of variables are written in rectangular boxes. The figure shows an instruction to assign to A the sum of the values in the locations of B and C. The arrow points backward to indicate that the value of B + C is assigned to A.

Decisions

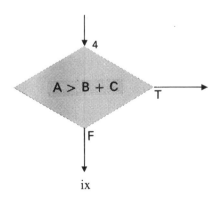

Decision instructions are written in diamond shaped boxes. Our decisions will usually be taken by determining whether a statement is true (abbreviated T) or false (F). Thus, the figure shows a decision whether the value of A is greater than the sum of the values of B and C.

Start and Stop

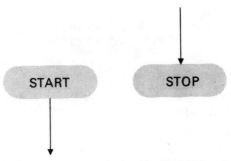

To be complete, a flow chart must contain both a START and a STOP box.

Iteration Boxes

Many computer programs involve a repetitive operation where the number of times that it has to be repeated is specified by a counter. Loops controlled by a counter occur so frequently and are so similar in their structure that it is convenient to use a special notation for them, which allows us to compress three boxes into one. Consider the fragment of a flow chart shown in Figure 1. The effect of boxes 6∅, 61 and 62 is to ensure that the loop is passed through N times. In our more compact notation the steps numbered 6∅, 61 and 62 in the flow chart fragment are written in just one box as

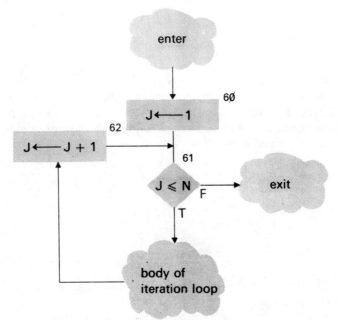

Figure 1   An iteration loop

in Figure 2. This notation may well seem strange to you at first, but it should soon become familiar and easy to use.

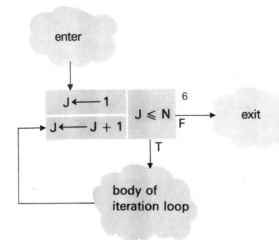

Figure 2   Compact notation for an iteration loop

Arrays

An *array* is a simple way of representing related items of data by the use of subscripts. An array using one subscript is also called a *list* or a *vector*.

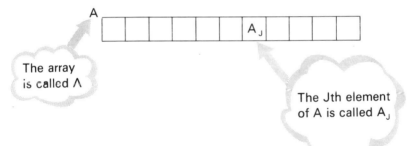

If two subscripts are used the array may also be called a *table* or a *matrix* (see Figure 3 on the next page).

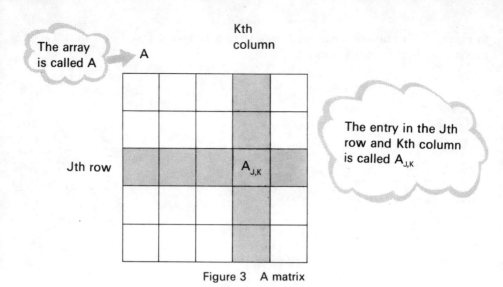

Figure 3   A matrix

Character Strings

The notation that we use for a variable whose value is a string of characters includes a method of referring to individual characters of a string and to substrings. Suppose that the value of a variable S is a string of characters. Our notation is as follows.

> S —the entire string.
> S(J)—the Jth character of the string S.
> S(J,K)—the substring which extends from the Jth to the Kth characters of the string S.

We shall also use arrays with string values. If S is a string array, the Jth string in the array S is denoted by S_J.

Special Symbols

To clarify the notation we use the following special symbols.

> $\emptyset$—denotes zero, as opposed to the letter O.
> ∇—denotes a space in a string of characters.

Any other flow chart notation that we adopt will be described when it is first used.

CHAPTER ONE

ALGORITHMS

Drawing a Flow Chart

Subroutines

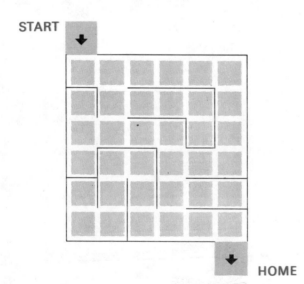

1.1 DRAWING A FLOW CHART

This first chapter sets the scene. If, as we hope, you have already had some experience in drawing flow charts and writing simple computer programs, this first chapter should contain little that is new to you. In it we describe our strategy for constructing larger programs. To solve a problem by computer you have to follow these stages.

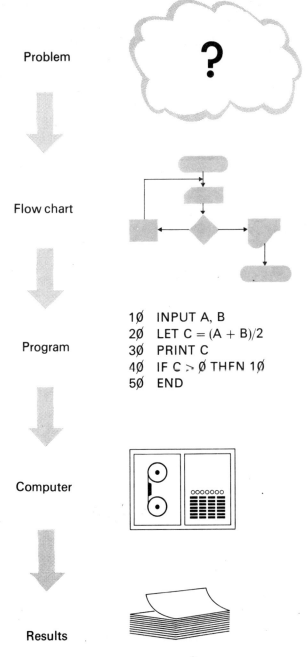

Problem

Flow chart

Program

```
1Ø   INPUT A, B
2Ø   LET C = (A + B)/2
3Ø   PRINT C
4Ø   IF C > Ø THEN 1Ø
5Ø   END
```

Computer

Results

3

The flow chart is the key to this process because it is the stage at which thoughts on the method of solution are first crystallized into a sequence of instructions. Such a sequence of instructions for carrying out some process step by step is often called an algorithm. Everybody has their own way of constructing an algorithm and, at first sight, it may not appear to be useful to give advice on how to do so. This chapter shows you *our* method of working so that you can follow our approach to the flow charts in later chapters.

If you have experience of writing large computer programs (one of several hundred instructions would count as large) you have probably noticed that methods of working which are suitable for small programs break down with large ones. With a small program the entire logic can be carried in your head, and, since you know the purpose of each variable, the loops and branches are relatively easy to get right. Bigger programs call for more careful treatment. A good parallel is found in human organizations. Almost invariably, an organization set up to tackle a complex task involves a hierarchy, with responsibility for specified tasks being passed down to subordinates where necessary. At each level of a managerial tree, the task in hand is split into

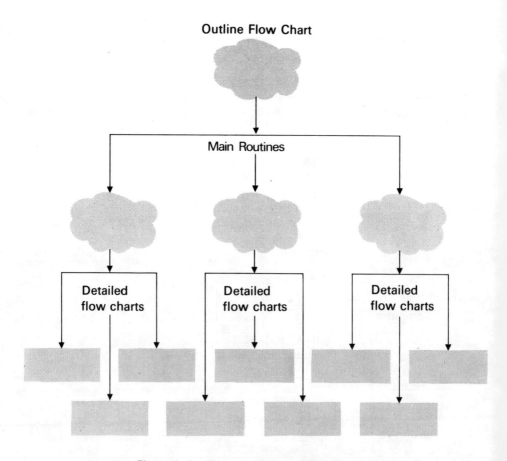

Figure 1—1   The various levels of flow chart

4

sub-tasks and passed down to subordinates on the level below. Eventually, simple tasks are allocated at the lowest level where they are carried out. The completed tasks are then marshalled at the next level up, to complete the next more complex tasks, and so on back up to the top of the tree.

The same sort of hierarchical organization can be used to construct computer programs. The hierarchy consists not of groups of people but of sections of program, each performing a specific task. These sections of program are usually called routines. Just as the proper delegation of responsibility is a mark of good management, so the correct division of a program into routines is a mark of good programming.

To solve a problem, we start by constructing an outline flow chart in which the purpose of each main routine is made explicit. Each main routine can then be broken down into smaller routines until eventually a detailed flow chart is obtained as in Figure 1–1. This method of solution gives a hierarchical structure similar to the management of a company. The use of outline flow charts is best grasped by looking at an example.

The Maze Problem

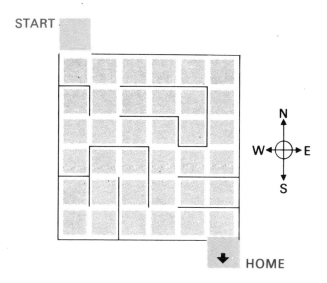

Figure 1–2   The maze

Suppose that we wish to instruct a man how to find his way through the maze given in Figure 1–2. Figure 1–3 gives two possible solutions. Either solution could be used as the basis for a computer program, but, whereas the first applies only to this particular maze, if you work through the instructions in the second, you will find that they do more. They can be used to guide a man through any maze for which the START and HOME positions are the only gaps in the perimeter. The second is an example of the constructive method of problem solving and it is this method that

1. Move 1 pace forward and turn left.
2. Move 1 pace forward and turn right.
3. Move 2 paces forward and turn left.
4. Move 2 paces forward and turn right.
5. Move 3 paces forward and turn left.
6. Move 2 paces forward and turn right.
7. Move 1 pace forward to HOME.

1. If you have reached HOME, stop.
2. If way ahead is blocked go to instruction 6.
3. Move 1 pace forward.
4. Turn to the right.
5. Go to instruction 1.
6. Turn to the left.
7. Go to instruction 2.

Figure 1–3   Two solutions to the maze problem

interests us in this book. Direct methods of solution like the one in the first sequence of instructions are usually less important in computing.

The constructive solution is based on a simple idea.

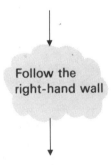

Follow the
right-hand wall

Figure 1–4 shows an outline flow chart based on this idea.

In the outline flow chart the entire strategy is laid out before you. The details of many of the steps are still vague, but any further detail that is added can (and must) be referred back to this original outline. The next stage is to decide how to represent the information in the problem. First, there must be some way to represent the maze. A matrix, M, with six rows and six columns suggests itself, so long as each entry in the matrix can in some way represent the possible moves that can be made from the corresponding square of the maze. Here is one representation that might not have occurred to you. To each entry in the matrix assign a four figure binary number according to the following rules.

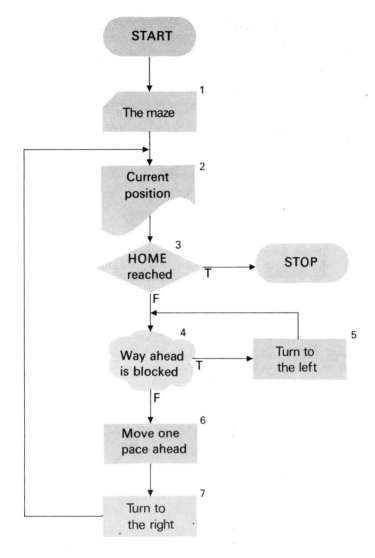

Figure 1–4   An outline flow chart for the maze problem

(i)   You can move west if the first digit is 1.
(ii) You can move south if the second digit is 1.
(iii) You can move east if the third digit is 1.
(iv) You can move north if the fourth digit is 1.

For example, in our maze we would assign the binary number

   Ø111

to $M_{2,2}$. This number could be stored in decimal form as 7. Using this technique, the entire matrix is given in Figure 1–5. This matrix is read in by box 1 of the outline flow chart.

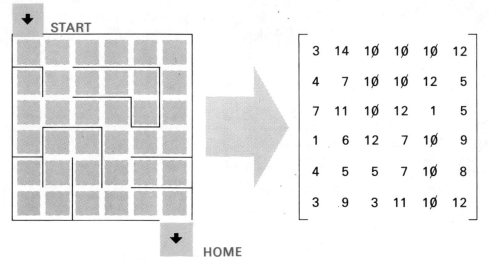

Figure 1–5   A representation of the maze

As well as requiring little storage space, this method of representing the maze is also handy for processing. This is important. Chapters 3 to 5 of this book look at many methods of storing data. In **those** chapters you will see how the kind of processing to be done influences the **way** that data is stored. The criterion for choosing one method as opposed to another is frequently a compromise between the need for fast processing and good use of storage space. For the moment it is important to bear in mind that processing and data storage are mutually dependent.

Suppose the variables J and K are used as subscripts for the matrix M. HOME has been reached when

J = 6 AND K = 6.

Box 3 of the outline flow chart can be expanded as shown in Figure 1–6.

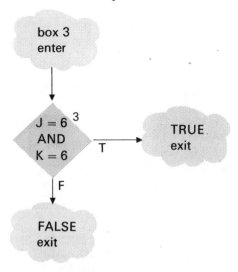

Figure 1–6   The details of box 3

For boxes 4 to 7 of the outline flow chart you need to know which way you are facing. You could use a variable F set according to the following rules.

(i)   If you are facing west F is 3.
(ii) If you are facing south F is 2.
(iii) If you are facing east F is 1.
(iv) If you are facing north F is $\emptyset$.

These values of F are related to the code used for the matrix M. Remember that, if we express $M_{J,K}$ as a binary number, each digit indicates whether a move is possible in a particular direction. If we number the digits 3, 2, 1, $\emptyset$ from left to right, the test in box 4 can be expressed as follows.

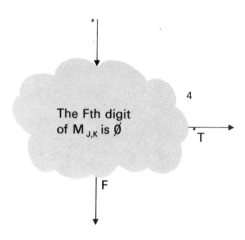

How this test is programmed depends on the programming language in which you are writing; we leave it as an exercise for you. Turning left in box 5 requires that F be reset. This can be done as given in Figure 1–7. Moving one step forward in box 6 requires that J or K be altered as in Figure 1–8. This leaves box 7, and the input and output boxes to be expanded. You should be able to handle these details on your own.

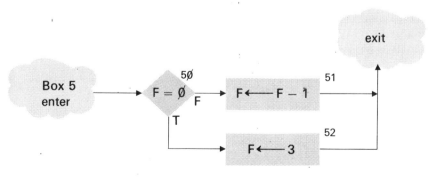

Figure 1–7   The details of box 5

9

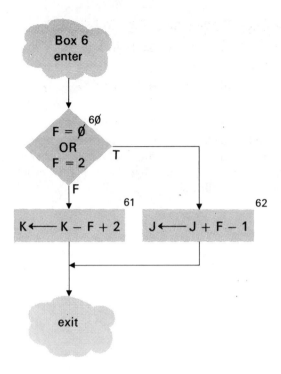

Figure 1–8   The details of box 6

In this example we have described the method of going from outline to detailed flow chart, but this is not the only effective way of solving a problem. It is sometimes best to start by fixing the key part of the processing; we call this the core of the algorithm. Once the core has been expressed in flow chart notation, the remainder of the flow chart is often relatively straightforward. In later chapters we shall find opportunities to make use of this bottom-up approach which has many applications. For example, many problems in numerical computing lend themselves naturally to this method of first developing the core of the algorithm. However it remains true that the best way to write a large computer program is usually from outline to detailed flow chart, the so called top-down approach. The process of isolating one step of the outline flow chart and expanding it in detail is one that you will see again and again in this book. An important benefit of the top-down approach is that no flow chart need consist of more than about ten boxes. Apart from being impossible to print, a large flow chart is very difficult to understand and should be avoided.

Questions 1.1

1. (i)   Expand step 4 of the maze flow chart (Figure 1–4) into a detailed flow chart.
    (ii) Construct a detailed flow chart of the maze algorithm discussed in this section.
    (iii) As it stands the flow chart in Figure 1–4 does not allow for the possibility that the maze has no solution. Amend your flow chart to allow for this possibility.

2. Consider a grid of dots and lines such as the following.

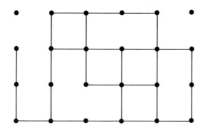

This pattern contains four squares with sides one unit long, three squares with sides two units long and one square with sides three units long. Devise an algorithm which has such a pattern as input and count how many squares of the various possible sizes that it contains.

3. The three numbers 192, 384, 576 are called *triad* numbers because they have the following properties:

   (i)   each is a three digit number,
   (ii) each of the digits, 1, 2, 3, 4, 5, 6, 7, 8 and 9 occurs in one and only one of the three numbers,
   (iii) the second number is twice the first and the third is three times the first.

   The problem is to find all triad numbers less than 1000. At first glance, this seems easy. All that is required is to write down all groups of three numbers which are each less than 1000 and test if they are triad numbers, but this is a clumsy way of solving the problem. Construct an efficient program to find them.

1.2 SUBROUTINES

The maze problem is quite small, yet it was helpful to draw an outline flow chart and to consider some of the individual boxes separately. With larger programs it is almost essential to break down the solution into a number of routines which can be tackled individually. When the basic routines have been isolated some of them may have a common look. Some may even occur more than once with no more than variations in the data that they process. It is best to keep routines of this kind separate from the rest of the program and, whenever one is required, to digress temporarily from the main stream of the program, execute it and return to the main program. Routines of this type are called subroutines. The writer of a program who wishes to use the subroutine does not need to copy the instructions into his program every time that he uses it, but writes a single instruction to call the subroutine into action. This means that a subroutine may be called from several different places. For example, Figure 1–9 shows a program which uses three different subroutines called A, B and Z. Subroutine A is called at two different places in the main program. Subroutine B is also called by A. Subroutine Z is a library subroutine, that is a standard routine written at some time in the past perhaps by a software house or by the computer manufacturer. Library subroutines are held in the computer system and attached to any program

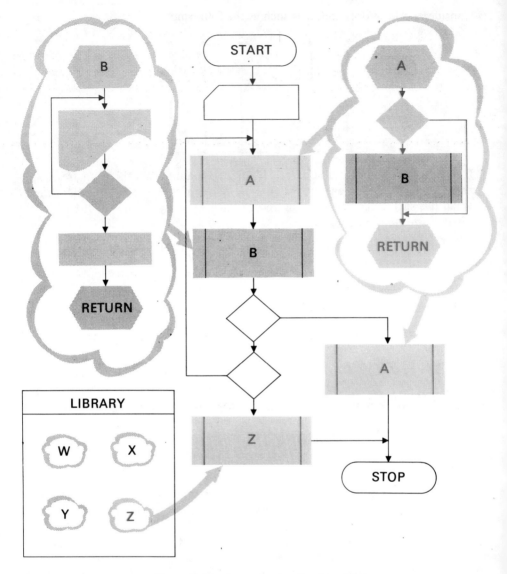

Figure 1–9   An example of subroutines

that calls them. In practical programming, library subroutines are very important and you will see frequent examples in this book.

The following are some of the advantages of subroutines.

(i) They save time and effort. The instructions for a particular task are written once and for all and can then be used whenever they are required.

(ii) Storage space is saved since only one copy is required of instructions that occur many times.

(iii) They help to make the programs easier to read and understand. Other routines are shortened, especially if many subroutines are used.

12

(iv) Subroutines are of great help in debugging a program, since they can often be written and tested independently of the rest of the program.

The way in which subroutines are implemented varies considerably from one programming language to another. We shall not be concerned with these variations, but we need an example to explain the conventions that we use. Consider the sequence of instructions to find the average or *mean* of N numbers stored in an array A given in Figure 1–10.

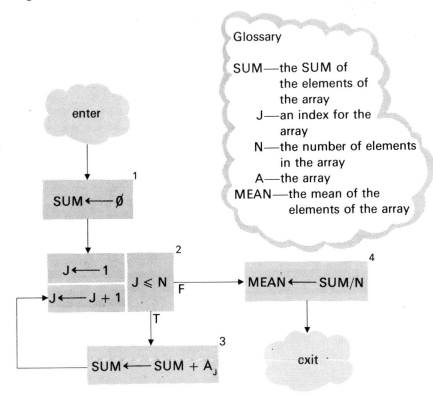

Figure 1–10   Instructions to find the mean

First, look at what information is needed to be able to execute these instructions, that is what needs to be known about the variables.

SUM and J: Nothing has to be known. These variables are assigned initial values within the flow chart; their values at the end are unimportant.

N and A: Before the instructions can be executed the value of N and the elements of the array A must be known.

MEAN: The result of the calculation is stored in MEAN. Any other routine that uses this sequence of instructions will need to know the value of MEAN.

Now suppose that you are drawing a flow chart in which you have to expand the following step.

13

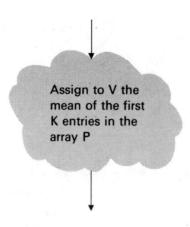

Assign to V the
mean of the first
K entries in the
array P

To save effort you decide to use the sequence of instructions in Figure 1–10. The variables K, P and V have to be identified with the corresponding variables used in Figure 1–10.

SUM and J: These variables are no problem, but it would be inconvenient if you had used the same variable names in your main routine and their values were altered. It is essential for variables to be protected from interference by a subroutine.

N and A: You want N to take the value of K and A to refer to the first K entries in P.

MEAN: You want the answer to be stored in V not in MEAN.

Two sections of a program are involved here and information must be passed between them.

Calling routine
K, P, V

information is passed between the sections

Subroutine
N, A, MEAN

Variables passed from one routine to another like this are called the parameters of the subroutine. It is possible to think in terms of two kinds of parameters, those which are passed to the subroutine and those which are returned from the subroutine but, since the same parameter is often used for both purposes, we shall make no such distinction and shall simply list the parameters. For the flow chart of a subroutine we use the notation shown in Figure 1–11. The first box contains the name of the subroutine and a list of parameters. The final box is an instruction to return to the routine that called the subroutine, whether the main program or another subroutine.

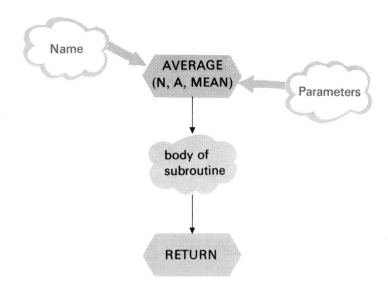

Figure 1–11   Notation for subroutines

The instruction in the flow chart that calls the subroutine is drawn as follows.

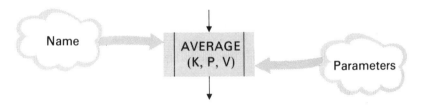

The parameters are listed in brackets under the subroutine name, with the variable names in the calling routine. The two lists are written in the order in which they are intended to correspond, but are usually lists of different names. In our example the names correspond as follows.

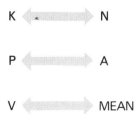

With this notation, the flow chart for the subroutine AVERAGE is given in Figure 1–12.

15

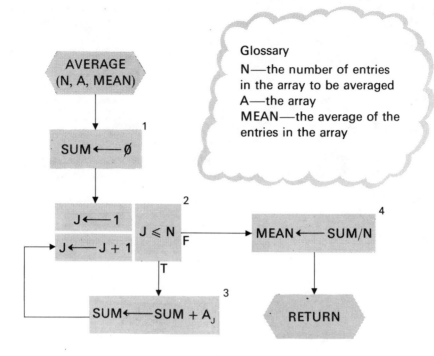

Glossary
N—the number of entries in the array to be averaged
A—the array
MEAN—the average of the entries in the array

Figure 1–12   The AVERAGE subroutine

When writing subroutines, two key ideas should be borne in mind. First, the call of a subroutine involves specifying parameters; these are variables in the calling routine which are to be processed by the subroutine. However, the call instruction need not use the same variable names as the subroutine. You can use whatever names seem appropriate in each routine. Second, the variables in the calling routine, apart from those specified as parameters, are protected from being altered by the subroutine. Again you can use whatever variable names seem appropriate. To complete this section, here are two examples of subroutines.

Example

You are asked to construct a subroutine called COUNT which counts the number of occurrences of a specified character in a string of characters. The first step is to decide what the parameters are. The values to be passed to the subroutine are

S—the string of characters,
N—the number of characters in the string,
C—the specified character.

The value to be returned is

X—the number of occurrences of the specified character in the string.

16

Figure 1–13 is a flow chart of the subroutine.

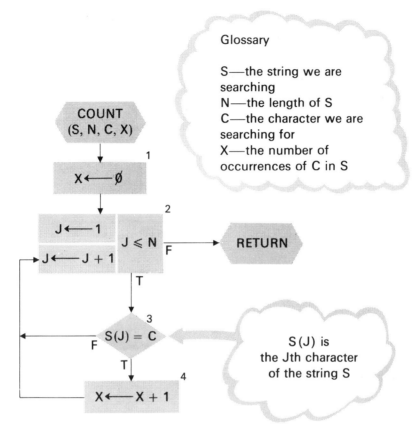

Glossary

S—the string we are searching
N—the length of S
C—the character we are searching for
X—the number of occurrences of C in S

COUNT
(S, N, C, X)

X ← Ø   1

J ← 1

J ← J + 1

J ≤ N   2

F   RETURN

T

S(J) = C   3

F

T

X ← X + 1   4

S(J) is the Jth character of the string S

Figure 1–13   The COUNT subroutine

Example

In a team sailing competition, six races are sailed and, in each race, each boat is allocated points for the position in which it finishes, the most points going to the winner. To calculate the final score for a boat, only its five best races are considered; the worst score for each boat is ignored. A team consists of four boats but only the three highest scoring boats are counted in the final total for the team. The problem is to draw a flow chart which reads the points scored by each boat in a team and calculates the total score for a team.

This method of scoring involves at each stage taking a list of numbers and adding them together except for the smallest which is ignored. This suggests a subroutine. A neat way of working is to add all the scores together and then subtract the smallest, as shown in Figure 1–14. The full flow chart, which uses the subroutine, is given in Figure 1–15.

17

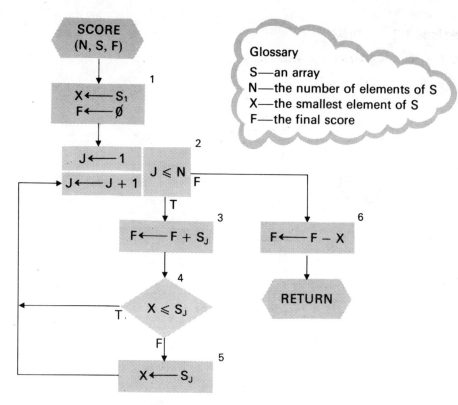

Figure 1–14   The SCORE subroutine

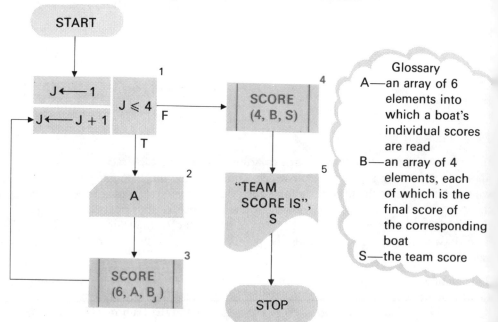

Figure 1–15   The boat scoring algorithm

18

Questions 1.2

1. A flow chart contains the instruction.

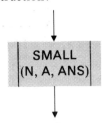

SMALL is a subroutine which assigns to ANS the smallest of the N entries in the array A.

(i) Draw a flow chart of SMALL.

(ii) What are the parameters and which variables are used only by the subroutine?

2. Construct a subroutine to reverse the order of the characters in a string.

3. One way of encoding and decoding messages, which consist only of combinations of the letters A, B, C, ..., Z and spaces is to represent these 27 characters by numbers as follows.

▽	A	B	C	D	E	F	G	H	I	J	K	L	M	N	O	P	Q	R	S	T	U	V	W	X	Y	Z
1	2	3	4	5	6	7	8	9	1∅	11	12	13	14	15	16	17	18	19	2∅	21	22	23	24	25	26	27

To generate the coded form of a message choose an arbitrary key word and perform a simple substitution. We illustrate this process by encoding the message CODED ▽MESSAGE, having chosen CODE as the key word. First use the table above to convert the key word CODE into its numerical representation 4-16-5-6 as shown in Figure 1–16. Draw a flow chart which uses the process described above to, on request, either encode or decode an input message. You will find that a subroutine fits naturally into the solution.

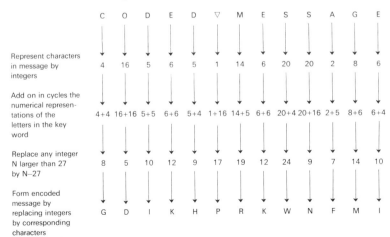

Figure 1–16   Encoding a message

CHAPTER TWO

LOW LEVEL PROGRAMMING

A Typical Computer

Machine Instructions

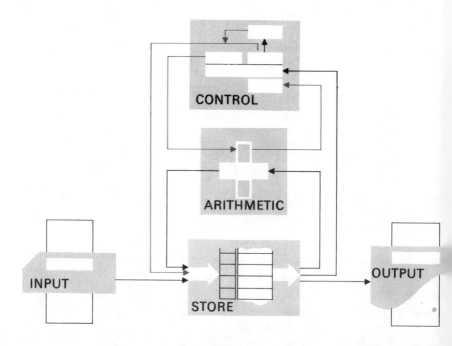

2.1 A TYPICAL COMPUTER

Most computer programs are written in high level languages, but if you want to understand computing you need to know a little about computer hardware and machine instructions. However, since we do not want to overwhelm you with the details of any particular computer, our discussion is based on an imaginary computer which has the key features of most actual machines without any of their complications. Figure 2–1 is a photograph of a typical medium sized computer used for data

Figure 2–1   A medium sized computer

processing. This photograph does not tell very much. Certainly the cabinet of the central processor gives no indication of what it might contain. We want to take the lid off and look at some features of the hardware that are important to a programmer. What we have to say is a simplification of the real thing, but we have concentrated on basic components that are shared by many types of computer.

Figure 2–2 shows these basic components and gives some indication of how they are linked to each other. At the bottom of the diagram is the store which is used to hold both data and program instructions. Connected to the store, is the arithmetic unit which accepts data from the store, processes it and returns the results to the store. At the top of the diagram is the control unit which interprets instructions and controls their execution. The control unit also keeps track of which instruction to execute next. In the diagram, the black lines show that data from store can be transferred to the arithmetic unit, that results from the arithmetic unit can be returned to store and that machine instructions from store can be passed to the control unit. The red lines show

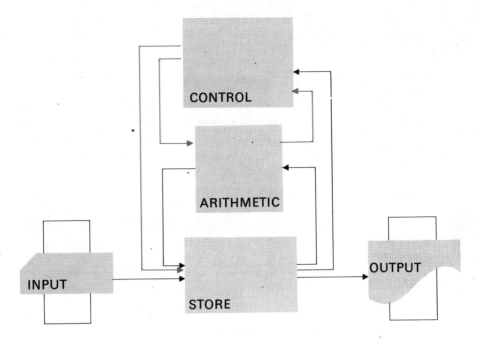

Figure 2–2 . The components of a computer

control signals issued by the control unit. The control unit, arithmetic unit and store are together called the central processor . Outside the central processor are peripheral devices used for input, output and supplementary storage, known as backing store. Typical peripherals are card and paper tape readers for input, line printers for output, and magnetic tapes and discs used as backing store. We shall discuss peripherals in later chapters and in this chapter concentrate on the central processor.

Store

You probably know already that data in store is held as a binary pattern, each digit of the pattern being called a bit. A code is used to give a meaning to a binary pattern. For this purpose the bits are usually grouped together, each group having an address to identify it. Each group is called a word and each word is identified by a unique address.. The number of bits in a word varies from computer to computer (16, 24, 32 and 36 are common). The number of words of data that can be held in store also varies from computer to computer. A small machine might hold four thousand words and a large one a million words or more. We shall use the following type of diagram to represent part of the store; it shows 32 bits per word.

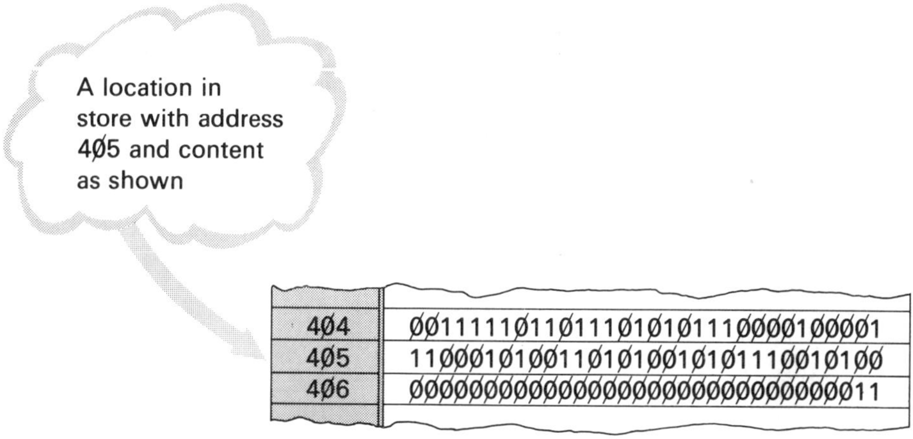

A location in
store with address
4Ø5 and content
as shown

4Ø4	ØØ111110110111010101110000100001
4Ø5	11000101001101010010101110010100
4Ø6	00000000000000000000000000000011

Since various types of data and instructions are all held in the same store, several codes are used to interpret what a particular binary pattern means. The three following codes are sufficient for our purposes.

Number Code

The simplest code is the number code in which the binary pattern within a word represents an integer. Thus in the above diagram the number $+3$ is shown stored in the location whose address is 4Ø6. It is represented by the corresponding binary number. If we are interpreting a word as a number, we shall write it in usual decimal form.

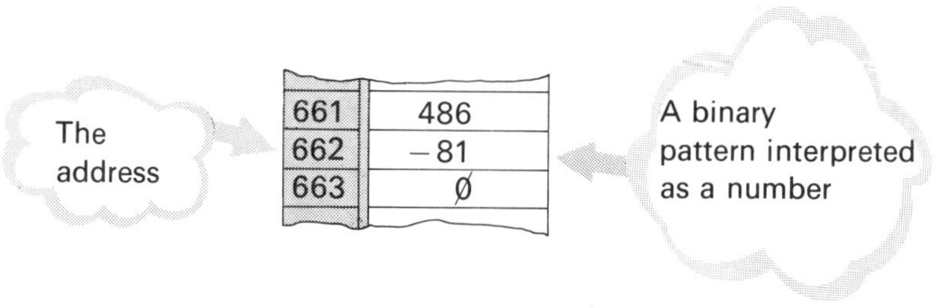

The
address

661	486
662	-81
663	Ø

A binary
pattern interpreted
as a number

Character Code

Using one word to store a number is a natural way of organizing store, but to store a string of characters a different code is needed, since it is wasteful of space to use thirty two bits for a single character. With eight bits, 256 different characters can be represented, which is sufficient to represent a wide variety of letters (capital and lower case), digits, mathematical symbols and control characters. The table in Figure 2–3 gives part of a code called EBCDIC which is used in many computers. Notice that a special code is needed for every character, even a space (which is denoted by $\triangledown$), and that the representation of a digit is different in the character code from the representation in the number code.

23

Binary Pattern	Interpretation	Binary Pattern	Interpretation
Ø1ØØ ØØØØ	▽	11Ø1 Ø1Ø1	N
Ø1ØØ 1Ø11	.	11Ø1 Ø11Ø	O
Ø1ØØ 11Ø1	(	11Ø1 Ø111	P
Ø1ØØ 111Ø	+	11Ø1 1ØØØ	Q
Ø1Ø1 11ØØ	*	11Ø1 1ØØ1	R
Ø1Ø1 11Ø1	)	111Ø ØØ1Ø	S
Ø11Ø ØØØØ	—	111Ø ØØ11	T
Ø11Ø ØØØ1	/	111Ø Ø1ØØ	U
Ø11Ø 1Ø11	,	111Ø Ø1Ø1	V
Ø111 111Ø	=	111Ø Ø11Ø	W
11ØØ ØØØ1	A	111Ø Ø111	X
11ØØ ØØ1Ø	B	111Ø 1ØØØ	Y
11ØØ ØØ11	C	111Ø 1ØØ1	Z
11ØØ Ø1ØØ	D	1111 ØØØØ	Ø
11ØØ Ø1Ø1	E	1111 ØØØ1	1
11ØØ Ø11Ø	F	1111 ØØ1Ø	2
11ØØ Ø111	G	1111 ØØ11	3
11ØØ 1ØØØ	H	1111 Ø1ØØ	4
11ØØ 1ØØ1	I	1111 Ø1Ø1	5
11Ø1 ØØØ1	J	1111 Ø11Ø	6
11Ø1 ØØ1Ø	K	1111 Ø111	7
11Ø1 ØØ11	L	1111 1ØØØ	8
11Ø1 Ø1ØØ	M	1111 1ØØ1	9

Figure 2–3   Part of the EBCDIC code

Using eight bits to represent each character, four characters can be represented in a single word. Thus in the following diagram the characters NATO are shown stored in a word whose address is 5Ø4.

5Ø4	11Ø1Ø1Ø1 11ØØØØØ1 111ØØØ11 11Ø1Ø11Ø

It is important to know that although up to four characters can be stored in a word the control unit can still retrieve individual characters. For example, the third position of word 5Ø4 above contains the character T. We could therefore redraw our store diagram as follows.

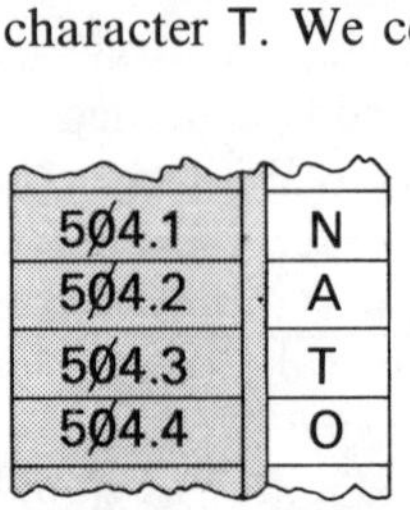

5Ø4.1	N
5Ø4.2	A
5Ø4.3	T
5Ø4.4	O

This emphasizes the fact that each character can be thought of as having a unique address.

Instruction Code

The third code is an instruction code, since instructions too are held in store. We have left a detailed description of the code used for instructions until the nature of the instructions which the computer executes has been explained. For the moment, all you need to know is that the machine instructions have two parts, an operator code which identifies the type of instruction and an operand address which is an address in store of a word or character of data or of an instruction. Since an instruction has two parts (an operator code and an operand address), you can imagine two numbers held in the one location.

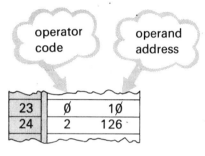

As well as the main store of a computer, there are small temporary stores in the other units of the central processor called registers. Operations, such as arithmetic, are carried out on data that has been copied from the store into a suitable register.

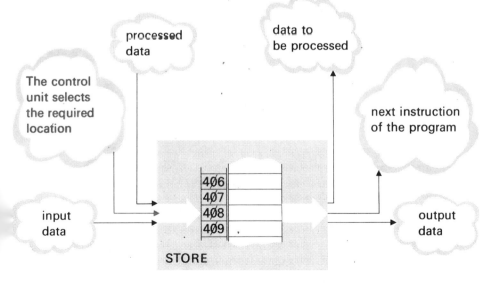

Figure 2–4   The store

25

This means that, apart from input and output, the only two operations that can be performed on a word of data in store are as follows.

(i) Copy the contents of a word into a register, that is *read*.
(ii) Copy the contents of a register into a word thereby destroying what was there before, that is *write*.

The word to be processed is selected by a signal from the control unit. For example, the signal might specify address 4Ø8, as shown in Figure 2–4. If the next operation were to copy a word of data from a register into the store, the word would be recorded in location 4Ø8 and the previous content of the location 4Ø8 would be destroyed. If at any later stage, the content of word 4Ø8 is wanted, the location can be read without its content being destroyed.

Other Arrangements of Store

The organization of store that we have described is by no means common to all computers. Remember that computers handle and store two types of information: instructions and data. Although in theory there could be separate stores for instructions and data, both types of information are usually held in a single store because of the flexibility that it provides. This means that the formats chosen for representing instructions and data must be compatible and in particular the method of addressing should be suitable for both. There are two commonly used ways by which symbols can be recorded in identified locations and retrieved when required. The two ways differ only in the number of bits to which a given address refers, but once that difference has been made the knock-on effect on the representation of numbers, characters and instructions is considerable.

A method of organizing the store, which is called a character organized store, is to give the location in which each character is stored a unique address and to group several locations together to hold each number. The range of characters which can be represented depends on the number of bits provided. For instance with 6 bits 64 distinct patterns can be formed and with 8 bits 256 different patterns. A typewriter keyboard usually has about 90 different characters including capital and small letters, digits and punctuation marks. When mathematical symbols and special characters to control the operation of peripherals are added even 7 bits (128 different characters) gives barely enough choice, so for a full character set at least 8 bits are needed.

A character organized store is convenient for handling individual characters and performing arithmetic operations on integers stored in decimal form. However, decimal arithmetic is slower than binary arithmetic, and not only is the hardware less efficient than for word organized stores, but programming has the added complication that each instruction must specify the number of locations that each operand occupies. The arrangement of the successful IBM 370 series computers, which has been copied by several other manufacturers, is a store which is addressed by 8 bit characters, where for fast arithmetic the characters are grouped into 32 bit words. Two sets of machine instructions are provided, one character based for character handling and the other word based for fast arithmetic.

The Arithmetic Unit

Instructions are executed by the arithmetic unit in response to signals from the control unit. As well as carrying out arithmetic operations, such as addition and multiplication, the arithmetic unit performs a wide variety of functions, many of which we have no opportunity to discuss in this book. The following are examples.

(i) Copying data into and out of store.
(ii) Testing data to see if it satisfies a specified criterion.
(iii) Carrying out logical operations on individual bits.
(iv) Translating data from one code into another.
(v) Editing data into a format suitable for printing.

Data which is being processed by the arithmetic unit is copied out of store into special purpose registers. Since an arithmetic operation, such as adding two numbers together, needs two items of data at the same time, the arithmetic unit contains registers for

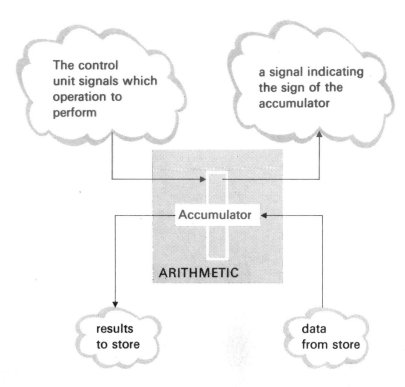

Figure 2–5   The arithmetic unit

the two operands. However only one register is of importance to the programmer. This is called the accumulator. The result of the operation just performed is left in the accumulator and from there can either be copied back into store, or is available for further processing. The operation to be performed is selected by a signal from the control unit and at the end of each operation a signal is passed back to the control unit indicating whether the content of the accumulator is now negative, zero or positive. These features are illustrated in Figure 2–5.

The Control Unit

In principle the control unit is nothing more than an intricate collection of switches. It breaks down every machine instruction into a sequence of tiny steps which are carried out by opening and closing switches at the correct moments which allows data to flow. The circuits in the control unit serve to interpret each instruction, send signals to other parts of the computer indicating what operation to carry out, and keep track of which instruction to execute next. You will see later that, by making use of the accumulator, all instructions can be reduced to the simple form.

operator code	operand address

For example, a typical machine instruction is as follows.

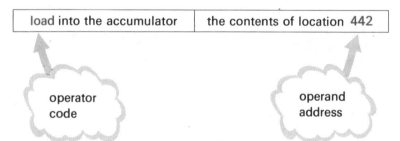

Such instructions are called single address instructions because there is only one operand which is specified by its address. The above instruction might be coded as two binary numbers which can be interpreted as follows.

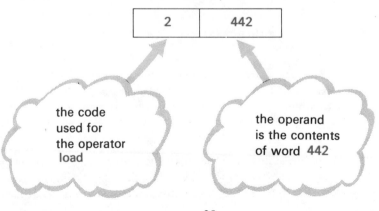

Since machine instructions are held in the store, the first stage of executing each instruction is to fetch it from the store and copy it into a register in the control unit called the instruction register; this is called the fetch cycle. The second part is to execute the instruction, this is called the execute cycle. As soon as the execution of one instruction is completed the control unit automatically fetches the next instruction, thus forming the complete operating cycle, see Figure 2–6. When the instruction

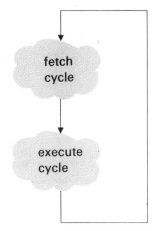

Figure 2–6   The operating cycle

has been fetched from store, the instruction register feeds a decoder which divides the instruction into two parts, the operator code and the operand address. Once decoded, the instruction can be executed.

The control unit has another special register called the sequence control register (SCR) which controls the order in which instructions are executed. The content of the sequence control register gives the address of the next instruction to be fetched from store. Normally, the machine instructions are held in store in the sequence in which the program is to be executed and every time an instruction is fetched from store into the instruction register, the address in the sequence control register is increased by 1 so that it contains the address of the next instruction in sequence. Branch or jump instructions are carried out by altering the content of the sequence control register. An unconditional branch uses an instruction such as the following.

Copy into the SCR the address 151

After this instruction has been executed, the next instruction will be fetched from location 151 in store. Conditional branching requires a test. This uses another register in the control unit called the indicator. The indicator is reset every time the content of the accumulator is changed. It indicates whether the content of the accumulator, interpreted using the number code, is negative, zero or positive. Thus the control unit contains the registers shown in Figure 2–7.

To complete the diagram of a computer, Figure 2–8 shows the connections between the store and the registers in the control and arithmetic units. Although this diagram is highly simplified, it does show the key features of any computer that uses single

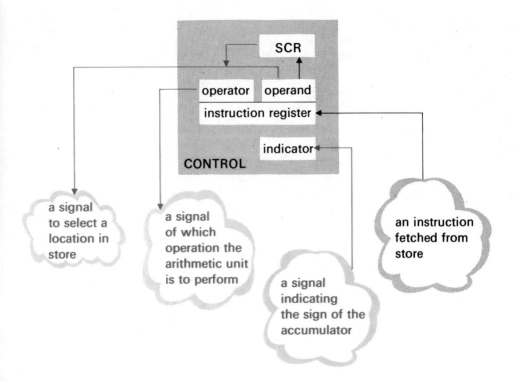

Figure 2–7   The control unit

address instructions. One feature that varies from computer to computer is the method of carrying out conditional branch instructions, but the differences are not major. Some computers have several accumulators and the programmer has the option of which is used for any specific instruction. Some computers allow instructions with two operand addresses. An accumulator is then unnecessary, since it is possible to write a single machine instruction for an assignment such as the following.

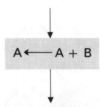

$$A \longleftarrow A + B$$

To give you a more accurate picture of the simplifications that we have made, the IBM 370 series computers have two sets of machine instructions. They have a set of single address instructions for which sixteen accumulator type registers are provided and an entirely separate set of two address instructions which address individual characters. Whether a computer uses single address or two address instructions, the sequence control register and instruction register are still required, as well as some form of indicator used for conditional branching.

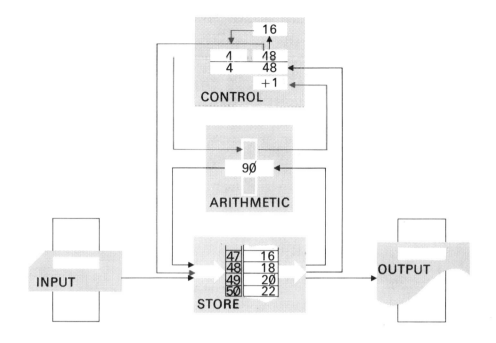

Figure 2–8   A conceptual model of a computer

Questions 2.1

1. Using the codes described in this section, what is stored in the following locations, interpreting each word as

    (i)   a number,
    (ii) four characters?

1663	ØØØØØØØØ Ø1ØØØØØØ 1111ØØØØ 1111ØØØØ
1664	ØØØØØ1ØØ 111ØØØ1Ø 111ØØØ1Ø 11Ø11ØØ1

2. What are the binary codes for

    (i)   43, 512 (use the number code),
    (ii) ROME, 8672 (use the character code)?

3. For a computer that you have used, find out the method of storing

    (i)   numbers;
    (ii) characters;
    (iii) machine instructions.

4. Look again at Figure 2–8, and imagine that an execute cycle has just been completed.

   (i)   What is the current operator code?
   (ii) What is the current operand address?
   (iii) From what address in store was the current instruction fetched?
   (iv) Where will the next instruction be fetched from?
   (v)   Why is the indicator +1?
   (vi) What is the value of the current operand?

   Suppose further that the current operator code specified an add instruction.

   (vii) What was the value of the accumulator before this instruction was executed?

2.2 MACHINE INSTRUCTIONS

Since our imaginary computer uses single address instructions, before a machine code program can be written each step of the flow chart must be broken down into a sequence of single address instructions. For example, an assignment such as

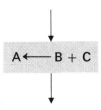

appears to be a single instruction which uses three operands. However, consider the following.

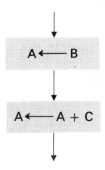

Each of these instructions has two operands, yet after they have been executed A, B and C will have exactly the same values as after executing the single three operand instruction. In fact, using the accumulator, the assignment can also be carried out using single address instructions as follows.

    load B into the accumulator
    add C to the contents of the accumulator
    store the contents of the accumulator in A

Thus the assignment can be expressed in three different ways,

(i)   as an instruction containing three addresses,
(ii) as instructions each containing two addresses,
(iii) as instructions each containing a single address.

Most computers use either one or two address instructions. Single address instructions are especially convenient for a word organized computer such as we introduced in the last section and so we shall restrict our attention to single address instructions.

Example

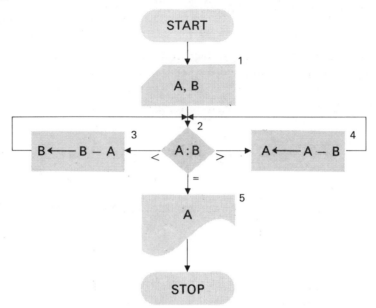

Figure 2–9   GCD: a flow chart to find the Greatest Common Divisor of A and B

The flow chart in Figure 2–9 finds the greatest common divisor of two positive integers. It uses the fact that any divisor of both the numbers A and B also divides their difference. The smaller number is subtracted repeatedly from the larger until the two numbers are the same. This flow chart is equivalent to the sequence of single

box 1	input A
	input B
box 2	load B into accumulator
	subtract A from accumulator
	if accumulator negative branch to box 4
	if accumulator zero branch to box 5
box 3	store content of accumulator in B
	goto box 2
box 4	load A into accumulator
	subtract B from accumulator
	store content of accumulator in A
	goto box 2
box 5	output A
	stop

Figure 2–10   Single address instructions for GCD

operand instructions given in Figure 2–10. Notice how the multiple branch in box 2 is carried out. The value of B − A is calculated in the accumulator which sets the indicator and tests are made on the value of the indicator. Since the value of B − A is in the accumulator when box 3 is entered, it does not have to be calculated again.

The binary pattern used to hold an instruction in store is coded in two parts, an operator code and an operand address. The operator code says what to do; the operand address specifies what to do it with. Remember that both are represented as binary numbers.

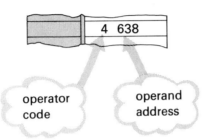

So far we have shown operator codes stored in the computer as numbers. However these numbers are particularly difficult to work with and instead we shall use a written form of operator code. In this written form each operator is referred to by a mnemonic, that is, a few letters which are chosen to be easily remembered. Here then is a basic instruction set which is sufficient to write simple programs.

First we have two instructions for copying data between store and the accumulator.

> LOAD—load a word of data from store into the accumulator.

> STORE—store the contents of the accumulator in the address given by the operand.

Next we have four arithmetic instructions each of which leaves its result in the accumulator.

> ADD—add the contents of the operand to the contents of the accumulator.

> SUB—subtract the contents of the operand from the contents of the accumulator.

> MUL—multiply the contents of the operand by the contents of the accumulator.

> DIV—divide the contents of the operand into the contents of the accumulator.

Each of the previous instructions has as its operand the address of a word of data in store. The next group of instructions are branch instructions. For each of these the operand is the address in store of the instruction to which the branch is made. This address is copied into the sequence control register to make the branch.

GOTO—branch to the specified instruction.

BP—branch if the indicator is positive to the specified instruction.

BZ—branch if the indicator is zero to the specified instruction.

BN—branch if the indicator is negative to the specified instruction.

The next three instructions are self explanatory.

INPUT—input a word of data into store.

OUTPUT—output a word of data from store.

STOP—stop.

These thirteen basic instructions allow a wide range of computer programs to be written, and any computer that uses single address instructions will have these instructions, or very similar ones, in its instruction set. The only exceptions are the last three, INPUT, OUTPUT and STOP. As you will see in Chapter 12, these have been deliberately simplified.

The machine instructions for handling individual characters vary from computer to computer and for this reason we shall introduce only three simple instructions. They have as their operands a single character in store and use only the eight right hand bits in the accumulator. The instruction to compare characters, CPCH, sets the indicator to negative, zero or positive depending on whether the specified character comes before, is equal to, or comes after the character in these eight bits of the accumulator. The three instructions are as follows.

LDCH—load a character from store into the accumulator.

STCH—store a character from the accumulator into store.

CPCH—compare a character in store with the character in the accumulator.

Machine Instructions

We now turn to the problem of writing machine code programs. First, there are a few simple points to bear in mind.

(i) The instructions must be stored in the correct sequence, for the next instruction will always be fetched from the address given by the SCR. Except after a branch instruction, this address will be

   address of current instruction + 1.

(ii) The binary patterns that make up the values of constants have to be stored explicitly.

(iii) No location allocated to a variable should be used before a value has been assigned to it by a STORE or INPUT instruction. It is not sensible to use an undefined value since it could be anything; it will be the value left there by the previous program!

Bearing these points in mind, here is how we would set about writing machine instructions for the flow chart in Figure 2–9. First we scan the flow chart and allocate storage space for all the constants and variables in the program. There are no constants involved; space only needs to be allocated for the variables A and B.

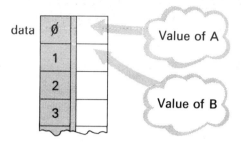

We can now work through the flow chart, box by box, generating machine instructions for each box in turn. This kind of methodical approach may not lead to a ruthlessly efficient program, but if the logic of the flow chart is correct, it will lead to a program that works. For the flow chart in Figure 2–9 we get the machine instructions given in Figure 2–11. To help you to understand the program, the interpretation of each instruction has been printed beside it.

		Machine Instructions		Interpretation
data	Ø			value of A
	1			value of B
box 1	2	INPUT	Ø	input A
	3	INPUT	1	input B
box 2	4	LOAD	1	load B into accumulator
	5	SUB	Ø	subtract A from accumulator
	6	BN	1Ø	if accumulator negative branch to box 4
	7	BZ	14	if accumulator zero branch to box 5
box 3	8	STORE	1	store content of accumulator in B
	9	GOTO	4	goto box 2
box 4	1Ø	LOAD	Ø	load A into accumulator
	11	SUB	1	subtract B from accumulator
	12	STORE	Ø	store content of accumulator in A
	13	GOTO	4	goto box 2
box 5	14	OUTPUT	Ø	output A
	15	STOP		stop

Figure 2–11   Machine instructions for GCD

Assembly Code

The form of writing down machine instructions given in Figure 2–11 is certainly straightforward but the result is not particularly easy to read or interpret and even simple alterations to the program may require a large number of instructions to be changed. This is because the operand of an instruction is expressed as a number, the actual address of the location involved. Using this form of operand is called **absolute addressing** and it has several drawbacks. People who worked with early computers had to use absolute addressing for their programs, but they soon began to look for ways of expressing their programs that were easier to read and in which mistakes could be corrected more easily. The technique which evolved is known as **assembly language**. Rather than use absolute addresses, in an assembly language every operand is a symbolic name, which corresponds to an address. Thus, the instruction that with absolute addressing was held as

is written in assembly code as

    STORE B

Where constants are used, their value is written explicitly between quotation marks, as follows.

    LOAD "1Ø Ø75"

When writing assembly code programs, the address of the location in which an instruction is stored is omitted. This simplifies programming, but special provision has to be made for branch instructions. Any instruction that is to be branched to is labelled. Thus, the program of Figure 2–11 includes a branch to the instruction stored in location 4. In assembly code the instruction in location 4 would be labelled as follows.

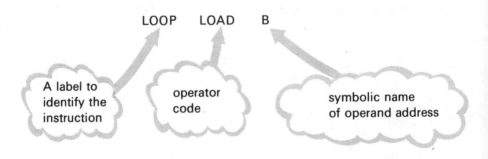

Since this instruction has now been labelled the subsequent instruction

    GOTO LOOP

has an obvious meaning. In Figure 2–12 you will find the assembly code equivalent of the machine instructions given in Figure 2–11.

Assembly Code Program   Machine Instructions

	Assembly Code		data		Machine address	Instruction	
					Ø		
					1		
	INPUT	A	box 1		2	INPUT	Ø
	INPUT	B			3	INPUT	1
LOOP	LOAD	B	box 2		4	LOAD	1
	SUB	A			5	SUB	Ø
	BN	NEG			6	BN	1Ø
	BZ	FOUND			7	BZ	14
	STORE	B	box 3		8	STORE	1
	GOTO	LOOP			9	GOTO	4
NEG	LOAD	A	box 4		1Ø	LOAD	Ø
	SUB	B			11	SUB 1	1
	STORE	A			12	STORE	Ø
	GOTO	LOOP			13	GOTO	4
FOUND	OUTPUT	A	box 5		14	OUTPUT	Ø
	STOP				15	STOP	

Figure 2–12   Assembly code program for GCD

The translation of an assembly code program into machine instructions is carried out by a special program known as an **assembler**. As well as the program instructions, input to the assembler must include statements which specify how much store to allocate for each variable and constant. In fact, modern assemblers are large programs which are almost as complex as the compilers used to translate high level programming languages and allow a wide range of facilities to make programming at assembly level simple. We discuss some of these facilities in Chapter 6.

Example

The flow chart in Figure 2–13 reads a sequence of positive numbers terminated by a negative number. It counts how many numbers have been read in and finds the smallest. The problem is to write an assembly code program from this flow chart.

The first step is to scan through the flow chart to identify the variables and constants used. At a first glance the program appears to use the following.

Variables	Constants
COUNT	
S	Ø
X	1

39

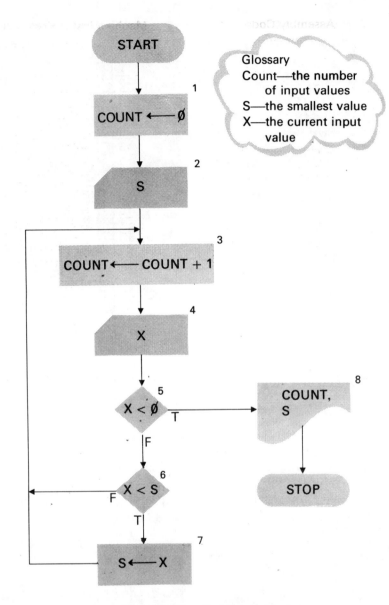

START

Glossary
Count—the number
of input values
S—the smallest value
X—the current input
value

1
COUNT ← Ø

2
S

3
COUNT ← COUNT + 1

4
X

5
X < Ø   T

6
X < S   F

7
S ← X

8
COUNT,
S

STOP

Figure 2–13   Find the smallest

40

	Assembly Code Program	

Assembly Code Program — Machine Instructions

Assembly label	Instruction	Operand	Addr	Machine Instruction	Operand
			0		0
			1		
			2		
			3		1
	INPUT	SMALL	4	INPUT	1
NEXT	LOAD	COUNT	5	LOAD	0
	ADD	"1"	6	ADD	3
	STORE	COUNT	7	STORE	0
	INPUT	X	8	INPUT	2
	BN	ENDATA	9	BN	16
	SUB	SMALL	10	SUB	1
	BN	SMALLER	11	BN	13
	GOTO	NEXT	12	GOTO	5
SMALLER	LOAD	X	13	LOAD	2
	STORE	SMALL	14	STORE	1
	GOTO	NEXT	15	GOTO	5
ENDATA	OUTPUT	COUNT	16	OUTPUT	0
	OUTPUT	SMALL	17	OUTPUT	1
	STOP		18	STOP	

Figure 2–14   Assembly code program and machine instructions for "Find the smallest"

However, look at box 1. The variable COUNT is set to the value $\emptyset$ at the start of the program. Rather than execute this assignment at the beginning of the program, when space in store is allocated to the variable COUNT, it is preset to the value $\emptyset$. This is another task for the assembler and requires a special statement. The test in box 5 can use the branch if negative instruction on the value of X and so the constant $\emptyset$ is not required. Thus the assembly code program begins with statements which specify to the assembler that the program uses the following.

Variables	Constants
COUNT—preset to $\emptyset$	1
S	
X	

The assembly code program and corresponding machine instructions are given in Figure 2–14.

Whilst we do not want to lay too heavy an emphasis upon machine instructions or assembly code programs, you will find that to write a few assembly code programs at this stage will help considerably in subsequent chapters. Your understanding of the many references we make to the computer at machine level will be immediate and the many ideas about software that we mention will be made easy to understand. For example, you should be accustomed to thinking of an assembly code program as

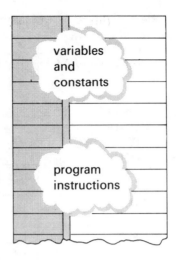

Figure 2–15   The layout of a program in store

having the layout in store that is given in Figure 2–15. This is the kind of picture that is helpful in Chapters 13 and 14 in which we discuss some techniques of compiling.

Questions 2.2

1. Figure 2–16 shows the contents of the registers in the control unit at the end of a fetch cycle, but before the instruction is decoded. What will be the contents of these registers after execution of this instruction?

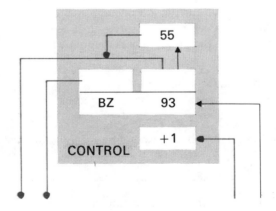

Figure 2–16   The control unit

2. Give the assembly code and machine instructions for the flow chart boxes of Figure 2–17.

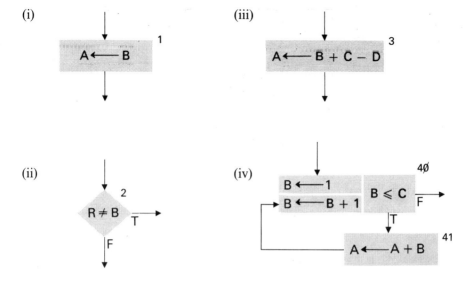

Figure 2–17   Some flow chart boxes

3. In translating a flow chart into assembly code the instructions used do not have to mirror the flow chart instructions exactly, so long as the effect of executing them is the same. Draw a flow chart fragment to represent the effect of executing the following sequence of instructions.

```
        LOAD    A
LOOP    SUB     B
        ADD     C
        BN      NEXT
        GOTO    LOOP
NEXT    STORE   A
```

4. Draw a flow chart to find the largest of an arbitrary set of input numbers. Write the machine instructions and assembly code for your flow chart.

CHAPTER THREE

DATA IN STORE

Fields and Records

Arrays

Access Vectors

Sequential Methods

Hash Coding

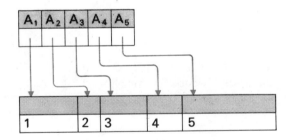

3.1 FIELDS AND RECORDS

The purpose of almost every computer program is to process information. This information must be held in the computer's store, but whereas the store consists of a sequence of locations with addresses, real life information is rarely presented in such a neat form. Items are liable to be of various sizes, not arranged in any particular sequence and with a complex of relationships between them. Before storing information in a computer it must be put in a form that is compatible with the structure of store.

Unstructured information about a problem → Structuring → STORE

The arrangement used to store information will depend on the processing, since much of the information contained in the problem may be irrelevant to the processing required, and many of the links between items may be superfluous. The information must therefore be structured in a way that preserves the links needed for processing and in a way that can be successfully held in store. The methods used are called data structures.

This is the first of three chapters in which we examine the kinds of data structure that are used when all the information relevant to a problem can be held in store. Chapters 7 to 10 look at the additional complications that arise when the store is not large enough and backing store devices such as magnetic tapes and discs have to be used to provide the necessary storage capacity.

We begin by looking at the basic components of data, and introduce some new terminology. In Chapter 2 we explained that whatever the organization of store each number or character is held in a location which can be referred to by its address. But whereas a number is a usable item of data, a single character is usually only part of a group of characters which together form an item of information. Consider the following.

TITLE
A PRACTICAL APPROACH TO COMPUTING

These characters can be stored in consecutive locations in store.

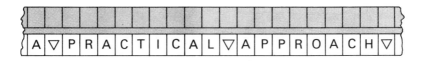

A ▽ P R A C T I C A L ▽ A P P R O A C H ▽

But when drawing a flow chart, you do not want to be concerned with the details of storage. You have a variable with name TITLE which at present has value A PRACTICAL APPROACH TO COMPUTING. If you write a program using a high level language you will rely on the compiler to make sure that the right amount of space is available and that it is properly used.

Several characters which together represent a single item of information as in the above example, are called a **field**. A field can be of any length, but everything within a given field is part of the same item of information. For example, each of the following is a field.

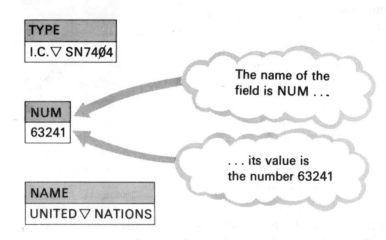

Most problems require that more than a single field of data be processed together. Several fields which are processed together are called a **record**. Records can also be of any length from a single field to many hundred. The important feature is that all the information is processed together. Precise definitions of the words field and record are difficult to make and not very helpful. As you read this book their meaning should become clear to you.

Example

An industrial firm has information about all the spare parts it holds in stock. For each part the following fields of information are held.

       Part Number
       Description
       Quantity held in stock
       Supplier (code number)

All the data held about each given part constitutes a record. A typical SPARE record might be the following.

Name of the record	SPARES			
Names of the fields	PART	DESC	STOCK	SUPP
Values	1Ø625	LENS-AØ6	146	7368

In the record in this example, the **PART** field is fixed at five characters; it is a fixed length field. The length of the **DESC** field depends on the part and will vary from record to record; it is a *variable length* field. As another example, a surname would normally be variable length,

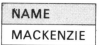

but a field containing a date would be fixed length.

YEAR
1877

YEAR
1984

A record consisting of a fixed number of fixed length fields is itself fixed length, otherwise it is variable length.

Since a record may have more than one field, we use a special notation to refer to an individual field of a record. For example, we refer to the **DESC** field in the **SPARES** records as follows.

DESC(SPARES)

The name of the field

The name of the record

To see how this notation works in practice, consider the following example.

Example

The industrial firm referred to in the previous example checks the **SPARES** records to find which parts are low on stock. Figure 3–1 is a flow chart to read the records

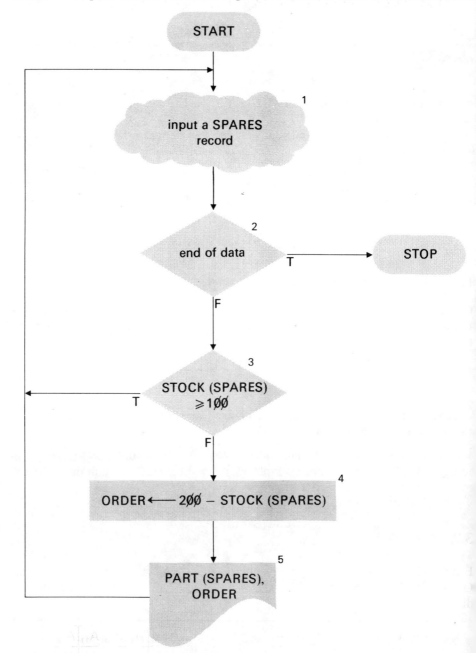

Figure 3–1   An example of the notation for record processing

one at a time and to list those parts for which an order must be placed. To input a record we could specify the individual fields.

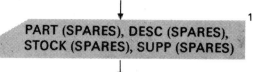

PART (SPARES), DESC (SPARES), STOCK (SPARES), SUPP (SPARES)

This is so unwieldy that for any operation using the entire record we write only the record name.

SPARES

This notation and the notation listed at the beginning of the book forms the basis of the flow charts in subsequent chapters. Although not directly related to any particular high level language we hope that you will find that the notation is easy to understand and that corresponding programs, in whatever language you use, are easy to generate.

Questions 3.1

Questions 1 and 2 are based on a library filing system. The information about a book on loan consists of a number which identifies the book, a number which identifies the reader and a date which specifies when the book becomes overdue.

1. Design a record for storing the information about each book on loan. What are the fields?

2. The library file can be searched and a list of books overdue printed. Draw a flow chart of this process.

3. In Chapter 2 only two types of data were discussed, characters and integer numbers. What other types of data are allowed in one programming language that you know?

3.2 ARRAYS

Even in simple programs there is an advantage in being able to store data in an array. One dimensional arrays, also called vectors, are thought of in terms of the following diagram.

Name of Vector	A											
Name of element	A_1	A_2	A_3	A_4	A_5	A_6	A_7	A_8	A_9	A_{10}	A_{11}	A_{12}
Values	17	10	5	16	23	11	12	14	6	5	21	22

A two dimensional array, or matrix, makes problem solving easier only in that it sometimes allows information to be expressed in a more natural way. However, the most important feature of arrays is that they are very straightforward to store because they are fixed length structures. For example, the elements of a vector of length 12 can be held in successive storage locations, as in Figure 3–2. The address of

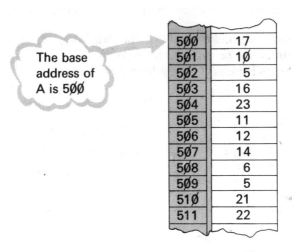

Figure 3–2   The vector A, as it might be held in store

the first element is known as the **base address** of the vector and the Jth element is stored in the location with address

base address + (J − 1)

Similar methods can be used for other fixed length structures. Consider the following artificial example. How do you store a list of three letter words?

        ANT
        BEE
        CAT
        DOG
        ELK
        FOX
        and so on.

The answer is simple; use an array of characters.

| A | N | T | B | E | E | C | A | T | D | O | G | E |

To specify where the Kth item of the list is stored, the group of elements that it uses is identified by the index of its first element. In our example, the address of the Kth item in the list is

base address + 3(K − 1).

Example

Often information that is not obviously in the form of an array, for example road or rail networks, can in fact be stored as an array. A standard example is found in the problem of the Seven Bridges of Königsburg. Seven bridges over the river Pregel link

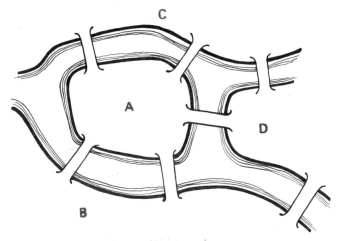

Figure 3–3   The seven bridges of Königsburg

the four sectors of the old city, as shown in Figure 3–3. The way the bridges link the sectors is shown by the following diagram.

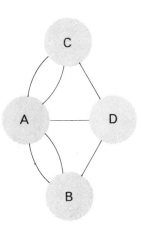

The problem facing the Königsburgers (in about 1730) was to find a walking tour through the city in which the walker returns to his starting point having crossed each bridge once and only once. The problem arose as a social one, and must have given considerable exercise (both physical and mental) to the people of that great city, before a mathematician, Leonhard Euler, chanced to hear of it and proved it impossible. His proof is based on a simple principle that what goes in must come out. If no route is used twice and if the journey ends where it begins, there must be an even number of routes entering each region. In Königsburg, regions B and C each have an odd number of routes entering them. However, our interest for the moment lies not so much in the problem as in the information it contains. This information can be represented by the diagram above, called a graph, but the graph cannot be held in store as it stands. One way of storing the information is to use a two-dimensional array, R, called a route matrix. The route matrix for Königsburg is shown in Figure 3-4.

$$
\begin{array}{c c c c c}
 & A & B & C & D \\
A & \emptyset & 2 & 2 & 1 \\
B & 2 & \emptyset & \emptyset & 1 \\
C & 2 & \emptyset & \emptyset & 1 \\
D & 1 & 1 & 1 & \emptyset
\end{array}
$$

Figure 3-4   The route matrix for Königsburg

The entry in $R_{J,K}$ shows the number of routes (bridges) connecting regions J and K. This data structure is easy to store and is often useful in problem solving.

Other examples of the use of arrays are given in the questions at the end of this section, but before finishing you should notice one further point. Processing arrays is so straightforward that it is often worth wasting storage space in order to hold information in an array. For example, consider the following problem.

Given a list of names and a value associated with each name, draw a flow chart to search the list for the value associated with a particular name.

NAME	VALUE

We might store the names in a vector **NAME** and the values in the vector **VALUE**. A name **QUERY** is input; we want to find the J for which

$$QUERY = NAME_J$$

and to print the corresponding $VALUE_J$. It is not a difficult flow chart to draw; our first version is given as Figure 3–5. The question we want to focus on is how

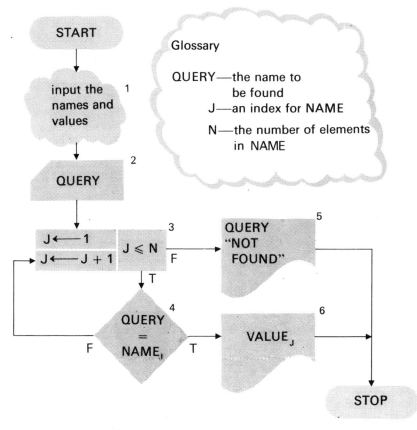

Figure 3–5   Searching for a given name

NAME can be stored. Let us take a particular example and assume the names to be

WASHINGTON
LONDON
PARIS
ROME
NEW YORK
and so on.

The associated values might be fares or times of a particular airline; their meaning need not concern us. The names vary in length, but, if plenty of space is available in store, a fixed number of elements in an array could be allocated to each name. This number would be the maximum number of characters in any one of them, see Figure 3–6.

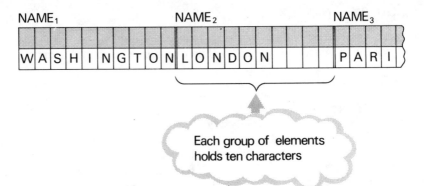

Figure 3–6   A fixed number of elements allocated to each name

Here fixed length fields are used to hold variable length data. This wastes storage space, but it is so much easier to process fixed length fields than variable length ones that it is often the most efficient way to proceed. In the next two sections we shall look at methods of storing variable length fields that are more efficient in their use of storage space. The price of saving space is paid by more complex processing.

Questions 3.2

1. (i)   Write down the route matrix of Figure 3–7, entering 1 in $A_{J,K}$ if town J is connected to town K and $\emptyset$ otherwise.
   (ii) Why is the route matrix not a very good data structure for the information?
   (iii) Construct a more efficient data structure (you may find it easier to answer this part of the question after reading the next section).

2. Six towns, and their distances apart, are given by the following table, in which a dash means that no connection exists because of mountains or rivers between the towns.

	A	B	C	D	E	F
A		2	—	5	4	—
B	2		3	—	—	9
C	—	3		—	—	7
D	5	—	—		5	—
E	4	—	—	5		6
F	—	9	7	—	6	

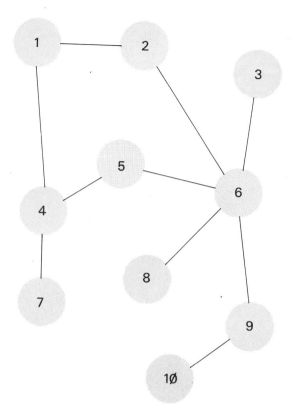

Figure 3–7   Towns 1 to 1Ø and the connections between them

The problem is to find the shortest route from A to F.

A practical solution to this problem is to imagine a set of rings (like the ones in the diagram in Question 1), joined by bits of string that are proportional in length to the distances between the towns. To find the quickest route from town A to town F, all you have to do is to pick up rings A and F and pull! The taut strings show you how to make the journey. Unfortunately this method of solution will not work on a computer. Devise a solution which *can* be programmed.

3.3   ACCESS VECTORS

We begin this section with a problem.

A computer is required to analyse the answers to a student questionnaire. For each of the five questions a limited number of replies are possible.

55

Question number	Question	Number of possible replies
1	Age category	8
2	Sex	2
3	Discipline of study	14
4	Course	1Ø
5	Examination mark	1ØØ

You want to write a program to read all the replies and analyse them for each question. What is an appropriate data structure?

You could allocate a hundred locations to each question and have a matrix with five rows and a hundred columns. This allows space for the answers to question 5, but it also allows one hundred locations for question 2 which has only two possible answers. Five hundred locations are set aside but only a hundred and thirty four are used. Using a two dimensional array for this problem is wasteful of storage space. To get round this, a data structure called a ragged array can be used. The ragged array for the questionnaire is illustrated in Figure 3–8.

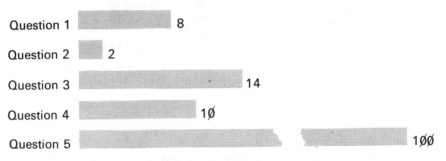

Figure 3–8   A ragged array

There are a number of ways in which this ragged array can be stored and the advantages of each depend very much on the exact kind of processing that the questionnaire analysis demands. One way is to think of the above data structure as being a collection of variable length records. These could be held in an array and, to speed processing, the addresses of the records could be held in another vector, A, as shown in Figure 3–9.

Used in this way, A is called an access vector, and, in this example, has the following entries.

$$A_1 = 1$$
$$A_2 = 9$$
$$A_3 = 11$$
$$A_4 = 25$$
$$A_5 = 35$$

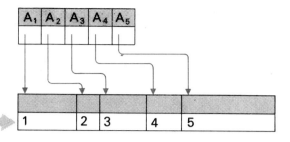

Figure 3-9   A method of storing a ragged array

The access vector, A, then points to elements of the array Q and the Kth response to the Lth question will be stored in Q_J, where

$$J = A_L + (K - 1).$$

Access vectors can be used in a similar manner for the problem about the list of names and associated values given on page 52. As the list is read in, a vector is set up which shows where the name of each city begins. In Figure 3-10, you see the names stored in an array, NAME. The elements of the access vector indicate where the name of the corresponding city begins.

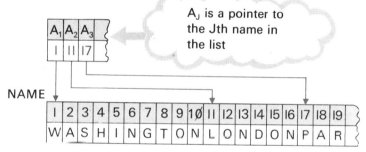

A_J is a pointer to the Jth name in the list

(a)   Each element of the access vector points to the first letter of a name

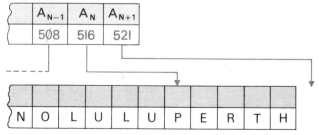

(b)   The last element of the access vector points to one beyond the end of the list of names

Figure 3-10   An example of an access vector

57

The Jth name stretches from character K to character L of NAME, where

K = A$_J$,

L = A$_{J+1}$ − 1.

In the notation we use for substrings, the Jth name is written as

NAME (K, L).

The last name in the list needs special attention. A simple method of dealing with it is to have the final element of the access vector pointing to just beyond the end of the list, as in Figure 3–10(b).

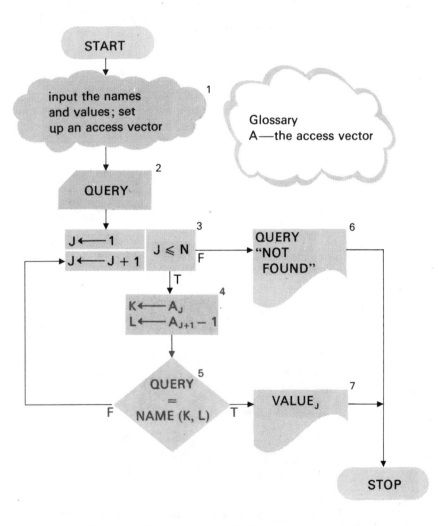

Figure 3–11   Searching for a name (using an access vector)

Compared with using an array of fixed length elements, this arrangement saves storage space, but, every time a name is required, the values of K and L have to be calculated. Also the flow chart given in Figure 3–5 needs minor modifications; these are given in Figure 3–11. There is the additional overhead of having to fill in the values of A during the input routine. If we want an efficient program, speed of execution must be weighed against storage space used and the most suitable data structure must be chosen.

Questions 3.3

1. A triangular array is stored in a vector.

 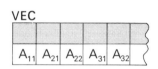

To refer to the element $A_{J,K}$ what index for VEC is needed?

2. The names

> ANN
> BILL
> CAROL
> DAVID

are stored in successive elements of an array.

What is the corresponding access vector?

3. A subroutine DELNAME has the following parameters.

> A—the access vector.
> N—the list of names stored in successive elements of an array.
> K—the number of names in N.
> M—a name known to be in the list.

DELNAME deletes the name, M, from the list, repositions the remaining names and adjusts the access vector accordingly. Draw a flow chart for DELNAME.

4. An unsorted list of names is held in successive elements of an array and an access vector points to each name in the list. A subroutine SORT has the following parameters.

A—the access vector.

N—the list of names.

a two dimensional array in which $S_{1,J}$ points to the Jth name in (sorted) sequence in the list and $S_{2,J}$ gives its length.

Draw a flow chart for SORT that sorts the access vector and leaves N unchanged.

3.4   SEQUENTIAL METHODS

So far we have discussed two ways of storing a list of variable length names, by treating them as fixed length and by using an access vector. Several other methods are in common use; we shall look at two of them.

Separators

Let us return again to the problem given on page 52 and suppose that the names are stored in an array with a special symbol, such as an asterisk, to separate one from the next. This symbol is known as a separator, see Figure 3–12. The search procedure

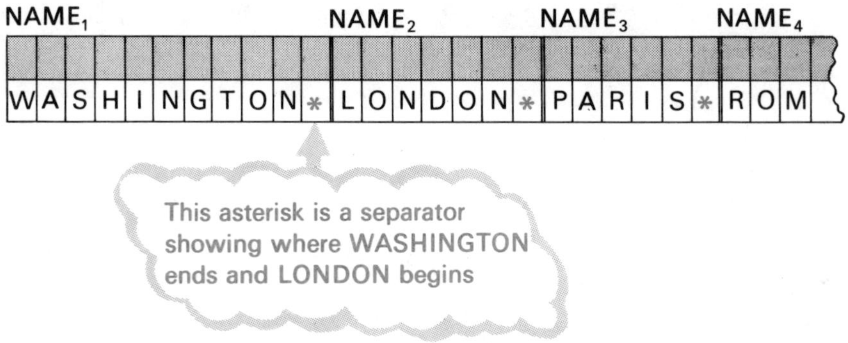

Figure 3–12   Separators

given in Figure 3–5 now requires quite a number of extra steps which are shown in Figure 3–13. Notice that the steps in boxes 5, 6, 7 and 9 of Figure 3–13 are needed just because the data is variable length.

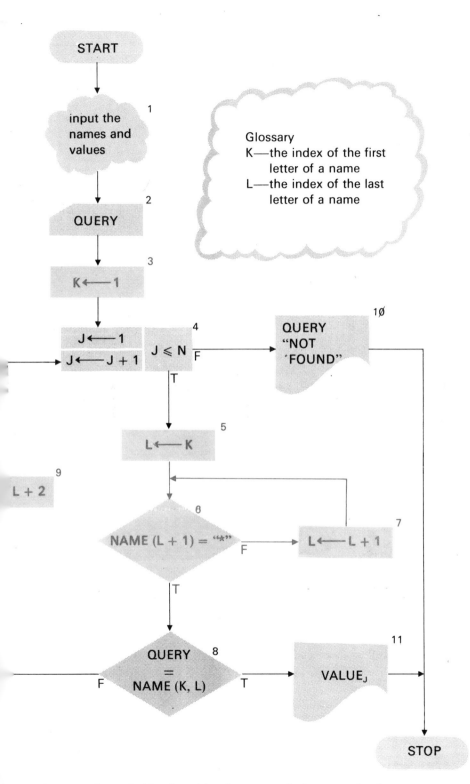

Figure 3-13   Searching for a name (using separators)

Length Fields

Another method of storing variable length data is to think in terms of records and to use a length field. For each item of data a record with two fields is created.

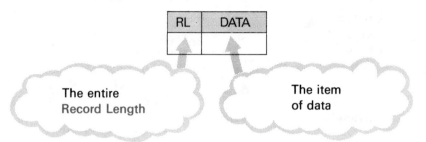

The list of names can now be stored in an array as follows.

RL	DATA	RL	DATA	RL	DATA	RL	DATA
11	WASHINGTON	7	LONDON	6	PARIS	5	ROME

Notice that in this arrangement, numbers and characters are interspersed in the same array. This may be awkward in some programming languages, but in general it is quite acceptable so long as you are sure of the code by which any given element is to be interpreted. Also, the flow chart to search the list for a specified name differs from the previous ones in that we are now thinking in terms of records. In the flow chart individual fields within records are examined. If K is the base address of a record our notation is

      RL (K)—the record length field of the record,
      DATA (K)—the data field of the record.

Using this notation, the flow chart is given in Figure 3–14.

The distinctive feature of the methods described in this section is that they do not rely on an index. The power of indexing is that it allows you direct access to items of data. If asked for, the Jth item can be found directly. Using separators or length fields denies direct access and forces you to work through the items in the order in which they are stored.

Indexing allows direct access to any item once its index is known, but if you look back to Figures 3–5 and 3–11, you will see that, even though indexing is used, the names still have to be searched sequentially. For example, given the name ROME there is no way of finding its index other than by a sequential search. This is because the index and the name have no connection apart from the historical accident of the order in which the names were read. If the list of names is long or has to be searched repeatedly the sequential processes described so far are inefficient, but apparently unavoidable. Improvements might be achieved by sorting the list. However, even

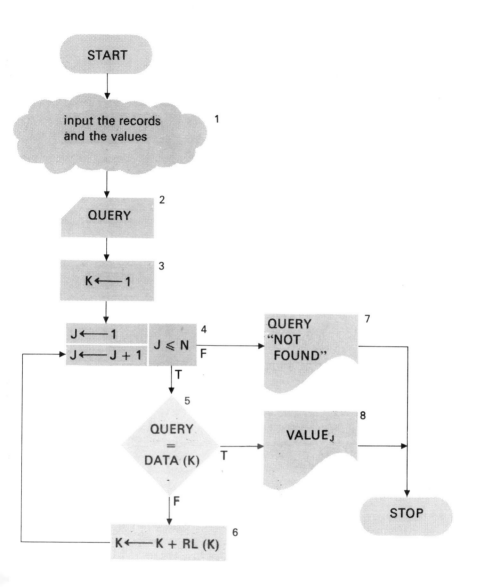

Figure 3-14   Searching for a name (using length fields)

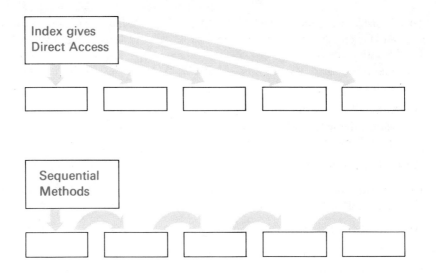

with sorted records, there is no immediate way, given a name held in an indexed list, to calculate where it is stored. A special search procedure will be required. In the next section we discuss a method of storage which partially overcomes this difficulty.

Questions 3.4

1. An array N contains names separated by separators.

N_1	N_2	N_3	N_4	⎫⎫	⎧⎧	N_{L-4}	N_{L-3}	N_{L-2}	N_{L-1}	N_L
A	B	*	C			*	X	Y	Z	*

The problem is to set up an access vector, A, in which A_J points to the first character of the Jth name in N. Draw a flow chart for a subroutine to do this. Assume that

(i)   the last entry in N is always an asterisk,
(ii) two asterisks do not occur as consecutive entries in N.

2. An unsorted list of variable length names separated by asterisks is held in an array A. The end of the list is marked by two asterisks.

A_1	A_2	A_3	A_4	A_5	A_6	A_7	⎫⎫	⎧⎧	A_{94}	A_{95}	A_{96}	A_{97}	A_{98}	A_{99}
J	O	*	J	I	M	*			J	O	H	N	*	*

(i) Construct a subroutine **NEXTNAME** which, given a variable J such that A(J) is an asterisk (not at the end of the list), returns values M and N such that the substring A(M, N) is the next name in the list. For instance, in the example shown, if J had the value of 3, M and N would have the values of 4 and 6 respectively.

(ii) Some of the names in the list appear more than once. Draw a flow chart to search the list to see if the first name in the list is repeated and print out a suitable message.

3. A list of names is stored as a sequence of records with length fields.

(i) Repeat Question 1, but using this storage arrangement.
(ii) Repeat Question 2, again with this storage arrangement.

4. An array R contains a list of names separated by asterisks as separators. You are required to create

(i) an array S consisting of the same names, but without the separators, and an access vector A pointing to the names now held in S,
(ii) an array T consisting of the same names but instead of separators, length fields.

In addition, any names duplicated in R should not be duplicated in either S or T. Draw a flow chart to read R and print out S, A and T.

3.5 HASH CODING

Hash coding is a method of storing a record which takes one of the data fields and from it calculates an address. The record is either stored in the location with address given by the rule or, if that location is occupied, in the first vacant location after the one first tried. Thus, searching for a record in a list stored by hash coding has two parts.

(i) Calculate an address from a suitable data field by means of a rule.
(ii) Try the specified location. If it is already occupied, try the next location.

The technique is illustrated by the following diagram.

The effectiveness of hash coding depends on the rule used to allocate an initial address. As far as possible, the records should be spread uniformly over the area allocated to them so that, if the location given by the rule is already occupied, the sequential search to find a vacant one will be quite short. If the records contain a numeric field a simple rule is to use the remainder after division. If n locations are available, the rule is to divide the value of the field by n and take the remainder. The remainder can then be used to find the base address of a record. If the value of the field is m, ordinary division gives

$$m = qn + r$$

where $\emptyset \leqslant r < n$, so that r can be used as the address.

Example

Hash coding is to be used to store $8\emptyset\emptyset$ records and space for $1\emptyset\emptyset\emptyset$ records is available. Each record has a six digit identity code.

CODE	Other data
63$\emptyset$ 341	

The address rule might be to take the remainder on division by $1\emptyset\emptyset\emptyset$. Thus for the record shown the rule would give address 341. Suppose that after reading several records part of the available storage space has been filled up as given in Figure 3–15(a).

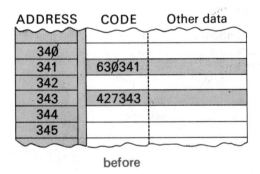

before

Figure 3–15(a)   An example of hash coding

The next two records to be read have codes 986341 and 21$\emptyset$342. For the first of these, the rule gives address 341, which is already occupied. The next space is free and therefore the record is inserted into it. For the second record, the rule gives address 342, but this space is now occupied. The next space is also occupied, but 344 is free and therefore the record is entered there. The final situation is given in Figure 3–15(b).

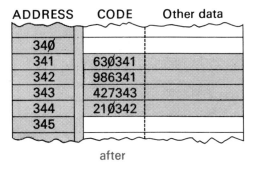

ADDRESS	CODE	Other data
34Ø		
341	63Ø341	
342	986341	
343	427343	
344	21Ø342	
345		

after

Figure 3–15(b)   An example of hash coding

On the face of it using the remainder after division as an address rule is possible only with a numeric field. However, remember that any field is stored as a binary pattern and it is possible to interpret any binary pattern as a number and do arithmetic on it. In computing jargon this is known as hashing; hence the term hash coding.

Let us see how hash coding can be used in the problem given on page 52. Suppose that, as the names and values are read in, a fixed length record is created.

NAME	VALUE

Since later we will be searching for a record given the value of its NAME field, we shall use the NAME field for the first stage of hash coding.

Suppose that there are about 2ØØ records in the list. Taking the first letter of a name, its position in the alphabet could be used to calculate an address. For example, we might allocate space for 26Ø records which allows 1Ø spaces for each letter of the alphabet. Using the variable L to denote the position in the alphabet of the first letter of a name, the address is

$$A = 1\emptyset(L - 1)$$

There is the added complication of relating this address to the way that records have been stored. One way of doing this is to allow each record a fixed number of elements in an array. Suppose each record needs ten elements. Then the address rule for a record with first letter in position A gives

$$1\emptyset A + 1,$$

which is

$$1\emptyset\emptyset(L - 1) + 1,$$

as the base address to try first. Using this method of storing the names, we get the flow chart of Figure 3–16 for the search procedure.

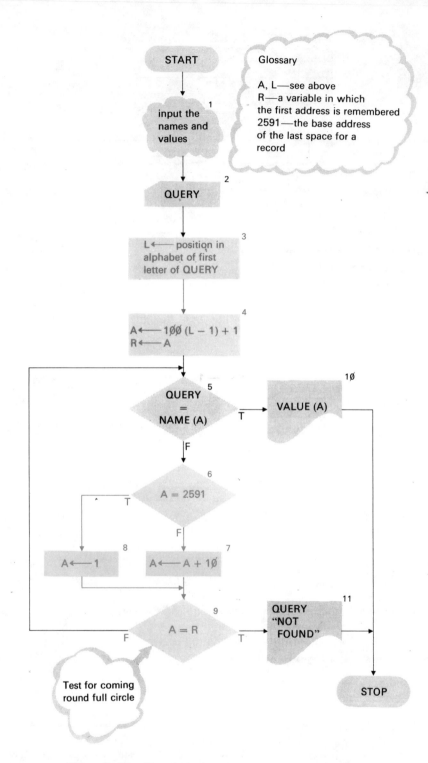

Figure 3–16   Searching for a name (using hash coding)

Questions 3.5

1. What complications can you foresee if variable length records are stored by hash coding?

2. Expand cloud 1 of Figure 3–16.

3. In box 9 of Figure 3–16 a test is made. It is the only check on whether the QUERY has been found. Why is it not the only possible one? Draw a more efficient flow chart.

4. Suppose that data from 1∅∅ interviews is gathered by 6∅ interviewers each of whom may carry out several interviews. Each interview record is of fixed length and the first field is the interviewer's code number. How would you store these records if 12∅ locations are available in store?

CHAPTER FOUR

LINKED LISTS

The Basic Concept

Simple List Processing

An Example

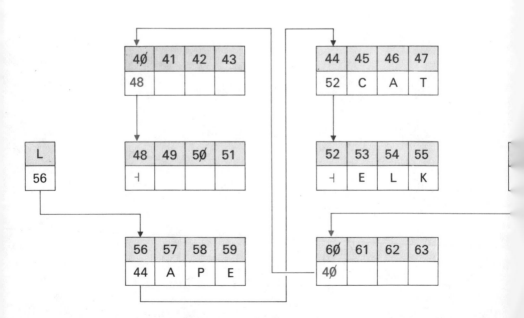

4.1 THE BASIC CONCEPT

In a sequence of records there are two orders that are important. These are the logical order, that is the sequence in which the records are processed, and the physical order, that is the sequence in which the records are stored. In most of the examples of the previous chapter, the logical and the physical order were the same. For instance, in an array the logical order of the elements is

$$A_1, A_2, A_3, \ldots, A_N.$$

This is the order in which the elements are usually processed. The logical order is the same as the physical order in which the elements are stored, because elements of an array would normally be held in successive locations in store (see Figure 3–2). However, imagine an ordered list of numbers and processing that requires repeated insertion of new items and deletion of existing ones. If the list is stored as an array, the numbers would be held in successive locations in store, and to insert or delete a number would require all subsequent numbers to be repositioned, as shown in Figure 4–1. The same kind of problem can exist for a sequence of records.

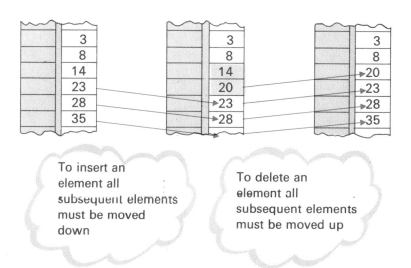

To insert an element all subsequent elements must be moved down

To delete an element all subsequent elements must be moved up

Figure 4–1   Insertion and deletion

Example

At an airline terminal the information on flight arrivals board is updated by computer. Information about each flight is held in a record with the following fields.

Flight Number	Time of Arrival	Gate Number

71

The list of flights due to arrive within the next hour needs to be updated continually, while still being sorted by flight number, so that when the list is displayed on the flight arrival board it can be easily scanned by the public.

This is an example in which we want to maintain the logical sequence of an ever changing list of records. The basic operations performed on the list are to

(i)   search for a specified record,
(ii) insert a new record,
(iii) delete an existing record.

While performing these operations, the list must be maintained in order. Using the storage structures of Chapter 3 the ordering would be achieved by using successive locations in store; the logical structure would be the same as the physical structure. As you can see from Figure 4–1, this is inefficient.

Linked lists are a way of storing data which avoids this inefficiency. In a linked list the records are stored in any convenient locations. The logical order of the records is indicated not by the physical sequence in which the records are stored, but by an extra field added to each record, called a pointer field. The pointer of each record contains the base address of the next record in the list. For instance, Figure 4–2 shows a simple linked list as it might be stored. An area of store has been divided into sections, each

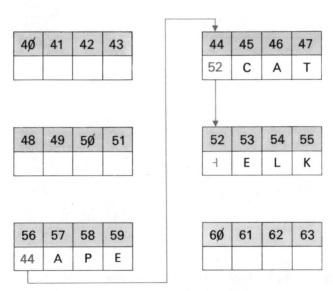

Figure 4–2   A linked list

the right size to hold one record. Some of these sections contain a record of the list and others are free. In this simple example each record consists of two fields.

72

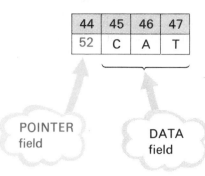

44	45	46	47
52	C	A	T

POINTER field

DATA field

The pointer indicates that the next record in sequence has base address 52. To follow through the records in their logical sequence, begin at the first record, which is APE, and follow the pointers from record to record as shown by the red lines in Figure 4–2. The end of the list is marked by a special end marker, ⊣ , in the pointer field of the final record. The list as shown in Figure 4–2 is not complete. Without scanning the whole store, there is no way of knowing where the list begins. The list needs a variable to hold the base address of the first record.

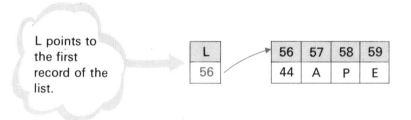

L points to the first record of the list.

L
56

56	57	58	59
44	A	P	E

The normal method of setting up a list from scratch is to create a free storage list. This is a linked list of free records, each of the same fixed length, covering the area allocated to the list. When a record is inserted into the list, space is taken from the free storage list and the space released by a subsequent deletion is returned to it. In our simple example the area that we set aside consists of all locations between 4∅ and 63. By the time that the linked list consists of

    APE
    CAT
    ELK

the free storage list might be as shown in Figure 4–3. The base address of the first record of the free storage list is given by a variable which we have called F. Whenever a free record is required the one whose base address is given by F is used and F is changed to point to the next free record.

The following basic steps are needed to insert a new record, say DOG, into the correct place in sequence.

73

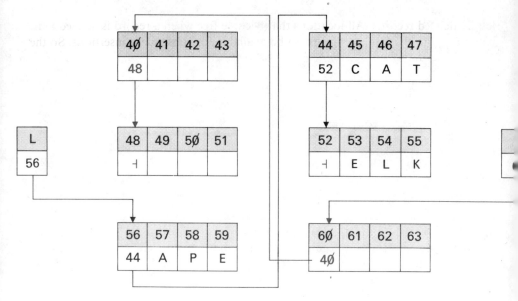

Figure 4–3   A linked list and free storage list

(i)   Copy **DOG** into the **DATA** field of a free record.
(ii) Search the list for the right place in the logical sequence to make the insertion.
(iii) Adjust pointers to link the new record into the list.

To delete a record is much the same. You might think that all that is involved in deleting the **CAT** record is to change the content of location **56** to the value **6Ø**. However, this does not cope with the problem of what to do with the gaps that are

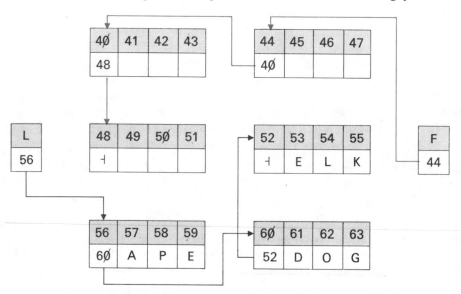

Figure 4–4   DOG inserted; CAT deleted

74

left by deleted records. All locations that become free when a record is deleted must be returned to the free storage list to be available for subsequent insertions. So the steps for deleting the record CAT are as follows.

(i) Search the list for the record CAT.
(ii) Adjust pointers to delete the record from the list.
(iii) Return the free locations to the free storage list.

Figure 4–4 shows the position when DOG has been inserted into and CAT deleted from the linked list given in Figure 4–3.

Using a linked list, records can be inserted or deleted indefinitely without ever altering the position of any other records in store. The only restriction is that the number of records must never exceed the area reserved for the list. Once the initial free storage list has been set up, the physical structure of storage remains fixed. But as processing proceeds, the logical structure of the sequence of records is able to vary.

Questions 4.1

In the example on page 71 we considered fixed length records such as the following.

FLIGHT	ARRIVE	GATE
PA 468	14.50	16

This record might occupy 11 locations in store, and the whole sequence might be held in ascending order of flight numbers. Figure 4–5 shows a free storage list of records each occupying 12 locations, of which 1 location is taken up by the pointer.

1. Enter the following list of flight arrivals into the free storage list.

Flight	Time of Arrival	Gate
PA 103	12.42	10
BE 201	14.16	6
AF 221	11.53	14
TA 302	13.50	8

2. The Air France flight AF 221 arrives and Pan Am flight PA 112, due to arrive at 14.45 from Gate 11 is added to the list. What alterations are needed?

4.2 SIMPLE LIST PROCESSING

In the previous section we looked at the basic list processing operations in the context of a simple example. In this section we shall turn these outline ideas into detailed flow charts. The underlying feature of a linked list is a record with a pointer field and one or more data fields. With a sorted list, the field that is used for sorting is called a key

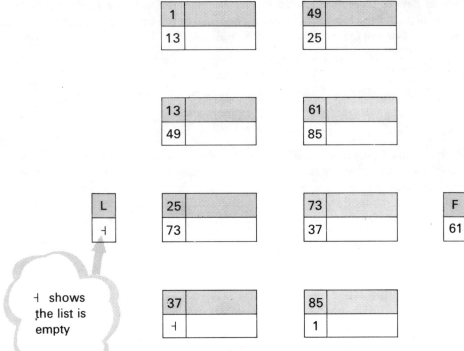

Figure 4–5   A free storage list

or sort key. The KEY field will normally be chosen on the grounds that it is the one best suited to the processing. All other data fields can be grouped together under the general heading of DATA. In this section therefore we shall think in terms of records with the following fields.

POINTER	KEY	DATA

The operations performed on a linked list of records are

(i)   the search for a record with a given key,
(ii) the insertion of new record and
(iii) the deletion of an existing record.

We shall discuss the first two in detail; the third is left as an exercise. Since these are operations that are performed repeatedly we shall treat them as subroutines and draw the flow charts accordingly. Since there is no index or rule by which the address of a given record can be calculated, all the flow charts involve sequential processing. The loop in Figure 4–6 appears in various guises in all three routines. A variable X is used to hold the base address of the current record of the list. Initially its value is set to L, the base address of the first record of the list. The end of list has been reached if X equals ⊣. To move to the next record of the list, box 3 involves copying the base

76

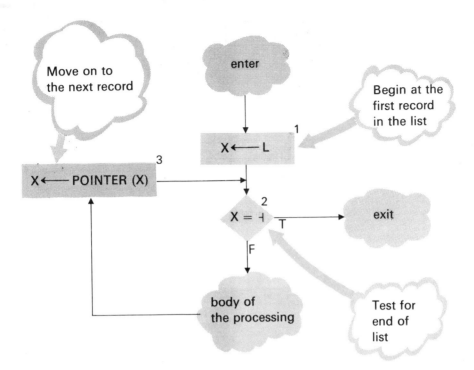

Figure 4-6   The basic search loop

address of the next record in sequence into X. This address is the contents of the pointer field of the current record for which the notation is

$$X \longleftarrow POINTER(X)$$

It is worth comparing Figure 4-6 with the flow chart box that we use for iteration (see page xi). This makes clear the difference between linked lists, in which the order is given by pointers, and a list held as a vector in which the order is given by using successive locations in store.

Search for a Record with a Given Key

Figure 4-6 is the basis of the search, but before it can be used in a subroutine, SEARCH, we need to be clear about what parameters must be used. They are as follows.

> L—the base address of the first record in the list.
> QUERY—the key of the required record.
> X—the base address of the required record.
> E—an error flag, set to 1 if QUERY is not in the list and to
> Ø if QUERY is in the list.

With these parameters, a flow chart for SEARCH is given in Figure 4-7.

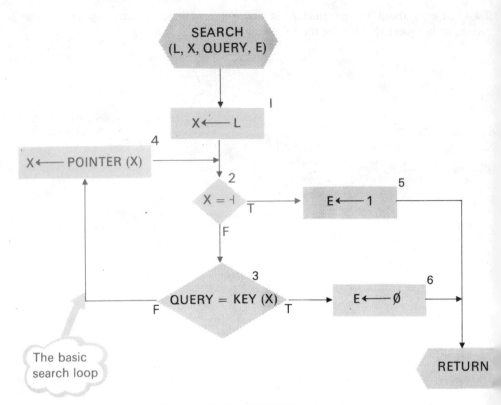

Figure 4–7   The SEARCH subroutine

This subroutine is very simple but does not make use of the fact that the list is sorted into a logical sequence. Question 1 at the end of this section suggests a possible refinement.

Insertion of a New Record

In the previous section we gave three steps that must be followed in order to insert a new record into a linked list.

(i)   Copy the new record into a free space.
(ii) Search for the right place to make the insertion.
(iii) Adjust pointers.

We shall look at each stage individually before giving the complete flow chart. But first, we need to give the parameters of the subroutine. These are

> NEW—the record to be inserted,
> L—the linked list,
> F—the free storage list,
> E—an error flag.

78

Two remarks about the parameter list are worth making at this stage. First, the record to be inserted will have the following fields.

NEW

KEY	DATA

When it has been inserted into the list it will have an extra field, which will hold a pointer. Second, we have included an error flag, E. It might be that there is no space

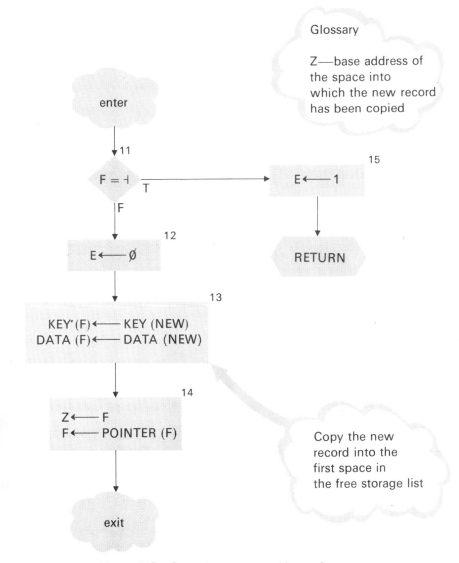

Figure 4–8   Copy the new record into a free space

for a new record. This would be the case if the free storage list were empty, indicated by the value F being ⊣. In Figure 4–8, the details of the first stage of the subroutine begins with a test for whether space for the new record can be found.

The second stage involves a search to find where in the logical sequence the record must be inserted. It is based on the same loop as was used in the SEARCH subroutine; the details are given in Figure 4–9.

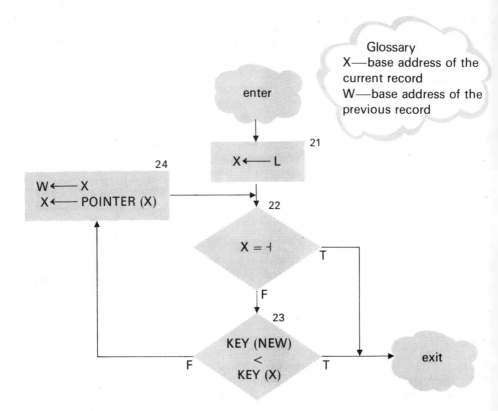

Figure 4–9   Search for the right place to make the insertion

As we work through the list to find where to insert NEW, we use two variables, W and X. The new record will be linked in sequence after the record with base address W and before the record with base address X. The last task is to adjust these pointers. Figure 4–10 shows what is involved in linking the record with base address Z between W and X in logical sequence. Only two pointers need to be altered; these are

POINTER(W) set to Z
POINTER(Z) set to X

The diagram shows the new record being inserted in the middle of the list. However, we have to be careful about an insertion at the beginning or end of the list. You should check that the Figure 4–11 accounts for all possibilities.

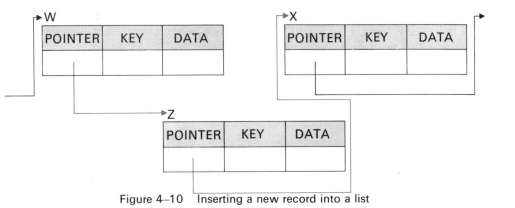

Figure 4–10   Inserting a new record into a list

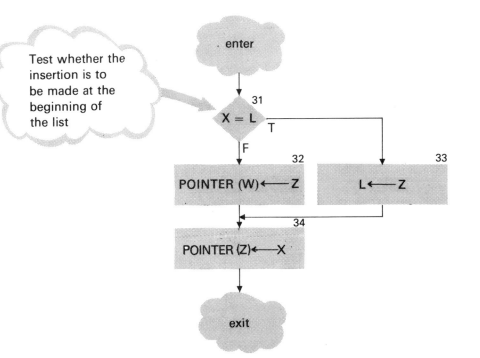

Figure 4–11   Adjust pointers

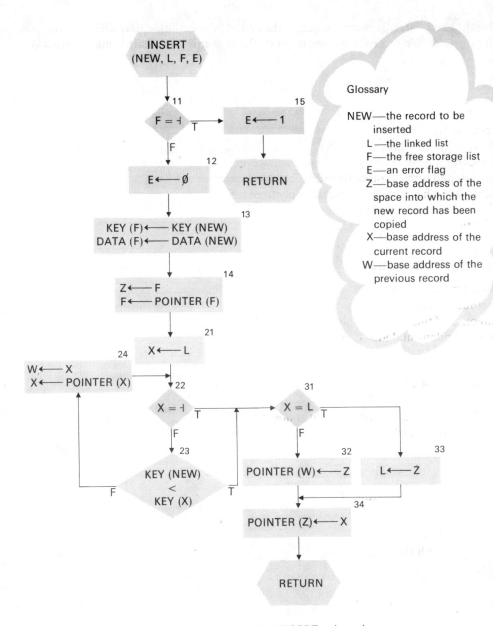

Figure 4–12   The INSERT subroutine

Putting these three fragments together the complete subroutine, INSERT, is given in Figure 4–12. We recommend you to work through this flow chart using Figure 4–3 as test data and insert a record with key DOG.

It would be wrong to get the impression that all linked lists are of the kind that we have been discussing in this chapter. Technically speaking we have only looked at one way linked lists; that is, lists with pointers only going one way. Depending on the processing to be carried out, it is sometimes useful to construct two way linked lists in which both NEXT and LAST fields are added to the basic information fields to complete the record in store. Lists can also have a hierarchy of pointers, some to sublists and some to other records. The possibilities are endless. The other simplification that we have made is to discuss only fixed length records. The main difficulty with creating a linked list of variable length records is how to organize the free storage list. The two basic techniques are to have a free storage list of

(i)   tiny free records and to take as many of these as are needed for each new record, or
(ii) variable length free records and take the best fitting space for each new record.

As so frequently is the case in computing there is no best method; you have to choose a method that fits the data and the processing in your problem. However, it is not the intention of this book to explore lists in great depth and so we have restricted ourselves to the fundamental idea of a one way linked list.

Questions 4.2

1. When searching a sorted list, it is not worth searching beyond the sort key of the required record.

   (i)   Modify the subroutine SEARCH to stop searching once past the required key.
   (ii) Discuss the advantages and disadvantages of the modification.

2. Construct a subroutine, DELETE, to delete a record with specified sort key from a linked list.

3. Modify the INSERT subroutine to check that the list does not already contain a record with the same sort key as the record to be inserted.

4. Consider the flight indicator board discussed in section 4–1. Periodically a program is run which deletes flights which have landed from the list and adds flights which are about to land. It may also change the details of flights that are already on the board. Draw a flow chart for this program.

4.3 AN EXAMPLE

Network planning is a technique for breaking down a complicated task into a number of activities so that a schedule of work can be drawn up. The simplest kind of network is a linear one.

To schedule this network is easy. For each activity we will be told its duration and the events at which it begins and ends. You can think of this information in terms of a record.

ACTIVITY$_J$

BEGIN	END	DUR

The purpose of the schedule is to work out the earliest possible date by which each event in the network can be completed and, then for each activity to print the day on which it must start. For example, the ACTIVITY data for the network we have given might be as follows.

ACTIVITY$_1$

BEGIN	END	DUR
1	2	3

ACTIVITY$_2$

BEGIN	END	DUR
2	3	7

To make up the schedule we need to be given some initial data. For instance, we have to know at which event to start, the starting day and at which event to stop. This again can be thought of as an input record.

INIT

STAGEA	DAY	STAGEZ
1	4Ø	3

With this input data the schedule is as follows.

```
ACTIVITY 1 MUST START ON DAY 4Ø
ACTIVITY 2 MUST START ON DAY 43
ALL ACTIVITIES ARE COMPLETE BY DAY 5Ø
```

As you can probably imagine, the flow chart to read this input data and to produce the corresponding output for a linear network is trivially simple, but networks are not always so straightforward. Figure 4–13 shows some of the complications that can be expected but gives little idea of the scale of things. In practice, a network might

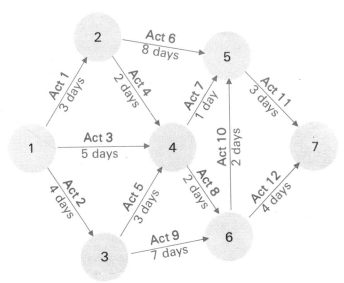

Figure 4–13   A scheduling network

consist of, say, ten thousand or more activities. Scheduling this kind of task can be a real headache.

The aim of scheduling is to calculate the earliest possible date by which each event can be reached. Basically the difficulty is that all activities that lead into an event must be completed before any activity that leads out of it can begin. For example, in Figure 4–13, event 4 must be reached before either of the activities that begin at event 4 can get under way. This means that we need to keep a record of the date by which event 4 can be completed. To calculate this date, we need to examine all the activities that immediately precede event 4 and, for each activity, calculate its

earliest beginning date + duration.

The earliest date for achieving event 4 is the *latest* of these.

To make this calculation the following information is needed for each event,

(i)   the earliest date by which this event can be achieved,
(ii) a list of all activities that precede this event.

85

Event number	Earliest date for achieving this event	List of immediately preceding activities
1	1	⊣
2	4	1,⊣
3	5	2,⊣
4	8	5, 4, 3,⊣
5	14	10, 7, 6,⊣
6	12	9, 8,⊣
7	17	12, 11,⊣

Figure 4–14   The information that must be held for each event in the network of Figure 4–13

For example, Figure 4–14 gives the information that must be held for each event of the network of Figure 4–13, assuming that event 1 begins on day 1. You can imagine this information being held in an EVENT record, one record for each event of the network. But, as you can see from Figure 4–14, if the information were to be held in this way the EVENT record would be variable length. An alternative arrangement is to store the list as a linked list.

The head of the linked list forms part of a record that is kept for every event of the network.

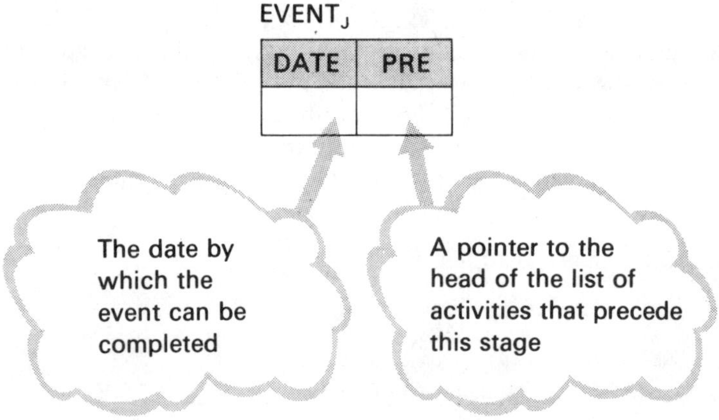

EVENT$_J$

DATE	PRE

The date by which the event can be completed

A pointer to the head of the list of activities that precede this stage

The list itself is stored by adding an extra field to every ACTIVITY record.

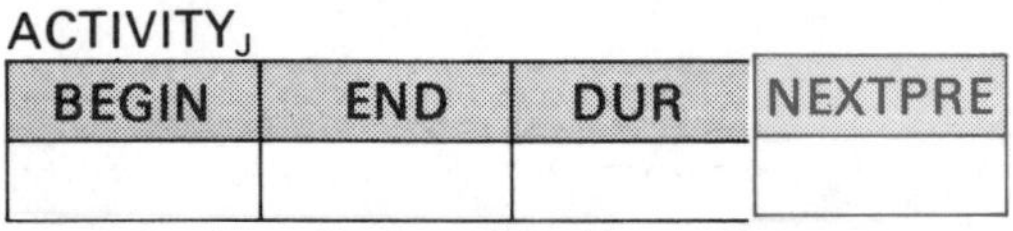

ACTIVITY$_J$

BEGIN	END	DUR	NEXTPRE

This holds a pointer to the next activity in the list of activities that precede the same event. Figure 4–15 gives the values of EVENT and ACTIVITY records for the network

EVENT		
	DATE	PRE
1	1	⊣
2	4	1
3	5	2
4	8	5
5	14	1∅
6	12	9
7	17	12

ACTIVITY				
	BEGIN	END	DUR	NEXTPRE
1	1	2	3	⊣
2	1	3	4	⊣
3	1	4	5	⊣
4	2	4	2	3
5	3	4	3	4
6	2	5	8	⊣
7	4	5	1	6
8	4	6	2	⊣
9	3	6	7	8
1∅	6	5	2	7
11	5	7	3	⊣
12	6	7	4	11

Event number   Activity number

Figure 4–15   The EVENT and ACTIVITY records for the network of Figure 14–13

of Figure 4–13. To see how the linked list is stored, start with the PRE field of event 4. This is a pointer to activity 5. The NEXTPRE field of activity 5, is a pointer to the next activity in the list, namely activity 4. The NEXTPRE field of activity 4 points to activity 3, and here the list ends because and NEXTPRE field of activity 3 is the end of list marker. These pointers indicate that the list of activities that precede event 4 is

5, 4 and 3,

as required.

Let us now look at what is involved in the scheduling algorithm. First, data about the network must be input. Then the earliest finish date must be worked out for each activity and event. Finally, the results have to be printed. Figure 4–16 is an outline flow chart of this process. At the input stage, the job of creating the linked lists has to be undertaken. This job might, of course, be carried out manually and included as part of the input list, but, with a large network this would be a considerable task, liable to error. It is better if the input routine creates the linked lists as the data about the activities alone is input. In cloud 4 of the outline the linked list of activities that precede event X must be updated. The problem is one of inserting a new record into linked list. The new record could be added to the bottom of the list but this involves threading down the list until its end is found. This is very inefficient compared with inserting the new record at the head of the list. For example, to insert a NEW record at the head of a linked list L only requires the following assignments.

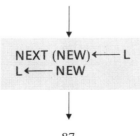

NEXT (NEW)⟵ L
L ⟵ NEW

87

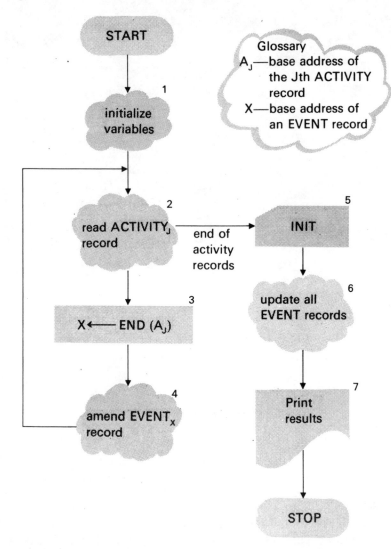

Figure 4–16   Outline of the scheduling algorithm

If you think about it, you will agree that there is no need to keep the activities within each list in any particular order. We should choose the most efficient method of creating the list. Accordingly, the details of clouds 2 and 4 of the outline are given in Figure 4–17. Compare the content of box 4∅ with the step given at the bottom of page 87. The pointer to the head of the list is

PRE(X)

and the pointer field in the new record is

NEXTPRE(A_J).

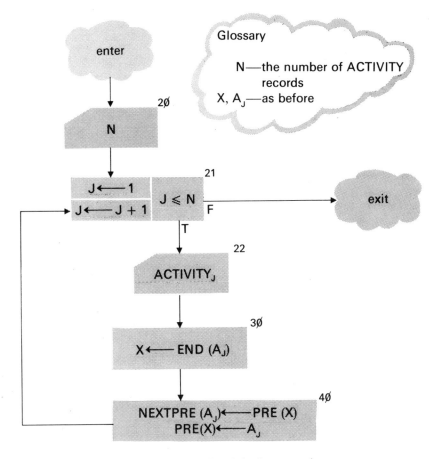

Figure 4–17   Details of the input routine

The next stage of the scheduling algorithm is to work out the earliest date by which each event can be finished. The basic idea here is to check an activity A, that begins at Y and ends at X. If

    date of Y + duration of the activity

is greater than the current date that we have for X then the date of X must be updated. This test must be made for every activity that immediately precedes event X. This basic idea is shown in Figure 4–18, but there are two important details that this flow chart misses. Firstly, event X can only be updated if there is one or more activity that precedes X. Secondly, it is possible that there will be an event before X that has not yet been updated. Event X can only be updated if all events that precede it have been updated. These two details have been incorporated with the basic idea to give the UPDATE subroutine of Figure 4–19. Our flow chart for UPDATE contains a programming technique that may be unfamiliar to you. In box 4, if there is a Y for which

    DATE(Y) = ⊣

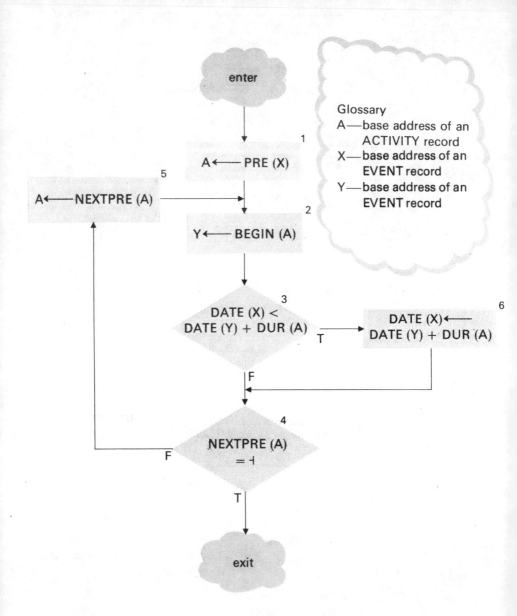

Figure 4–18　Basic idea of UPDATE

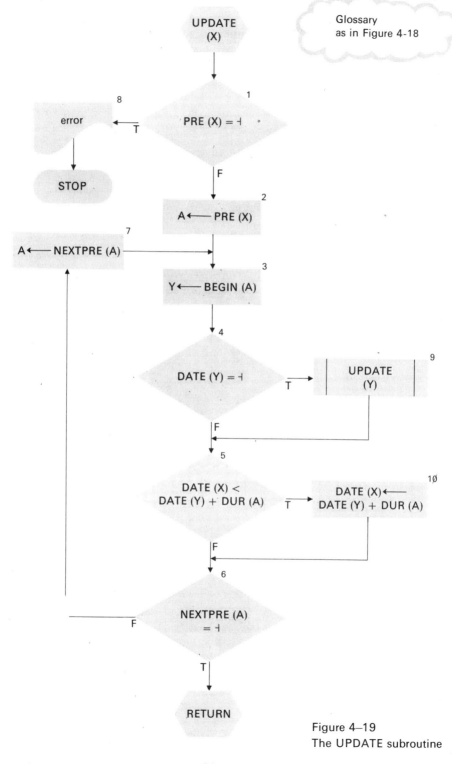

Figure 4–19
The UPDATE subroutine

91

the subroutine is called before it has been completed. The technique of a subroutine calling itself is called recursion and it is a particularly powerful tool for dealing with linked structures. Not all programming languages allow this technique, and in Chapter 5 we give a version of UPDATE which does not use recursion. In our example, using a recursive subroutine raises the interesting question of where to start the updating process. Rather than start from the beginning and work forwards, we can start at the end and let the subroutine work backwards as and when it needs to. This means that the details of the rest of the outline flow chart for the scheduling algorithm are relatively simple; they are given in Figure 4–20.

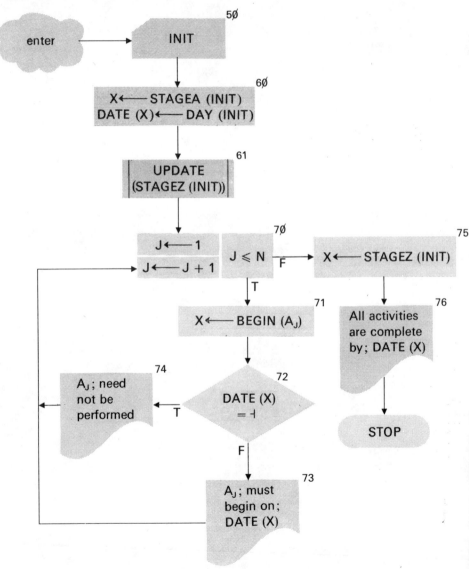

Figure 4–20   Details of the process and print routines

Apart from showing a use of linked lists, this example has a message we would not like you to miss. Frequently a flow chart can be broken down into three stages, input, process and output. The input and output stages should always be organized to be convenient to the users of the program. This may mean that time must be spent during the input routine to convert the data from a form that is convenient for the user to data structures that are needed for processing. Wherever possible you should make the input data as simple as possible. In this example the input data only refers to the activities that make up the links in the network. The records for the events and the linked lists of activities that precede each event are not input data but are built up by the input routine.

Questions 4.3

In our example of network analysis, we discussed only the situation of working out a schedule given a starting date. In practice, it would be normal to specify a finishing date as well and, for each activity to specify

(i) the date after which it could start, given the initial starting date,
(ii) the date by which it must start, if the finishing date is to be met.

This will show up how much slack there is in the network and which activities need careful watching. The second date is found by working backwards from the finishing date, using a process almost exactly the same as for working forwards from the start date.

1. What extra fields are needed for the

       ACTIVITY, EVENT and INIT records

   to allow for the additional processing.

2. Amend the UPDATE subroutine so that it can be used for forwards or backwards processing.

3. Draw a flow chart for this improved scheduling algorithm.

CHAPTER FIVE

OTHER DATA STRUCTURES

Stacks and Queues

Trees

A Discussion

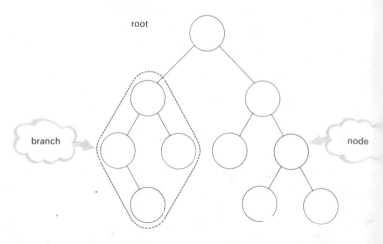

5.1 STACKS AND QUEUES

A particularly easy type of list to process is one in which all insertions and deletions are made at an end of the list. This may be because the records have no particular sequence and can be processed in any order that is convenient. For example, in Chapter 4 the sequence of the records in the free storage list was unimportant and so we always worked from one end, as you would with a stack of plates. Alternatively, the processing may require records to be processed in the order in which they joined the list, as in a canteen queue.

Stacks

Look back at the flow chart that we drew to instruct a man how to find his way through a maze. It is given in Figure 1–4, page 7, and, although representing an acceptable first attempt it has drawbacks. Not the least of these is that the man is guided up every blind alley that the procedure searches. For instance, suppose that the current position is printed as the pair

     J, K

where J and K are indexes of M, the matrix which represents the maze.

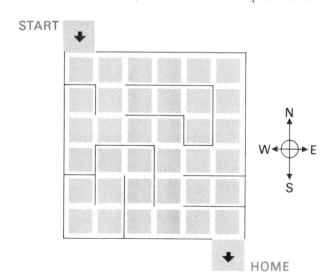

The flow chart in Figure 1–3 produces the following output list for this maze.

1, 1   1, 2   2, 2   3, 2   3, 1   2, 1   3, 1   4, 1   3, 1   3, 2   3, 3   . . .

A blind alley

It would be an improvement if the route did not include walks up these blind alleys. A technique that can be used here is to suppose that, instead of being printed, the current position is entered in an array S, the whole to be printed once HOME is reached. A pointer, P, can be kept to show where in S the current position has been entered. Used in this way, S is a stack.

S

S_1	S_2	S_3	S_4	S_5	S_6		
1, 1	1, 2	2, 2	3, 2	3, 1			

P points to the top of the stack.

To enter the current position into S the assignments

$$P \longleftarrow P + 1$$

$$S_P \longleftarrow (J, K)$$

are sufficient but before they are made a test is needed to find whether an alley is being searched. The test is remarkably simple (see Figure 5–1). Using this technique the stack S grows and collapses as follows.

1, 1

1, 1   1, 2

1, 1   1, 2   2, 2

1, 1   1, 2   2, 2   3, 2

1, 1   1, 2   2, 2   3, 2   3, 1

1, 1   1, 2   2, 2   3, 2   3, 1   2, 1

1, 1   1, 2   2, 2   3, 2   3, 1

1, 1   1, 2   2, 2   3, 2   3, 1   4, 1

1, 1   1, 2   2, 2   3, 2   3, 1

1, 1   1, 2   2, 2   3, 2

1, 1   1, 2   2, 2   3, 2   3, 3   and so on.

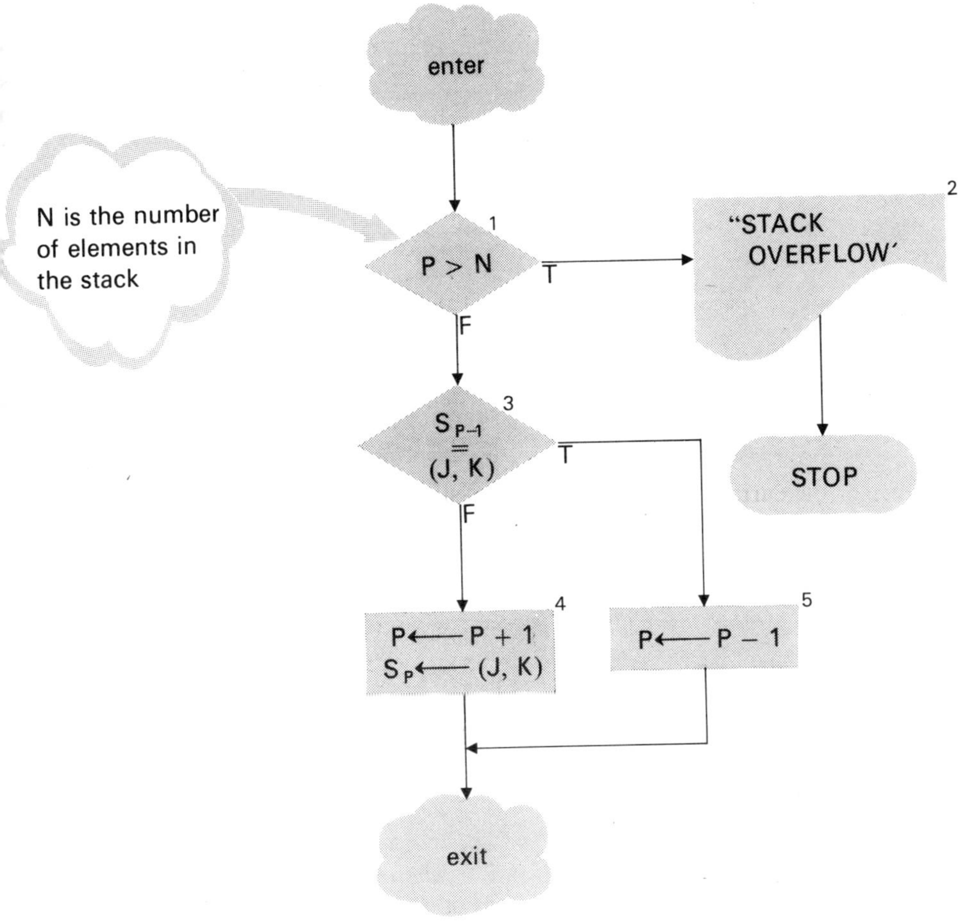

enter

N is the number
of elements in
the stack

P > N   1   T → "STACK
                    OVERFLOW"   2

F

S_{P-1}
$=$
(J, K)   3   T

F

STOP

P ← P + 1
S_P ← (J, K)   4

P ← P – 1   5

exit

Figure 5–1   Test for a blind alley

As you can see, new items are always added to the one end of the list and deletions are always made from that end. This is how stacks are used in processing. Two basic ingredients are involved,

(i)   a list in which the items are stacked,
(ii) a pointer to the top of the stack.

Something to watch out for if you are using a stack is overflow. For example, you might store the items in a vector and have as pointer the index of the top item. Remember that a vector is fixed in size and that the stack might grow so large as to fill the available space. A test like the one in Figure 5-1 is often needed.

We have only discussed stacks of single items of information, but stacks can also be used to store records. If the records are of fixed length, they can be held in successive locations, either in store or in an array. A stack pointer points to the top of the stack; the stack itself can be referred to by its base address (see Figure 5-2).

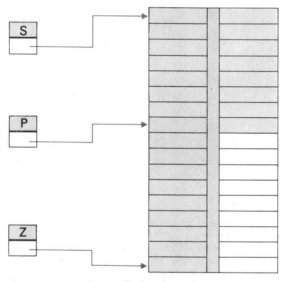

Figure 5-2   A stack

For each record inserted, the pointer will be increased; for each record deleted, the pointer will be decreased. The stack is full when P = Z and empty when P = S. As is so often the case, fixed length records present few difficulties.

Stacks are especially valuable for holding variable length records, since at any given moment the available storage space is divided into two sections. The first is solid with records and the second is completely empty; insertions and deletions are always at the same end and do not change this situation. Using a stack avoids the fragmentation of store that occurs if insertions and deletions of variable length records are allowed anywhere which often results in there being no area large enough for a long record even though the available space is far from full (see Figure 5-3).

We now pose you the problem of how to store a stack of variable length records. As with many problems of data storage there is no fixed solution. You might use

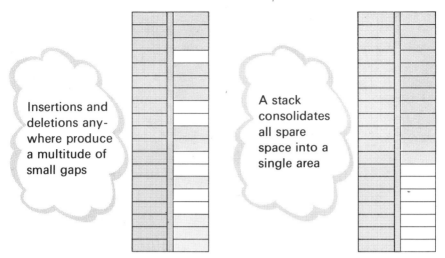

Figure 5-3   Storage of variable length records

separators and have the pointer point to the first free location. Or you might use length fields. If you do, you will find that the best arrangement is to have the length field as the last field of the record (see Figure 5-4). Using separators or length fields are both satisfactory. It is up to you which you use.

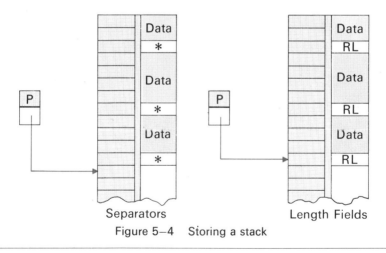

Separators   Length Fields

Figure 5-4   Storing a stack

Example

To construct a subroutine to insert a new variable length record into a stack, suppose that the stack is stored with the final field of each record a length field and that the pointer points to the length field of the top record on the stack.

The new record will have base address **NEW**.

When it is stored in the stack we need another field.

DATA	RL

and, assuming that this field can be held in one location, its value is

length (NEW) + 1

The subroutine begins with a test for overflow (see Figure 5–5).

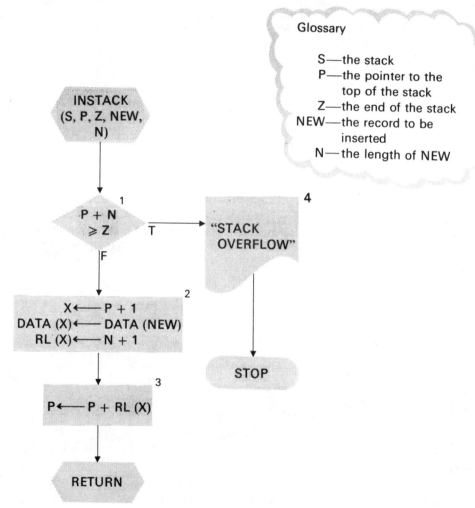

Figure 5–5   The INSTACK subroutine

Stacks are frequently used within large programs to keep track of the processing. For example, examine the UPDATE flow chart in Figure 4–19. This is a recursive subroutine, but many programming languages do not provide for recursion. Using a stack, the subroutine can be modified to avoid recursion. This is shown in Figure 5–6.

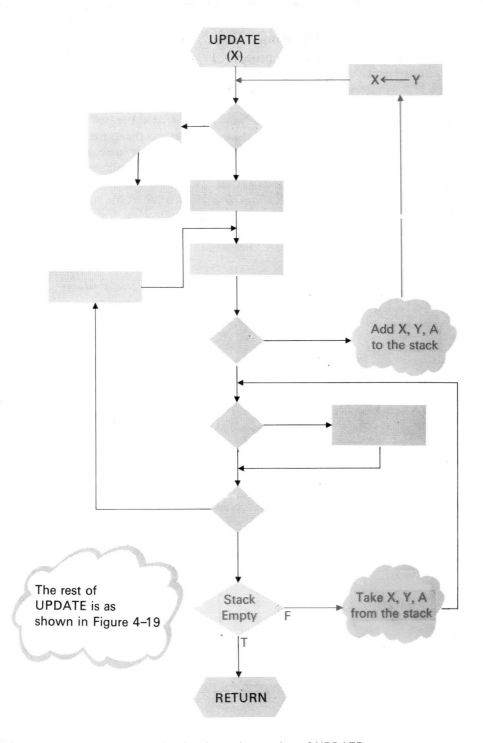

Figure 5–6   An alternative version of UPDATE

101

Queues

Queues are used to hold data that is processed in the order of its arrival. The natural way to store a queue is to hold all records in a continuous area, adding new records at one end and deleting records from the other. In a canteen queue, when somebody leaves the head of the queue everybody behind him moves up one place. If this were mirrored in store, the head of the queue would always be at the base address of the locations and every time a deletion was made every item in the queue would have to be moved up one location. For long queues, this is obviously inefficient and so it is normal to move the position of the head of the queue by adjusting a pointer rather than moving every item in the queue. The effect of this is that the position of the queue moves through store. Since the locations allocated to the queue must be fixed in number, when the queue reaches the end of the space allocated, it starts again at the beginning. Pointers are required for the head and tail of the queue, and for the base address and last location of the space allocated to it. These points are illustrated in Figure 5–7.

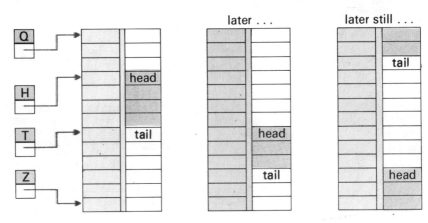

Figure 5–7   Storing a queue

If the records are of fixed length they can be held as a one dimensional array. For a queue of variable length records a simple method of storage is to have the first field a length field (unlike stacks where the last field is used). The pointer to the head of the queue points to the record that has been in the queue longest and the pointer to the tail points to the first free location. Adding a record to this kind of queue is complicated by the need for a test for when to jump back to the beginning of the allocated space, but basically the routine has the following assignments at its core.

$$RL(T) \longleftarrow N + 1$$
$$DATA(T) \longleftarrow DATA(NEW)$$
$$T \longleftarrow T + RL(T)$$

N is the length
of the new
record

102

We have shown you insertion for a stack; this time we examine the details of deletion.

Example

Before constructing a subroutine OUTQ to delete a record from a queue of variable length records, the problem of wasted space at the end of the locations must be settled. We shall use the following conventions.

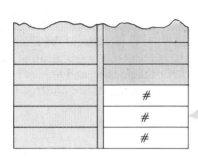

If there is insufficient space to hold a complete record, the wasteland is filled with special characters

The subroutine tests whether the wasteland has been reached. The flow chart is given in Figure 5–8, on the next page.

Our description of stacks and queues gives you little insight into their application. Probably the most useful are stacks, especially when keeping track of a complicated sequence of operations. Frequently a stage is reached in the execution of a program when several possibilities have to be looked at. The program can look at only one at a time, but makes a note of the others to remind itself to look at the others later. This note can take the form of a record added to a stack. Queues are sometimes needed in simulation programs or real time situations. For instance, items might need to be serviced in the order in which they are input. Another possible misconception that you could get from this section is to imagine that stacks and queues always use contiguous areas of store. This is the case when the logical structure of a stack or queue is mirrored in the physical structure of their storage. However, it is common to use the logical structure for processing and to use the physical structure of a linked list for storage. This is how the free storage list was organized in the previous chapter. Finally, we have followed the traditional approach of discussing stacks and queues at the same time. Logically, they are similar, but you will find that they have very different applications.

Questions 5.1

1. (i)   Why is the RL field of a variable length record held in a stack best held at the end of the record?

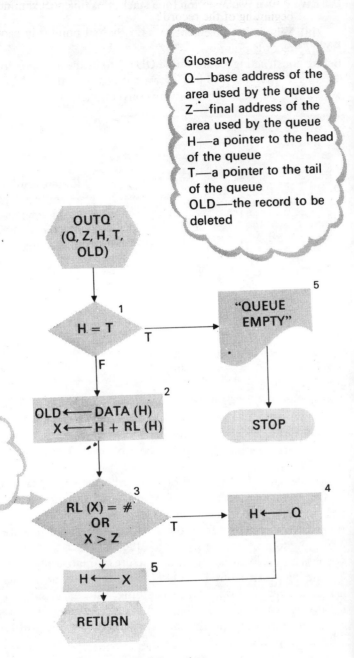

Glossary
Q—base address of the area used by the queue
Z—final address of the area used by the queue
H—a pointer to the head of the queue
T—a pointer to the tail of the queue
OLD—the record to be deleted

OUTQ
(Q, Z, H, T, OLD)

H = T   1

T → "QUEUE EMPTY"   5

→ STOP

F

OLD ← DATA (H)
X ← H + RL (H)   2

Test whether
wasteland or
end of area
has been reached.

RL (X) = #
OR
X > Z   3

T → H ← Q   4

H ← X   5

RETURN

Figure 5–8   The OUTQ subroutine

104

(ii) Why is the RL field of a variable length record held in a queue best held at the beginning of the record?

(iii) Why is it convenient to have the tail pointer in a queue of variable length records pointing to the first free location?

2. Variable length records are held in a queue. Construct a subroutine INQUEUE to insert a new record into the queue.

3. Take a critical look at your solution to Question 1 on page 10, in the light of the discussion at the beginning of this section. What amendments are needed to improve your solution?

5.2 TREES

Most of the data structures studied so far have been linear. That is, given any particular record there is one that immediately precedes it and the one that immediately follows it, except for the first or the last items.

The problem of converting such structures into a form that can be stored is relatively straightforward, but unfortunately information does not always occur in this convenient form and it is often the case that records are linked by more than one backward and one forward link.

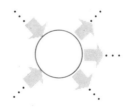

Since a structure like this exhibits no natural order in which to store the records, we are almost forced to store them in a sequence other than the order in which they are processed. The links are then represented by pointers and each record has as many pointers as there are links. These structures are called nonlinear, and in this section we shall consider one such nonlinear structure, a tree. It is so called because its pictorial representation looks like a family tree, and much of the other terminology used in the description of tree structures—parent, branch, etc.—is derived in the same way. Figure 5–9 gives a summary of the terminology that we shall use.

In Figure 5–9, each node of the tree has no more than two descendants; it is called a binary tree. At each node of the tree imagine the key of a record. In addition to the key and other data fields, there are three pointers that can be associated with each

105

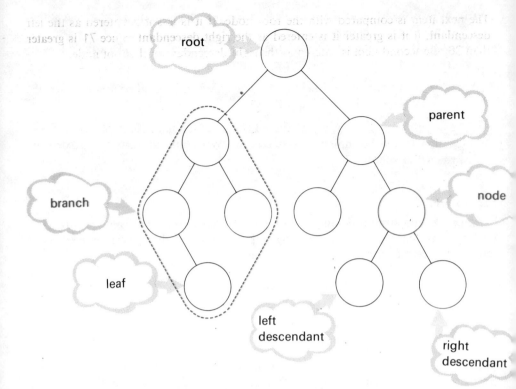

Figure 5–9   Some terminology used with trees

node, one to the left descendant, one to the right descendant and one to the parent. This information can be held in the fields of a record,

KEY	LEFT	RIGHT	PARENT	Other data

but often the processing does not demand that all three pointers be stored.

An interesting application of binary trees is in sorting data. The first part of the process is to construct a sort tree, which we shall discuss now; later we show how to retrieve information from this kind of tree.

Example

Consider the following list of numbers.

36, 71, 16, 27, 92, 13, 11, 46, 24, 85.

The first item in the list is entered at the root node.

The next item is compared with the root node. If it is less it is entered as the left descendant, if it is greater it is entered as the right descendant. Since 71 is greater than 36, the second item is entered as the right descendant of the root node.

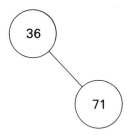

The next item is also compared with the root node and, being less than 36, it is entered as the left descendant.

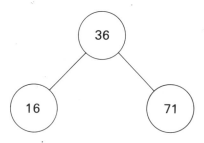

The next item is again compared with the root node. It is less than 36, but, since there is already a left descendant it cannot be entered there. Instead, 27 is compared with the left descendant and, since 27 is greater than 16, it is entered as the right descendant of 16.

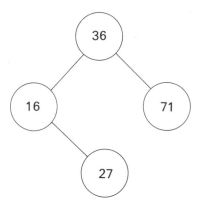

This process is repeated for all subsequent items in the list. Finally, the complete sort tree for this list is given in Figure 5–10(a). Notice that in this diagram the value at every node is greater than its left descendant and less than its right descendant.

Suppose that we now add the value 48 to the tree. To find where to put it we start at the root node.

48 > 36 and so go to the right descendant of 36.
48 < 71 and so go to the left descendant of 71.
48 > 46 and so add 48 as the right descendant of 46.

The new sort tree is given in Figure 5–10(b).

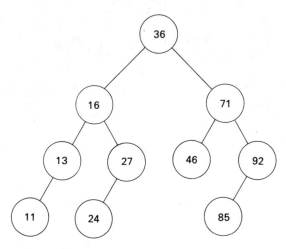

(a) The sort tree for the list 36, 71, 16, 27, 92, 13, 11, 46, 24, 85

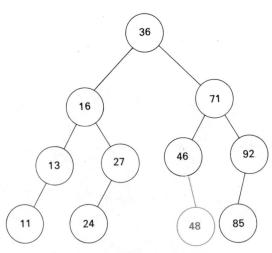

(b) Adding the value 48 to the tree

Figure 5–10   An example of a sort tree

108

The steps given in the above example are similar to the steps for inserting an item into a linked list. With a linked list there is only one possible next record and so the instruction to go to the next record is easy to write in coded form. It is as follows.

X ⟵ NEXT(X)

With a binary tree there are two possible next records and the step to the next record needs a test to find which must be chosen. The details are as follows.

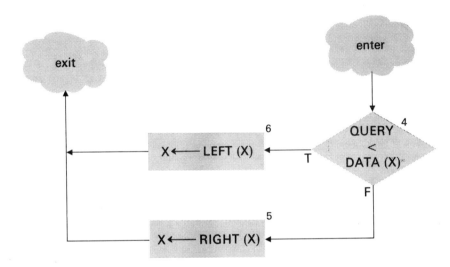

Apart from these instructions, the flow chart of a subroutine to search a tree for a record with a given KEY is the same as the one to search a linked list. You should compare flow chart in Figure 5–11 with the one given in Figure 4–7, page 78. In the SEARCH subroutine of Figure 5–11 the PARENT field is never used. There are in fact quite a number of processes that can be performed on trees without the PARENT field ever being needed and, if these are the only processes required, the records used to store the tree need only have the following fields.

KEY	LEFT	RIGHT	Other data

The great advantage of linked lists is that insertions and deletions can be made without disturbing the physical position of any other records in store. This advantage is shared by all linked structures such as lists or trees. Basically, the procedure for insertion is as follows.

Take space from a free storage list, find where to make the insertion and alter pointers as necessary.

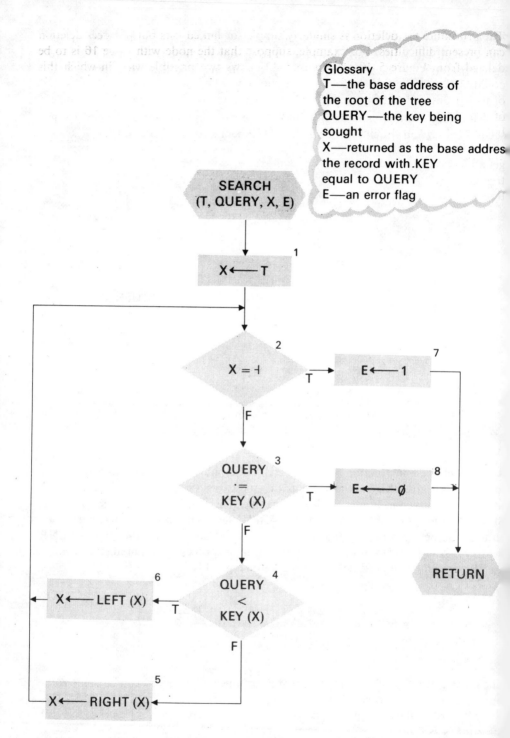

Figure 5–11   The SEARCH subroutine

110

The procedure for deletion is similarly simple for linked lists but for trees deletion can present difficulties. For example, suppose that the node with value 16 is to be deleted from Figure 5–10(a). Figure 5–12 shows two possible ways in which this could be done. The first way is to hang the right hand branch of 16 onto the right of its left descendant; the second way is to hang the left hand branch onto the left of its right descendant. There is nothing to choose between either of these methods, but they do illustrate an important property of trees. Trees are efficient to search only if they are fairly well balanced. With random data you can reasonably expect to get a balanced tree, but if either of the above ways of deleting a record are used the tree can become unbalanced quite quickly. Redraw Figure 15–12(b) as a proper tree and you will see what we mean. Possibly the simplest way to overcome this

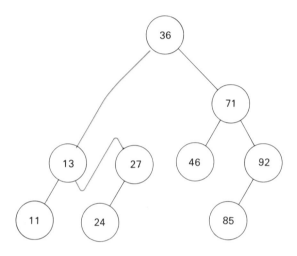

(a) Hanging the right descendants onto the left descendant

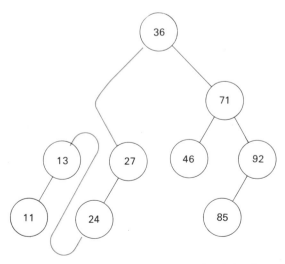

(b) Hanging the left descendants onto the right descendant

Figure 5–12   Two methods of deletion

111

difficulty of balance is to leave the pointer fields of a deleted record intact but to make a note that the record has been deleted (see Figure 5–13). This means that during processing a tree might contain a number of dummy records that have been left behind by previous deletions. However, there is always the chance that the dummy spaces can be refilled by subsequent insertions.

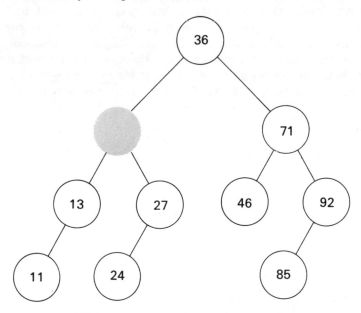

Figure 5–13   Another method of deletion

This has implications for the routine to insert a record into a tree that we take up in the next section, but it means that deleting a record is particularly simple. As Figure 5–14 shows, the routine for deletion is much the same as the SEARCH subroutine. In the DELETE subroutine each record of the tree has an extra field which is set to ∅ if the record has not been deleted, but which is set to 1 if the record has been deleted.

KEY	LEFT	RIGHT	DEL	Other data

This field shows
whether the record
has been deleted

112

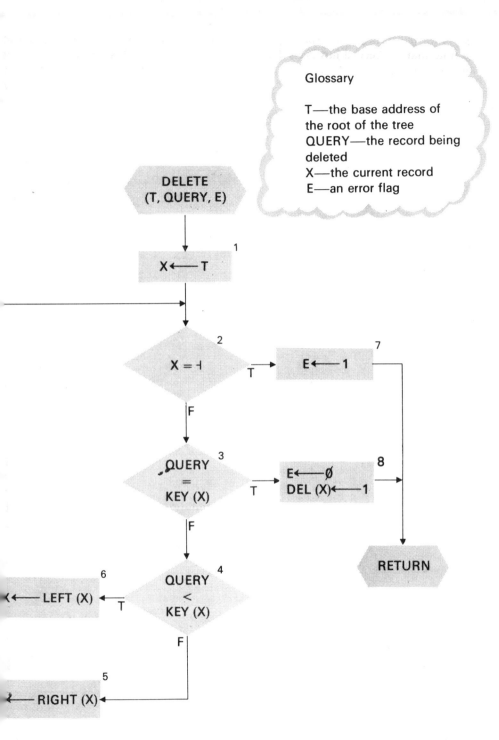

Figure 5–14   The DELETE subroutine

113

Finally, not all trees are binary trees. For instance, it is possible for a node to have more than two descendants.

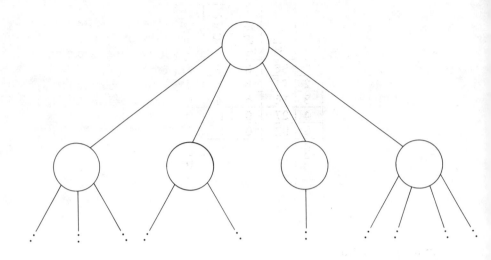

Trees of this kind present a problem of storage. If a note were kept of each descendant of a given node, the records used to store the tree would be variable length. One solution to this difficulty is to use different pointers. For each node two pointers are kept, one to its left most descendant, the other to its right hand neighbour.

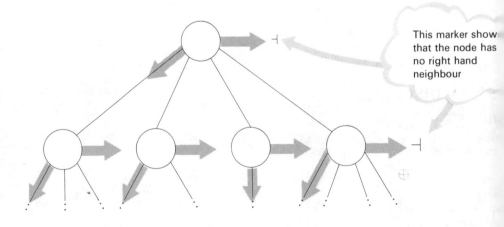

This marker shows that the node has no right hand neighbour

Using this method of storage a complicated tree structure is broken down into a binary tree. This has the advantage that the algorithms for processing binary trees often apply to the more complex structures.

Questions 5.2

1. The sort tree of Figure 5–10(a) can be stored in an array as follows.

	KEY	LEFT	RIGHT	DEL
1	36	3	2	Ø
2	71	8	5	Ø
3	16	6	4	Ø
4	27	9	⊣	Ø
5	92	1Ø	⊣	Ø
6	13	7	⊣	Ø
7	11	⊣	⊣	Ø
8	46	⊣	⊣	Ø
9	24	⊣	⊣	Ø
1Ø	85	⊣	⊣	Ø

Assuming that deletions are made in the manner of Figure 5–14, what alterations have to be made to

(i)   insert a new record with key 51 into the sort tree,
(ii) delete first the record with key 11 and then the record with key 16?

2. (i)   What alterations have to be made to the SEARCH subroutine to check that the record being sought has not been previously deleted.
   (ii) What assumption has been made about the keys of the records stored in the tree for the DELETE subroutine to work?

3. Construct a subroutine NEXTNODE which, given the base address of a record in a binary sort tree, returns the base address of the next record in sort sequence. Assume that no records have been deleted.

5.3   A DISCUSSION

In this and the last two chapters you have seen quite a number of data structures. We began the discussion with some general remarks, one of which is so important that we feel that it is worth repeating.

> *"The information must therefore be structured in a way that preserves the links needed for processing and in a way that can be successfully held in store."*

To complete the discussion we shall look at a typical problem and will try to show you how to choose the best data structure for processing and for storage.

The Problem

Imagine that a list of records is to be held in store and that during processing the list will be constantly searched and updated by deleting old records and inserting new ones.

Choosing a Data Structure

There are a number of ways of storing records. Possibly the simplest method is to use separators or length fields. This means that the links between records are implied by using successive locations in store.

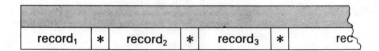

But how suitable is this method for the processing required in the problem? Searching for a record with a given key needs a sequential search which is not particularly efficient. The efficiency of the search can be improved if the list is maintained in the order of sort keys. In fact, if there were no insertions or deletions to be made, the structure of an ordered list using separators or length fields might be acceptable—at least it has the benefit of simplicity. However, if the records were large the difficulties of moving records up and down the space reserved for them would probably outweigh any advantages that mere simplicity has to offer.

An effective way of storing a list of records that has to be searched is to use hash coding. In hash coding a first guess at the location of a record in store is calculated from its key and a sequential search is used from there on.

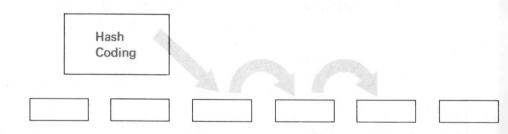

Hash coding is a valuable technique, well worth considering for our problem. In order to be effective, the sequential search has to be kept reasonably short. This usually means that about 20 per cent more space than will ever be filled needs to be made available. If space is at a premium this may be too large an overhead to be acceptable.

There is also a rather severe drawback with hash coding. Although insertions can be made at any time, deletions can be a real headache. Basically hash coding is most effective if a list of records is set up at the start of processing and if no subsequent changes are made to the list.

To cope with some of the processing demands of the problem we could try some kind of linked structure. Here, the logical order of the records is indicated by pointers and not dictated by the physical order in which they are stored.

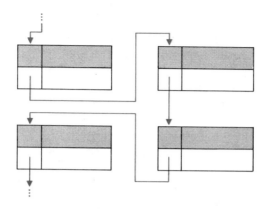

Insertions and deletions can be made without altering the physical position of other records in the list. However there is still the problem of searching the list to find a record with a given key. For a large number of records it is often worth giving up a certain amount of storage space to hold the keys in a way that can be searched efficiently. A simple but remarkably effective method of searching an ordered list is the binary search—which we expect you have met before. To hold a copy of the keys in an ordered list while the complete records were held in a linked list would require a two dimensional array in which

$A_{1,J}$ is the key of the Jth record,

$A_{2,J}$ is a pointer giving the base address of the Jth record.

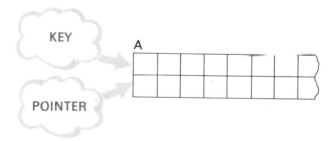

Using an array in this way is a simple extension of the concept of an access vector. Certainly the speed of searching is improved if an access vector is used, but, as we noted at the beginning of Chapter 4, insertions and deletions cause a problem (see Figure 4–1). If possible we ought to set up the means of access as a linked structure, that can be searched efficiently. A natural choice is to use a sort tree as an index to the linked list. This kind of tree is called a tree index. Since this is a structure that meets almost all the requirements of the processing without making excessive demands on storage space, it is the one that we shall use for the problem on hand.

To sum up, we suggest that the records be held as a linked list and that a copy of the keys be entered in a tree index.

Details of Storage

Having decided on which data structures to use the next step is to look a bit more closely at what form the various structures will take. First, for the linked list of data records a slightly more sophisticated list than the simple one way linked list discussed in Chapter 4 is needed. For example, to delete a record, the tree index is searched to find its base address. To make the deletion the pointer from the previous record in the list must be altered. Thus two pointers are needed for each record in the list.

PRE	NEXT	Other data

To make the deletion, the NEXT field of the previous record must be set to the base address of the next record in the list.

The following assignments carry out these steps.

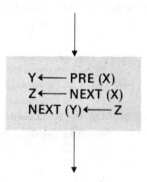

$$Y \longleftarrow PRE\ (X)$$
$$Z \longleftarrow NEXT\ (X)$$
$$NEXT\ (Y) \longleftarrow Z$$

In this linked list each record has two pointers, one to the previous record and one to the next record. This is an example of a two-way linked list.

The records used for the tree index have the following fields.

KEY—the key of the record
POINTER—a pointer to the base address of the record
LEFT— a pointer to the left descendant
RIGHT—a pointer to the right descendant
DEL—a marker to show whether the record has been deleted.

Even though there are five fields, none need occupy more than one location in store and so the index is not likely to occupy a very large proportion of the available space.

Initially the storage space for data will be divided into two areas, one for the linked list of data records and the other for the tree index. Since both areas will be used for linked structures they must first be organized as free storage lists. In Chapter 4 we suggested that a free storage list is easy to handle if it is held as a stack. This requires only one pointer to the top of the stack. Space for insertions is always taken from the top of the stack and space released by a deleted record is also returned to the top of the stack. You may have noticed that records deleted from the tree index do not release any spare space since they are left behind to preserve the balance of the tree. This is not an important point but it might cause trouble later on.

The Processing

Now that the details of data storage have been decided we can look in more detail at the processing. The routines to insert and delete data records into the linked list are relatively straightforward and we have already discussed routines to search the tree index (see Figure 5–11 with amendments suggested in Question 5.2.2) and to delete a record from the tree index (see Figure 5–14). To complete the picture, let us look at the problem of inserting a new record into the tree index. In many ways this routine is similar to the INSERT subroutine of Figure 4–11 but the problem of coping with deleted records presents an interesting challenge. An outline flow chart of the procedure for insertion is given in Figure 5–15. Steps 1 and 2 of the outline flow chart are a bit more complicated than a simple search because, to make the insertion, a note must be kept of whether the current node is the right or left descendant of its parent. This can be done by means of a variable A which is set to

$\emptyset$—insertion to be made at the root node,
1—insertion to be made as a left descendant,
2—insertion to be made as a right descendant.

Using A in this way, the details of steps 1 and 2 of the outline are given in Figure 5–16. If the search reveals that the new record is to be inserted as a leaf of the tree, space has to be taken from the free storage list to accommodate it. Thus the details of step 5 of the outline begin by creating a new record out of the first free record in the free storage list. Testing the value of A will tell whether the new record is to be the root or the left or right descendant of its parent. These steps are included in Figure 5–17. Alternatively it might be possible to insert the new record into the place of one that has been deleted—see steps 3 and 4 of the outline flow chart in Figure 5–15. For this replacement to be made, the key of the new record must be sandwiched between the keys of the left and right branches of the deleted record.

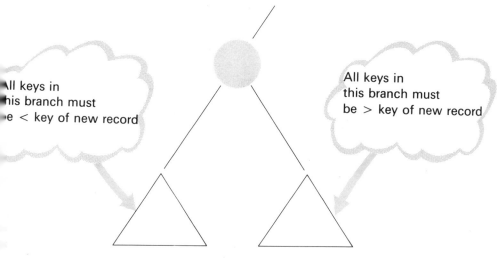

All keys in this branch must be < key of new record

All keys in this branch must be > key of new record

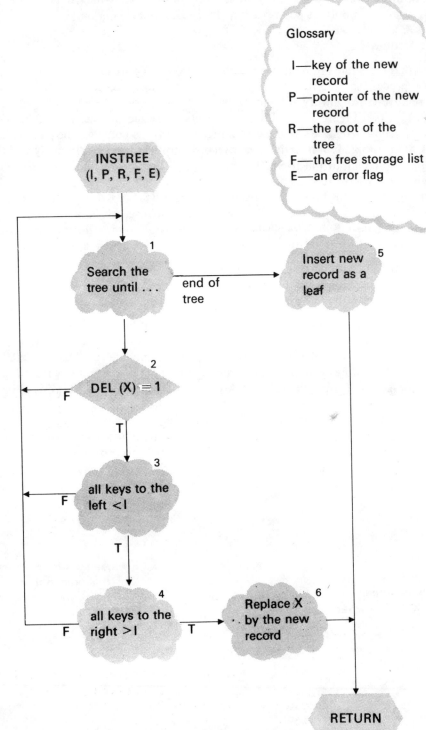

Figure 5-15   Outline flow chart for INSTREE subroutine

120

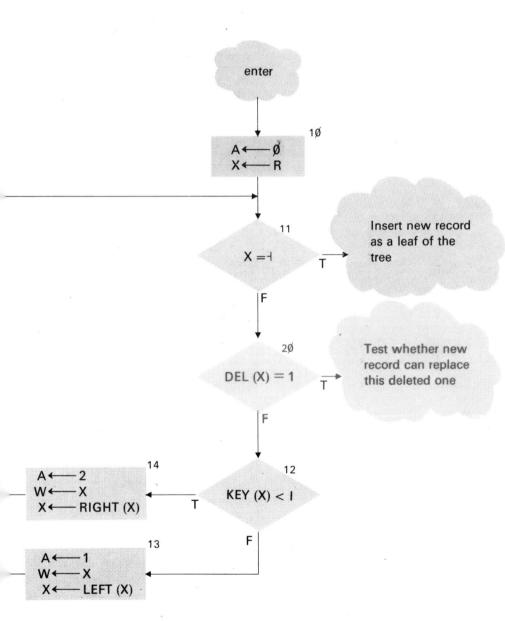

Figure 5–16   Steps 1 and 2 of INSTREE

121

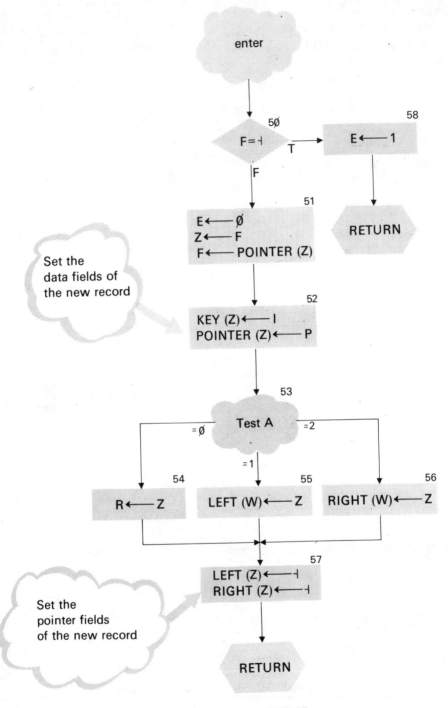

Figure 5-17   Step 5 of INSTREE

122

At first sight you might think that to make this test involved testing every node of each of the branches. Fortunately this is not the case. All that has to be found is the largest key in the left branch or the smallest key in the right branch. A simple property of sort trees can be used, one that is also true for any branch of a tree. To see the property for yourself, try the following example.

Example

Where on the following tree would you expect to find the largest key and where the smallest key?

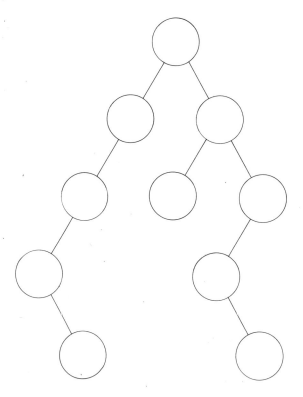

To find the smallest you go as far to the left as possible; to find the largest you go as far to the right as possible.

We have used this property to produce the details of steps 3 and 4 of the outline. These, as well as the details for step 6 of the outline are given in Figure 5–18. Notice how the steps are simplified by an initial test to find out whether it is the left or the right branch that needs to be searched—see box 15. We shall leave our discussion of the processing here. There are many more details that you might like to look at for yourself.

In a section as brief as this we have not tried to cover all aspects of the problem that we began with. Our aim has been to show you some of the steps in solving a problem

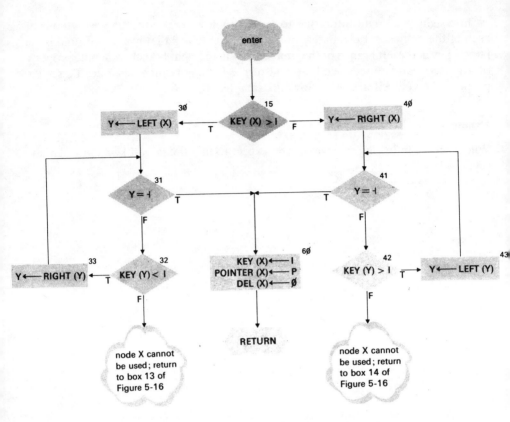

Figure 5–18   Steps 3, 4 and 6 of INSTREE

both at the general level of choosing an appropriate data structure and at the detailed level of a flow chart for one of the key processes. Unfortunately there is no recipe for immediate success at problem solving. The best training is to practise; the best attitude is an open mind. But still you might not succeed!

CHAPTER SIX

FURTHER LOW LEVEL PROGRAMMING

The Index Register

Indirect Addressing

Subroutines

Assembly Code

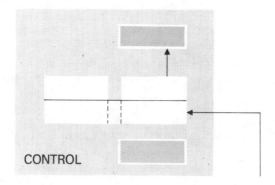

CONTROL

6.1 THE INDEX REGISTER

In Chapter 2 we introduced a number of machine instructions, sufficient to write simple algorithms, but the instruction set of a modern computer is much larger than suggested in that chapter. Many of the extra instructions are natural extensions of those seen already: further arithmetic instructions, floating point arithmetic, extra branch instructions, etc. Not yet mentioned are the kind of machine instructions that are used for processing indexed variables. To process a one-dimensional array a program needs to be able to access the address given by

BASE ADDRESS + INDEX − 1.

Since this calculation is being made all the time, most computers provide a special hardware facility called an index register. You will remember that a machine instruction is represented as follows.

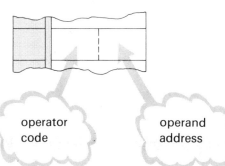

Although not mentioned in Chapter 2, the bits which give the operand are divided as follows.

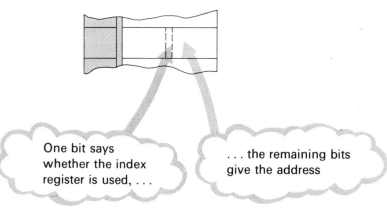

The index bit says whether the index register is used. It is set as follows.

    ∅—the register is not used,
    1—the register is used.

When writing instructions which use the index register, the number 1 is put between the operator and the operand. For example, the instructions

ADD(1) 7ØØ   or   ADD(1) B

specify the use of the index register. You will remember that, before an instruction is executed, it is fetched from store into the instruction register, where it is decoded. The decoding of an instruction which uses the index register is slightly more complicated than usual in that the decoded operand address is the sum of the contents of the index register and the address part of the instruction (see Figure 6–1).

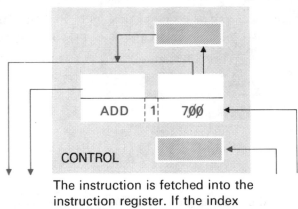

The instruction is fetched into the instruction register. If the index register currently has the value 48, ...

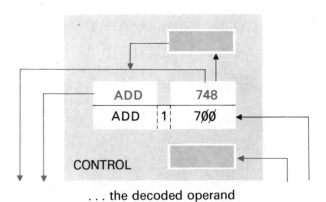

... the decoded operand will have the value 748.

Figure 6–1   The index register

Clearly some way of changing the value in the index register is needed. The way th this is done varies very much from computer to computer. Some have a full range arithmetic instructions which operate on the index register; some computers eve provide several registers. But even with very few instructions for changing its conten the index register gives great flexibility. We shall only introduce one such instructio since it is quite sufficient for our purposes.

The instruction to load a number into the index register has operator code LIR. Here are some examples.

Machine Instructions		Assembly Code	
LIR	6Ø	LIR	J1
LIR	16	LIR	"1"
LIR(1)	7ØØ	LIR(1)	B

The third example uses the index register. When it is decoded the current content of the index register is added to the address of B to give a new address. On execution of the instruction the content of the new location is then loaded into the index register.

To see how the index register is used to process one dimensional arrays, suppose that a flow chart contains the following assignment.

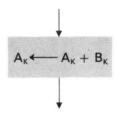

$$A_K \longleftarrow A_K + B_K$$

To translate this assignment into machine instructions requires the base addresses of the arrays A and B (assuming that the elements of each occupy just one location). If these addresses are 6ØØ and 7ØØ respectively and the value of $K - 1$ is stored in the index register, the following instructions carry out the assignment.

Machine Instructions		Assembly Code	
LOAD(1)	6ØØ	LOAD(1)	A
ADD(1)	7ØØ	ADD(1)	B
STORE(1)	6ØØ	STORE(1)	A

Look at the execution of one of these in detail. The instruction

ADD(1) 7ØØ

is fetched into the instruction register. The presence of the 1 indicates that when this instruction is decoded the contents of the index register will be added to the base address, 7ØØ, and the instruction becomes

LOAD the contents of (7ØØ + K − 1).

Figure 6–1 shows the execution of this instruction when the index register contains the value 48. As you can see, the index register can be used with both machine instructions and assembly code. For ease of reading, we shall use assembly code for the rest of this section. You should however be able to write the corresponding machine instructions with little difficulty.

129

Example

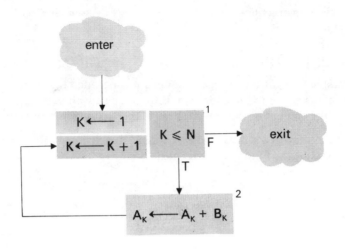

Figure 6–2   A typical flow chart loop

Figure 6–2 gives a typical flow chart loop. At machine level the assignment in box 2 uses the index register. Each time round the loop the value of K − 1 in the index register must be increased by 1. The instructions are as follows.

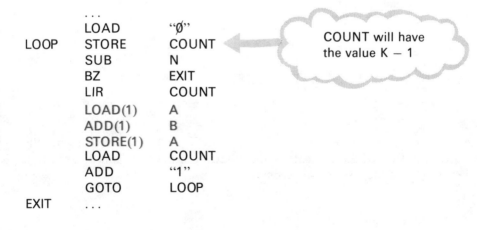

As well as being used with machine instructions to process arrays, the index register is also valuable for processing records. Suppose that two records are stored in locations called **REC1** and **REC2** respectively. If the length of the records is known to be **N**, they can be compared by means of the following instructions.

```
          LOAD       "Ø"
LOOP      STORE      K
          SUB        N
          BZ         SAME
          LIR        K
          LDCH(1)    REC1
          CPCH(1)    REC2
          BZ         INCR
          GOTO       DIFFRNT
INCR      LOAD       K
          ADD        "1"
          GOTO       LOOP
```

The index register can be used with character-handling as well as word-handling instructions. The details vary from one machine to another but we shall not make any distinction between the two.

In this sequence of instructions the individual values of the locations in which the records are stored are compared one by one. We have assumed the values to be characters. In practice it would not be necessary to do so since the only purpose of the instructions is to compare the binary patterns in two sets of locations. The code used to interpret the patterns is irrelevant.

Example

Figure 6–3 gives part of the flow chart to search a list of names for a QUERY (see Figure 3–14). The storage structure used for the list of names, in this case, was to store them as records with two fields, as shown on the next page.

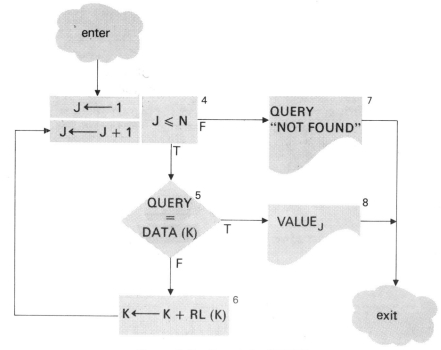

Figure 6–3   Search for QUERY

131

RL	DATA

The records are stored in successive locations starting at a base address called NAMES. Supposing that the QUERY record is also stored in this format, the instructions for box 5 of the flow chart are as follows.

```
BOX5    LOAD      "1"
LOOP    STORE     Q
        SUB       QUERY        ◄——  The first location of
        BZ        BOX 8             QUERY is the record length
        LIR       Q
        LDCH(1)   QUERY
        LIR       K
        CPCH(1)   NAMES
        BZ        INCR
        GOTO      BOX 6             Glossary
INCR    LOAD      K                 Q—an index for
        ADD       "1"                   the QUERY record
        STORE     K                 K—an index for
        LOAD      Q                     the list of NAMES
        ADD       "1"
        GOTO      LOOP
```

Note that this section of code only covers box 5 of the flow chart.

The use of the index register as we have described it in this section is a simplification of the real thing. For example the IBM 370 series of computers have sixteen registers which can be used for indexing. There is a complete set of instructions which have these registers as their operands and large sections of program can often be written in which all variables are stored in registers rather than in store. However the basic concept remains the same: to process arrays efficiently some sort of indexing facility is essential.

Questions 6.1

1. Draw the flow chart that corresponds to the following sequence of assembly code instructions.

```
        . . .
        LOAD      "∅"
LOOP    STORE     K
        SUB       N
        BZ        EXIT
        LIR       K
```

```
           LOAD(1)     B
           SUB(1)      A
           BP          BOX 3
           LOAD(1)     A
           GOTO        ASSIGN
BOX 3      LOAD(1)     B
ASSIGN     STORE(1)    C
           LOAD        K
           ADD         "1"
           GOTO        LOOP
EXIT       . . .
```

2. The flow chart in Figure 6–4 finds the largest element of a vector A. Write the corresponding assembly code instructions.

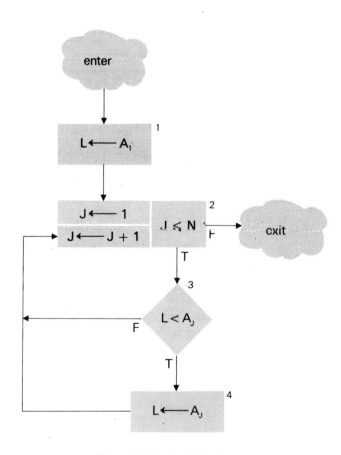

Figure 6–4   Find the largest

3. What are the assembly code instructions for boxes 4, 5 and 6 of Figure 6–3?

6.2 INDIRECT ADDRESSING

Indexing is best suited to processing data that is stored sequentially. To move on to the next item of data the value of the index register is increased by one. When data is not stored sequentially and pointers are used, a different technique is needed. To understand what is involved, have another look at the search loop that formed the basis of the flow charts in Section 4.2 (see Figure 6–5).

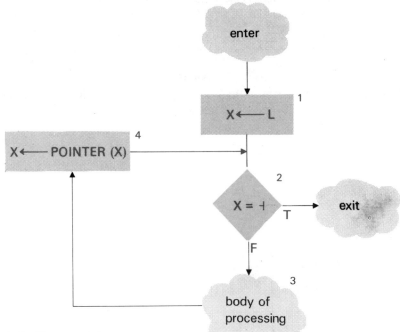

Figure 6–5   The search loop

Here the variable X is used as a pointer to locations that hold a record in the list.

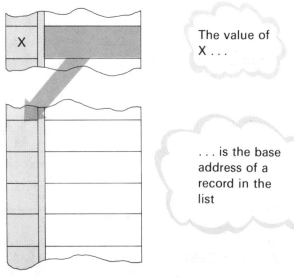

The value of X . . .

. . . is the base address of a record in the list

134

If the first field of the record is the pointer field, the following instructions are needed for box 4 of the flow chart.

> LOAD (value to which X points)
> STORE X

The first of these instructions has the usual format of an operator and operand, but the operator will be stored in one location and the actual operand in another.

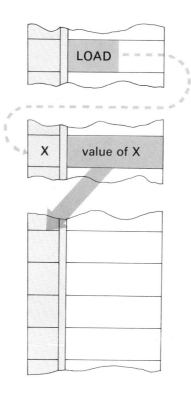

This is an example of indirect addressing. To show that **indirect addressing** is required, the letter I is written before the operator mnemonic. For example, the instructions for the search loop are as follows.

	LOAD	L
TEST	STORE	X
	SUB	"−1"
	BZ	EXIT
	. . .	
	body of loop	
	. . .	
BOX 4	I LOAD	X
	GOTO	TEST

We have assumed that the end of list marker is the number −1

The instruction

ILOAD   X

uses indirect addressing. When this instruction has been fetched from store, the operator code is decoded. Since indirect addressing is specified, the operand part of the instruction register is replaced by the corresponding bits from the address given by the operand. The operand is now decoded and the instruction is executed as normal. These steps are illustrated in Figure 6–6.

Assume that X has been stored in location 11
and that the value of X is 6Ø6.

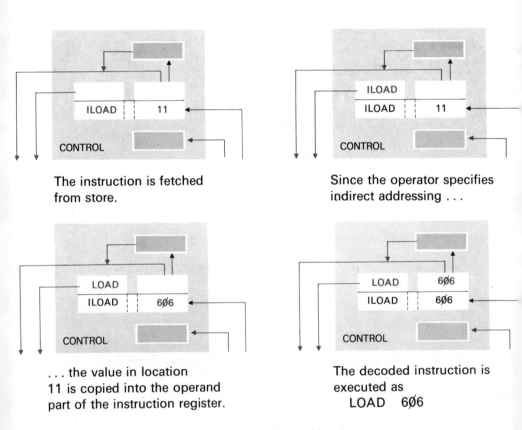

The instruction is fetched
from store.

Since the operator specifies
indirect addressing . . .

. . . the value in location
11 is copied into the operand
part of the instruction register.

The decoded instruction is
executed as
LOAD   6Ø6

Figure 6–6   Indirect addressing

Indirect addressing is the natural machine code counterpart of pointers and, as such, presents no real conceptual difficulties. What is harder to grasp is how to interpret a machine instruction that uses both indirect addressing and indexing. However such instructions are so useful that it is worth considering an example in which they occur. The body of the SEARCH subroutine, is given in Figure 6–7.

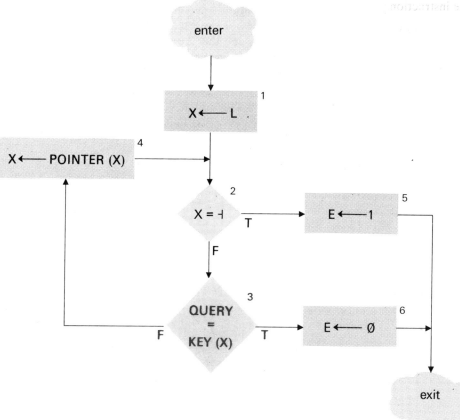

Figure 6–7   Part of the SEARCH subroutine

Suppose that the linked list is the one given in Figure 4–3 in which each record has two fields, a pointer in the first followed by a sort key of three characters. For the test in box 3, all characters in the sort key must be compared with the characters of the query record. A simple loop is needed.

```
                ...
BOX 3    LOAD       "1"
TEST     STORE      K
         SUB        "4"
         BZ         BOX 6
         LIR        K
         ILDCH(1)   QUERY
         ICPCH(1)   X
         BN         BOX 4
         BP         BOX 4
         LOAD       K
         ADD        "1"
         GOTO       TEST
BOX 4    ...
```

137

The instructions that use both indirect addressing and indexing look rather complicated. Let us see how the second of them is executed. Suppose the instruction has
been fetched into the instruction register and that 2 is the value currently held in the
index register. Figure 6–8 shows what happens next. If you follow through these
steps carefully you should find that the instruction is really quite simple to interpret.
It is important to remember that the indirect addressing part of the instruction is
decoded before the index is added to the operand. Indexing and indirect addressing
are the only additions that need to be made to the simple model of a computer given
in Chapter 2 to allow quite sophisticated low level programs to be written.

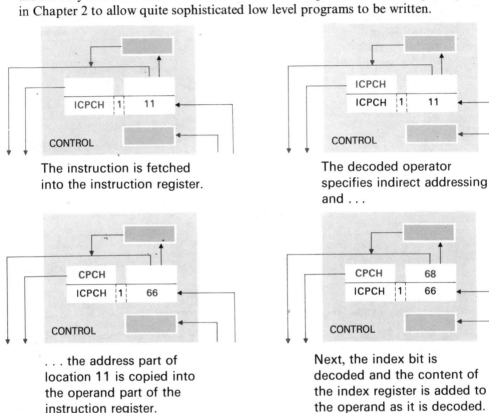

The instruction is fetched
into the instruction register.

The decoded operator
specifies indirect addressing
and . . .

. . . the address part of
location 11 is copied into
the operand part of the
instruction register.

Next, the index bit is
decoded and the content of
the index register is added to
the operand as it is decoded.

Figure 6–8   Indirect addressing and indexing

Questions 6.2

1. Records stored as a linked list have the following fields.

Write assembly code for a print routine for this list (see Figure 6–9).

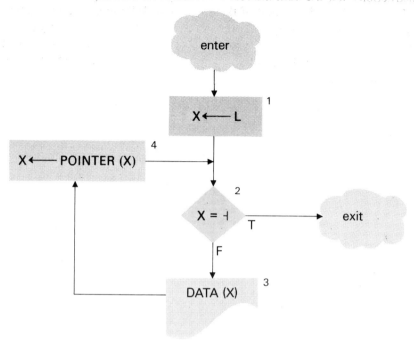

Figure 6–9　A print routine

2. In each part of this question we have given two sequences of instructions. Which of them are equivalent?

(i)　IBN　　　　LOOP　　　　　　　　　　LIR　　　　　LOOP
　　　　　　　　　　　　　　　　　　　　　　BN(1)　　　"∅"

(ii)　LIR　　　　K　　　　　　　　　　　LIR　　　　　K
　　　LOAD(1)　AVECT　　　　　　　　　LIR(1)　　　AVECT
　　　STORE　　TEMP　　　　　　　　　　LOAD(1)　　"∅"
　　　ILOAD　　TEMP

(iii)　LIR　　　　COUNT　　　　　　　　　LIR　　　　　COUNT
　　　ILOAD(1)　A　　　　　　　　　　　LOAD(1)　　A
　　　　　　　　　　　　　　　　　　　　　STORE　　　TEMP
　　　　　　　　　　　　　　　　　　　　　ILOAD　　　TEMP

6.3　SUBROUTINES

In Section 1.2 we emphasized two simple ideas about subroutines, first that a subroutine is a sequence of instructions that can be called from anywhere, and second that information, or parameters, must be passed between the calling routine and the subroutine. The way in which both these ideas are implemented varies tremendously from one programming language to another, but there are a few basic ideas that are worth discussing independently of any particular high level programming language.

The best way to think about the ideas is in terms of the model of a computer that we have developed in this and previous chapters.

To call a subroutine a special instruction is used. The operator mnemonic is CALL.. One purpose of the CALL instruction is to get the subroutine going; the other is to enable the subroutine to return to the calling routine once execution is complete. Suppose that the instructions of a subroutine have been stored in locations from 8Ø1 onwards. The effect of the instruction

CALL 8ØØ

is first to copy the value of the sequence control register into location 8ØØ, then to overwrite the SCR with the value 8Ø1 (see Figure 6–10). Notice how both purposes of the CALL instruction are carried out. First, the next instruction will be fetched

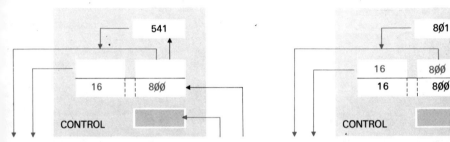

The instruction is fetched into the instruction register.

When executed, the value 541 will be stored in location 8ØØ.

Figure 6–10   Executing the CALL instruction

from location 8Ø1. This is the first instruction of the subroutine. Second, it is the address of the next instruction in the calling routine that has been loaded into location 8ØØ. This is the return address that the subroutine needs to know. The last instruction to be executed within the subroutine will be

IGOTO   8ØØ

which is an indirect branch. When executed, the operand 8ØØ will be replaced by the contents of location 8ØØ. This is the return address, left there by the CALL instruction. Thus effectively the instruction is

GOTO   return address.

This is what is needed to return from the subroutine. All this means is that you should think of a subroutine as having the layout in the store as shown in Figure 6–11.

140

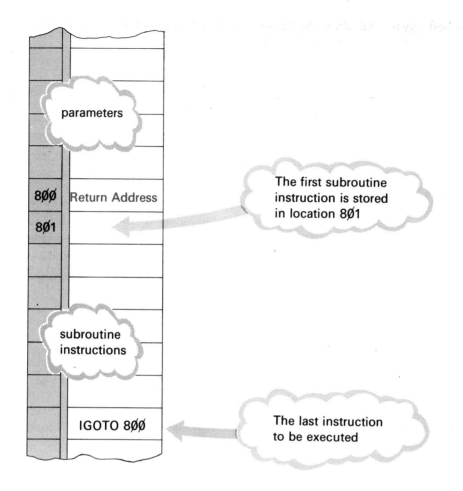

Figure 6–11 A subroutine in store

Calling a subroutine and the return from it are relatively straightforward. It is more difficult to get a clear understanding of how information is passed to and from the subroutine. We shall describe three techniques; in practice other methods can be used. First, consider the parameters of the SEARCH subroutine.

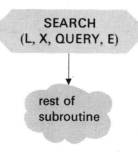

An instruction that calls **SEARCH** might be as follows.

The various techniques for passing these parameters are illustrated in Figure 6–12. The first parameter, P, in the calling routine corresponds to L in the subroutine. In both cases the parameter is a variable whose value is the base address of the first record of a linked list. This is said to be a call by value. To make the transfer, the following instructions are needed in the calling routine before the call instruction is executed

```
LOAD    P
STORE   L
```

When the subroutine has been executed, the calling routine must pick up the value of X that has been calculated and assign it to the variable Q. This is another call by value.

A different method of parameter passing is more appropriate for the query record. Instead of transferring the value of REC, it is sufficient to transfer its base address. This is a call by address. Note that when instructions are needed to process the QUERY record within the subroutine, they will have to use indirect addressing, since the value of QUERY is an address.

The last parameter in the list is the error flag E. It would be typical of many programs to have E held in a location that was used by all routines in the program. Parameter variables handled in this way are called global; notice that information does not need to be passed explicitly which makes the use of global parameters an attractive proposition wherever possible.

Thus we have three basic methods of handling parameters, call by value, call by address and using global variables. Within the body of the subroutine there are also variables and constants that are not parameters. This data is local to the subroutine and space must be provided for it. Again, the methods of providing for local data varies from one programming language to another. We will not go into these details here, but you will find some of these ideas followed up in Chapter 13.

In the previous sections you will find most of the bits and pieces needed to write assembly code for the **SEARCH** subroutine. The flow chart is given in Figure 4–7 the machine instructions using absolute addressing are given in Figure 6–13. However to complete the assembly code for **SEARCH**, you need to know how to declare parameters in assembly language. This is one of the topics of the next section Questions on this section are given at the end of the next section so that you can write the programs in assembly code.

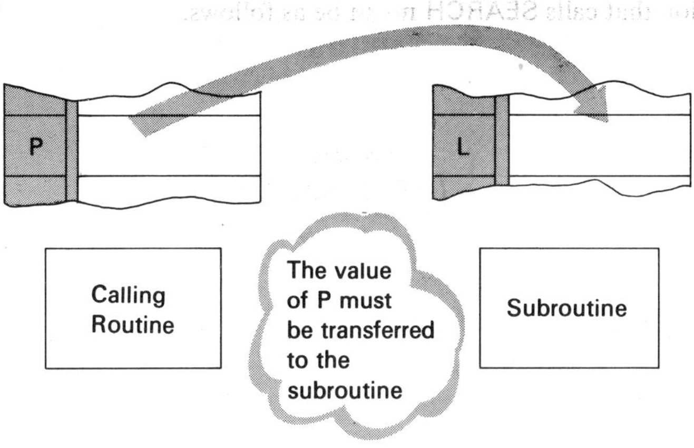

(i) A call by value

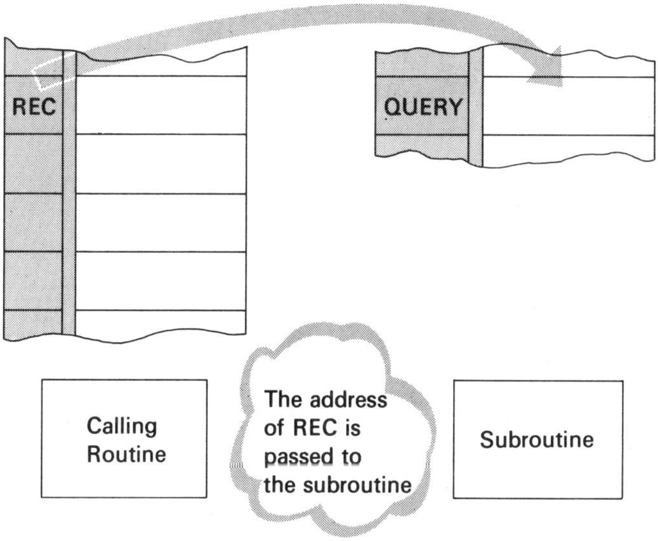

(ii) A call by address

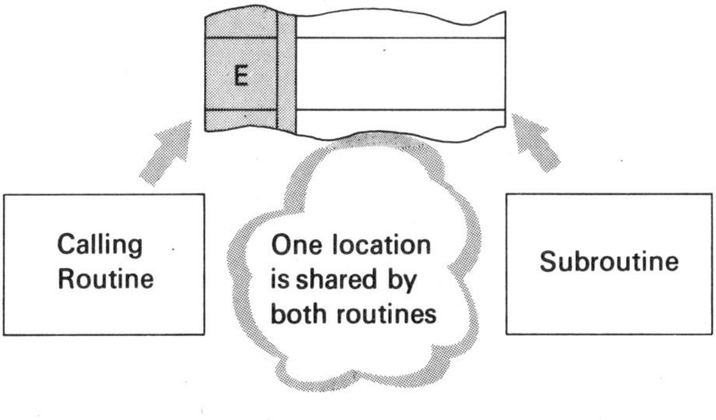

(iii) A global variable

Figure 6–12 Three techniques for passing parameters

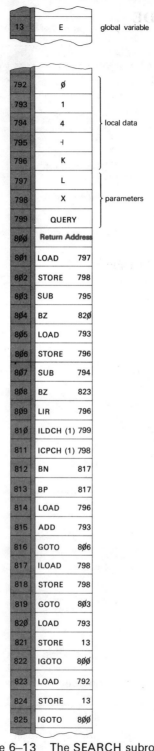

13	E	global variable

Address	Contents	
792	Ø	
793	1	
794	4	local data
795	-l	
796	K	
797	L	
798	X	parameters
799	QUERY	
8ØØ	Return Address	
8Ø1	LOAD 797	
8Ø2	STORE 798	
8Ø3	SUB 795	
8Ø4	BZ 82Ø	
8Ø5	LOAD 793	
8Ø6	STORE 796	
8Ø7	SUB 794	
8Ø8	BZ 823	
8Ø9	LIR 796	
81Ø	ILDCH (1) 799	
811	ICPCH (1) 798	
812	BN 817	
813	BP 817	
814	LOAD 796	
815	ADD 793	
816	GOTO 8Ø6	
817	ILOAD 798	
818	STORE 798	
819	GOTO 8Ø3	
82Ø	LOAD 793	
821	STORE 13	
822	IGOTO 8ØØ	
823	LOAD 792	
824	STORE 13	
825	IGOTO 8ØØ	

Figure 6–13   The SEARCH subroutine

144

6.4 ASSEMBLY CODE

Any high level programming language such as COBOL, FORTRAN or BASIC provides for some but not all of the data structures we have discussed in the last three chapters. If you are writing in a high level language you are constrained to use the data structures provided and the range of structures available is an important factor when choosing a language. Only by writing machine instructions or assembly code can you have the flexibility and precision to arrange your data in whatever way is most efficient for your purpose. If you try to write programs to manipulate the data structures that we have looked at you will find that you need a wider range of machine instructions than those described in Chapter 2. In this chapter we have discussed, we have looked at two important extensions, indexing and indirect addressing; finally we want to have a more detailed look at assembly language.

An assembly code program consists of a sequence of program statements. When a program has been written, each statement is usually punched onto a single card. These cards are read by the assembler, which is a program that reads and converts the cards into machine instructions in binary form. This form of the program is usually output by the assembler onto a magnetic tape or disc. Before the program can be run, the binary version has to be read into store by a special software program known as a loader, but more of that in Chapter 13. The assembly code statements are of two basic types, those that correspond directly to machine instructions and directives to the assembler.

Program Instructions

Since, in general, every assembly code instruction corresponds to one machine instruction, each will have the same number of operands as the corresponding machine code. In Chapter 2 we described single operand instructions and mentioned that some computers are organized to process double operand instructions or both. We shall continue to discuss single operand instructions, but the same extension to double operand instructions applies. As input to the assembler each assembly instruction often has a fixed format which might be as follows.

LABEL	OPERATOR	OPERAND	COMMENTS

5 character field   1Ø character field   15 character field   4Ø character field

The use of a fixed format usually helps to make the resulting code readable. The operand can be a symbolic address (such as A), an absolute address (such as 6ØØ) or a literal (such as " −1Ø").

Directives to the Assembler

Before being able to translate program instructions, the assembler must be told how to interpret the symbols that are subsequently used for variables, constants, etc. This is done by means of declarations which use records of the same format as program instructions, but whose fields have different names and purposes.

NAME	TYPE	EXTENT	COMMENTS

The two simplest types of declaration are used to describe variables and constants. Here are the declarations required for the assembly code program on page 40 (Figure 2–13).

NAME	TYPE	EXTENT	COMMENTS
COUNT	CONSTANT	W 'Ø'	HAS BEEN PRESET TO Ø
SMALL	VARIABLE	W	
X	VARIABLE	W	

Each of the variables used is one word long, indicated by W. The COUNT variable i preset to the value Ø. This is achieved by setting up a constant called COUNT. The assembler will give this constant the initial value Ø, but this does not prevent program instructions from changing its value when the program is executed. Similar declara tions can be used to specify other types of storage required by the program. In typical assembly language these might include the following.

(i)   Character variables or constants of any specified number of characters in length
(ii) Arrays in which each element is a word in length.
(iii) Double precision variables each occupying two words.
(iv) Floating point numbers used for scientific calculations.

Other directives to the assembler specify which peripherals the program uses, give th program a name and inform the assembler which is the final program statemen Thus the first statement of any program is a directive giving the name of the program

VETA is the name of the program →

NAME	TYPE	EXTENT	COMMEN
VETA	PROGRAM		

The final statement is always an **END** statement.

NAME	TYPE	EXTENT	COMMENTS
	END		

This tells the assembler that there are no further statements.

Macros

Subroutines involve a branch out of the main program to a closed body of instructions followed by a return to the main program. Since it is clearly inefficient to repeat large chunks of program the facility to branch out of the main routine is fundamental to most programming languages. However, if the subroutine consists of only a few instructions it may in fact be more efficient (though more tedious) to write the few instructions into the main program each time they are required. This is especially true of assembly languages where the same sequence of operators is frequently repeated with different operands. To speed up this process, most assembly languages allow macros. Here is a typical example of a macro declaration.

```
DECR    MACRO
        LOAD        @1
        SUB         @2
        STORE       @1
        END                 END OF MACRO
```

If subsequently in a program we write the instruction

```
        DECR N, K1
```

which is called a macro call, this is taken as a directive to the assembler to insert the three statements

```
        LOAD        N
        SUB         K1
        STORE       N
```

into the assembled program. In the macro definition, the operands @1 and @2 are dummy operands and are replaced by the first and second parameters of the macro call; N and K1 in our case. Note that macros are dealt with when the program is assembled into machine code, not at the time of execution.

Macros are a means of simplifying the writing of programs in that sequences of instructions used repeatedly can be dealt with once and for all by one macro declaration. Typically, macros are used for generating subroutine calls and for input and output routines. Another application is described by the following example. Suppose that a program has been designed to be run using terminals for input and output. The same program might run equally well using cards for input and a line printer for output; it might work with magnetic tape for input and magnetic disc for output. One way to give such a program this kind of flexibility is to use macros for generating

147

the input and output instructions. By altering only the macros declarations, the program can change from one kind of peripheral to another without any amendments to the body of the main program.

Apart from alleviating the tedium of creating correct programs, macros are typical of the sort of facility that makes programming a practical proposition. Every facility that a programming language offers which allows a complicated problem to be broken into tasks and subtasks is welcomed by the programmer. Each one helps to make easier the writing, correcting and testing of large programs.

Example

Let us use these ideas to write assembly code for the ADDV subroutine given in Figure 6–14. You have seen most of the program instructions before since we gave them in Section 6–1. In this example, the arrays A and B can be anywhere in store. It would be inefficient if, before executing the subroutine, the entire arrays were copied into

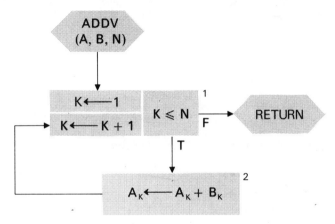

Figure 6–14   The ADDV subroutine

specified locations. What can be done efficiently is to pass the base addresses of A and B to the subroutine as parameters, by loading them into two specified locations which we shall call AX and BX.

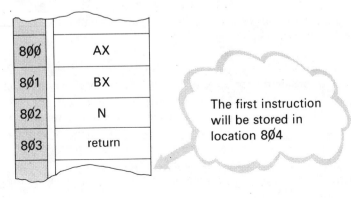

148

Suppose that we want to load A_K into the accumulator. Even if the value of $K - 1$ has been loaded into the accumulator, the instruction

LOAD(1)   AX

is not good enough because AX is a pointer. Indirect addressing must also be used. The program instructions that we need are as follows.

```
           LOAD       "Ø"
LOOP       STORE      COUNT
           SUB        N
           IBZ        RETURN
           LIR        COUNT
           ILOAD(1)   AX
           IADD(1)    BX
           ISTORE(1)  AX
           LOAD       COUNT
           ADD        "1"
           GOTO       LOOP
```

The program instructions must be preceded by directives to name the subroutine and declare the parameters (and variables) that it uses.

```
ADDV     SUBROUTINE
AX       VARIABLE      W
BX       VARIABLE      W
N        VARIABLE      W
RETURN   VARIABLE      W
```

Suppose now that we wanted to use the subroutine to add the vectors with base addresses P and Q each with ten elements. The calling routine needs the following statements.

```
           LOAD       PX
           STORE      ADDV
           LOAD       QX
           STORE      ADDV + 1
           LOAD       "1Ø"
           STORE      ADDV + 2
           CALL       ADDV + 3
```

Since this sequence of seven instructions is cumbersome to write every time a subroutine with three parameters is called, a macro might be used. The single macro call

SUB3   ADDV, P,Q, "1Ø"

will generate the required calling sequence when the program is assembled.

In this brief introduction to assembly language we have done little more than hint at the range of instructions that are available. We have, however, tried to concentrate on some of the fundamental ideas that are common to many assembly languages.

Questions 6.4

1. What parameters would be suitable for the SCORE subroutine given in Figure 1–14.

2. Write assembly code for the boat scoring algorithm given in Figure 1–15.

3. Write assembly code for the SORT subroutine given in Figure 6–15.

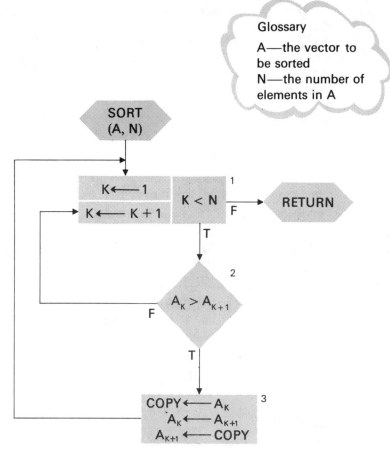

Figure 6–15   The SORT subroutine

CHAPTER SEVEN

SERIAL FILES

Magnetic Tape

Serial File Processing

Errors

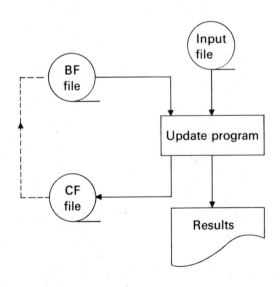

7.1 MAGNETIC TAPE

The last four chapters have introduced various ways of storing and manipulating data in the central processor. However, many programs are required to process quantities of data that are too large for all of it to be held in store at the same time. In this chapter and the next three we look at peripheral devices and how to use them, since by making use of peripherals the store can be augmented to cope with large amounts of data.

An organized collection of records which are processed together is called a file. We have seen a number of small files already. For example, on page 52, there is a list of the names of cities. This list forms a file in which each record contains the name of a single city. On page 72 there is a list of flight information for an indicator board. This list forms a file in which each record contains the information about a single flight. Although technically files, these examples are not typical of the files that we shall be looking at, because all the files that we have seen have been small enough to hold entirely in store. We shall concentrate on large files held on backing store devices, such as magnetic tapes, discs and drums. The term file processing is often used as a blanket term to describe the techniques for using backing store. Files are held on backing store for two main reasons.

(i)   Data can easily be stored for long periods and used again.
(ii) For the same amount of data, a magnetic tape or disc store is many hundreds of times cheaper than storing the data in the central processor.

Three examples of files which are too large to be held in the store of even a large computer are a list of the customers of a mail order company, a catalogue of the books in a library and a telephone directory. Here is yet another example.

Example

At the beginning of Chapter 3 we discussed the example of an industrial firm which held information about a stock of spare parts by means of records with the following fields.

SPARES

PART	DESC	STOCK	SUPP
1Ø625	LENS – AØ6	146	7368

The records for all the spare parts form a file; we shall call it the stock file in later examples and exercises.

Backing store devices in most modern computers record data on magnetic surfaces. This is cheap and reliable provided that good quality surfaces are used and that the devices are manufactured to high precision. The drawback is that before data held on backing store can be used by the central processor, it must be transferred into store. This means that using an item of data from backing store takes much longer (perhaps 10,000 times longer) than using an item already in store.

Although a wide variety of backing store devices are in use, as far as the methods of processing are concerned there are two main types: serial devices and random access devices. To understand this distinction consider the difference between using microfilm and the printed page for storing the written word (see Figure 7–1). Both can be read,

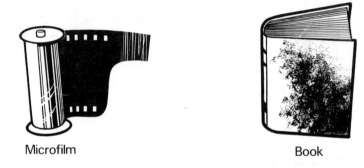

Microfilm   Book

Figure 7–1   Two ways to store words

but whereas microfilm is suitable for a novel, which is read from one end to the other, it is unsatisfactory for a dictionary. Looking for a word in a dictionary, the reader might want to refer to an entry in the middle or to skip from place to place. Neither of these operations is easy with microfilm. Books are more flexible. The reader can begin to read at any page; he can skip back to refer to something he has already read or he can jump to anywhere in the book, using an index if there is one. In the language of computing, microfilms can be used serially, but are not suitable for random use; books can be used either serially or randomly. In this chapter and the next we shall discuss serial devices and some methods for using them; in Chapters 9 and 10 we shall turn to random access devices. We have no intention of making these chapters a list of different types of peripheral, but to appreciate how they are used requires some knowledge of what they do.

The most common form of serial backing store is magnetic tape. Figure 7–2 shows a magnetic tape unit, which looks rather like an ordinary tape recorder. The tape is wound past an electronic head which can either read the data stored on the tape or write fresh data onto the tape, thereby erasing what was there before. Whichever operation is being performed, the data will be stored on tape as a long string of characters.

2	3	O	C	T	O	B	E	R	1	9	4	3

Figure 7–2   A magnetic tape unit

The characters are stored as binary patterns, but the exact manner in which each character is coded is not important to a programmer. The important point is that the data is stored sequentially and is read or written character by character beginning at one end of the tape and working through to the other.

The speeds at which the magnetic tape travels and the density at which data is stored on a tape mean that it is impossible to read a single character at a time, since starting and stopping cannot be too abrupt if the tape is not to be stretched or broken. For this reason, characters are read or written in data blocks which are separated by inter-block gaps on which no data is stored (see Figure 7–3). Reading a single block of data from a magnetic tape involves the following. Initially the tape is stationary with the head over an interblock gap, at A say. When the tape starts to move in the direction of the arrow the section of tape from A to B passes the head while the tape is accelerating. The tape is moving at full speed as point B passes the head. As the data block,

155

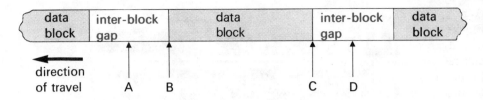

| data block | inter-block gap | data block | inter-block gap | data block |

direction of travel

A   B   C   D

Figure 7–3   Interblock gaps

B to C, passes the head it is read character by character into store. When the end of the block passes the head the brake is applied and the tape stops with the head near the middle of the next interblock gap at D. If another data block is to be read immediately, the tape is not stopped but continues straight on to the next block.

An important consideration when using magnetic tape is the number of characters to be held in one data block. Transferring a block of data into store takes a very long time in comparison to the time taken by the central processor to execute instructions, the time for each transfer having three parts.

start time + read time + stop time.

Dividing the number of characters read by the time taken for the transfer gives the effective transfer rate which is often measured in thousands of characters per second (k ch/s). Figure 7–4 shows the relationship between block size and effective transfer

Block Size (characters)	Effective Transfer Rate (k ch/s)
500	60
1000	81
2000	97

Figure 7–4   Effective transfer rates

rate for a magnetic tape deck with a peak transfer rate of 120 k ch/s. As the table shows, the larger the block, the higher the effective transfer rate. The effective transfer rate is also improved if more than one block is read without stopping the tape, but time is still wasted reading interblock gaps. For speed, it is clearly advisable to choose the largest block size possible. Against this has to be weighed the cost of allocating space in store to hold the records in a given block. A programmer is usually restricted by the amount of store available (fifty thousand characters would be typical for a commercial program) and part of this space must be reserved for building up output records. As so often in computing no solution is ideal and you must look for the best compromise that the practical details allow.

A programmer normally thinks of files stored on magnetic tape in terms of records. Blocks are made necessary by the physical characteristics of magnetic tape, whereas records are determined by the logic of processing data. Although at first glance blocks and records seem to be different concepts, in practice the two are closely related. From a logical point of view, to process a record efficiently the whole of it needs to be in store; it is no good having part in store and part on backing store. From the physical point of view, data is transferred to and from magnetic tape in units of one block. The actual size of the blocks is usually determined by the programmer and he can often establish a suitable relation between block size and record size. The simplest arrangement is to let each block contain a single record. This arrangement is easy to program, but if the records are short most of the magnetic tape is then used for inter-block gaps. The storage capacity of the tape and the effective transfer rate are thereby substantially reduced. If storage capacity and transfer rates are important, several records can be held in each block in order to increase the block length. With variable length records, if several are stored in each block, it is necessary to use length fields or separators to determine the extent of a record. The important point to appreciate is that the relation between block size and record size is completely flexible and at the programmer's disposal. The following diagrams show some of the possible arrangements. In these diagrams, data is stored on the red shaded areas; the blank areas represent interblock gaps.

(i)

Fixed length records, one to a block.

(ii)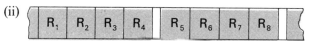

Fixed length records, a specified number to a block.

(iii)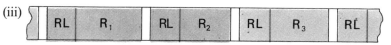

Variable length records, one to a block. The first field is RL, the record length.

(iv)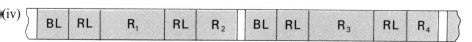

Variable length records, as many as convenient to a block. Each block is headed by a BL field giving the block length and each record is headed by an RL field giving the record length. This is a very common arrangement in commercial data processing.

The relation between files and reels of magnetic tape is equally flexible and is also under the programmer's control. For example, a large file may extend over several reels of tape. This flexibility is useful, but it does mean that some way is needed of

157

labelling both tapes and files. A tape is normally identified by the first block written on it, called a tape header block. It will contain fields for the following information.

(i)   Tape identity, to identify the actual reel of tape.
(ii) File identity, including an indication as to whether this is a one reel or multi-reel file.
(iii) Tape security, including fields giving a date showing when the tape was last written and how long after this date before the tape can be overwritten.

A tape is terminated by a final block, called the tape trailer block. This contains fields for the following information.

(i)   Status information, such as an indication that this is the end of a one reel or multi-reel file.
(ii) Checking information, such as the number of blocks written onto the tape.

Example

Each record of a library loan file contains the following fields.

> The TITLE of book—a variable length field.
> The NAME (and address) of borrower—a variable length field.
> The DATE on which the book becomes overdue—a fixed length field.

Since two of the constituent fields are variable length, the record as a whole is variable length. Within a record, the standard arrangment is to put any fixed length fields at the beginning and to use separators between variable length fields. Two points need to be considered when deciding how to store this variable length record on magnetic tape. These are the relation between records and blocks on the tape, and the processing which is to be performed on the record. Since processing is performed when the record is in store you might think that the second point has little to do with how it is stored on a magnetic tape, but this is not the case because if the formats of the record on tape and in store is radically different the program will waste time converting the record into its tape or store format each time it is written or read respectively. To make good use of magnetic tape requires as large a block length as possible, for this will give both a high effective transfer rate and allow as many records as possible to be held on a tape. The last of the four arrangements on page 157 suits this situation. Whatever size blocks are allowed sufficient space must be reserved in store to hold the longest block that can occur. It is therefore convenient to decide on a maximum block size and to fit as many variable length records as possible into each block. Most blocks on the tape will be shorter than the maximum. A typical block on tape has the form shown in Figure 7–5.

Since the programming required to read and write variable length blocks involve awkward details, computer manufacturers provide special software routines, called housekeeping routines, to help the programmer. These housekeeping routines are an integral part of many high level programming languages such as COBOL. They mean

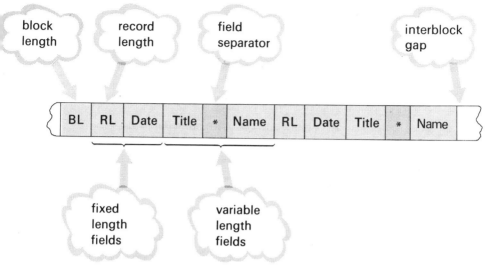

Figure 7–5   A block of the library file

that a programmer can write a single instruction corresponding to the following flow chart step.

Read a record
from the stock
file into a
specified area
in store

The housekeeping routine will pass the next record in sequence to the main program and the programmer need not concern himself with deciding when to read a new block and how to separate out individual records.

Questions 7.1

1. Data is stored on a magnetic tape at 800 characters per inch and the speed of travel is 75 inches per second. Each block of data is 1000 characters long and the interblock gap is 0·6 inches.

    (i)   If the start up and stop times (including time to pass over half the interblock gap) are both 0·005 seconds, what is the average number of characters transferred into store per second when 1, 2 and 4 blocks, respectively, are read from the tape? Express your answers in thousands of characters per second (k ch/s).

(ii) Draw a graph to show how the effective transfer rate varies with block size if only a single block is read.

2. Describe how to store the stock file (discussed on page 153) on magnetic tape.

3. Describe a structure for the following transaction records, suitable for a file held on magnetic tape. Each record contains the following fields.

> Customer code
> Salesman code
> Date of order
> Commodity code ⎫
> Order quantity ⎭ *these two fields are repeated as many times as necessary*

Each customer is identified by an eight digit numerical code. The first digit, restricted to the range Ø to 4 inclusive, represents the class of customer. Each salesman is identified by a four digit numerical code, of which the first two digits are an area code and the last two digits identify which salesman in the area made the transaction. Each commodity is represented by a two digit number.

7.2 SERIAL FILE PROCESSING

Constraints of Magnetic Tape

Suppose that a file is held on magnetic tape and that an extra record has to be added somewhere in the middle of the file. To insert the new record all subsequent records must be moved up to make room for the addition. This would involve winding through the tape reading data from it and writing new data simultaneously, which is impossible for engineering reasons. Deleting a record and closing up the gap is similarly difficult. Replacing several characters on a tape by an equal number causes problems in making sure that new characters are written in exactly the same place as the ones being replaced and in practice no attempt is made to alter the data on a magnetic tape once it has been written. At any given time a tape is specified as being available for input or for output but not for both. Thus to alter a file on a magnetic tape it is read and another version is created on a different magnetic tape. A program which reads a file and writes a new version with alterations is called an updating program The old version of the file is called the brought forward file (abbreviated to BF file) and the new version the carried forward file (abbreviated to CF file). The carried forward file written by one program is the brought forward file used the next time the file is read. This is shown in Figure 7–6. Another constraint that magnetic tape imposes on the use of serial files is that when being used for output a magnetic tape can be wound in one direction only. Thus the updating program must be organized to process all the records in the sequence in which they are to be written onto the carried forward file

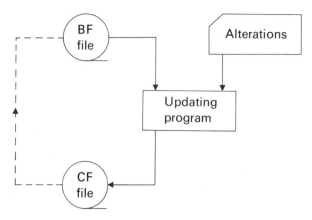

Figure 7–6   Updating a brought forward file

System Flow Charts

A chart such as Figure 7–6 is called a system flow chart. Superficially it looks much like an ordinary flow chart, but whereas a flow chart is concerned with the processing within the computer, a system flow chart emphasizes the flow of data before and after processing. The system flow chart shows a brought forward file being read, a carried forward file being written and alterations being read from punched cards. The broken

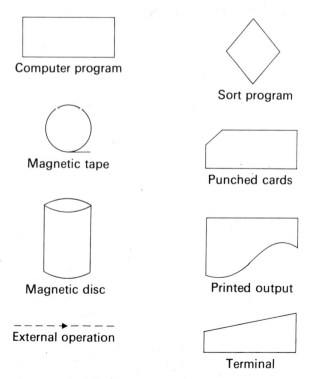

Figure 7–7   Symbols used on system flow charts

lines indicate that next time the file is read, the carried forward file written by this program will be used as the new brought forward file. Some of the common symbols used on system flow charts are shown in Figure 7–7.

Consider the stock file introduced as an example on page 153 and suppose that the file is held on magnetic tape. As spare parts are issued from the company's store records have to be altered. Since a serial file cannot be altered except by writing a new file, the tape is read and the records, some amended, are copied on to another tape. If there are only a few alterations the updating program is easy to construct. All the punched cards are read into store. The brought forward file is read one record at a time. For each record, if there is an alteration, the record is changed and the amended record is copied to the carried forward file. If there is no change to be made the unaltered record is copied to the carried forward file. However this method will not work if there are so many changes to be made that all the data from the punched cards cannot be held in store at the same time. Under these circumstances, the stock file would normally be held on magnetic tape as a sorted sequence of records and, before updating, the alterations are sorted into a sequence that matches the stock file. For instance the stock file and alterations could both be sorted by part number. Whatever the means of sorting, one important part of any record on a file is the field or fields by which the record is identified. This field is called the key or, in particular, the sort

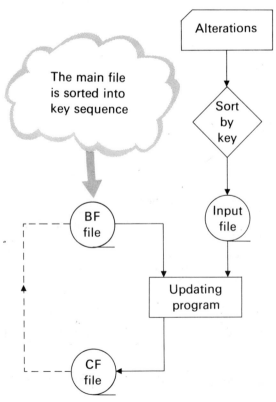

Figure 7–8   Sorting the alterations

162

key if it is used to sort the records on the file. The system flow chart for updating the sorted stock file is shown in Figure 7–8.

This style of processing, in which many records are updated together is known as batch processing. In practice a wide variety of batch processing systems can be represented as variations of the system flow chart shown in Figure 7–9.

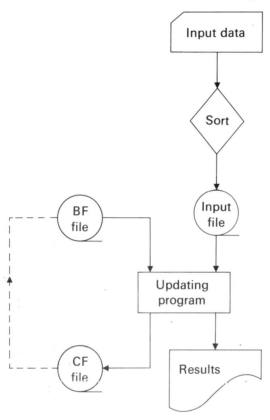

Figure 7–9 A common system flow chart in batch processing

Example

Here is a typical example of a commercial problem. The industrial company whose stock file is described on page 153 also maintains a file of the suppliers from whom it purchases spare parts. Each record on this supplier file contains the following fields.

SUPP—the code number of the supplier
NAME—the name and address of the supplier
PART—part number
PRICE—unit price
QUANTITY—purchase quantity
ORDER—oustanding orders

These fields are repeated for each part supplied by this supplier

The file is sorted by the supplier code.

Once a week the company updates the stock file from punched cards which specify the quantities which have been issued from stock. If the stock of any part falls below a specified level an order has to be placed with the supplier. The program that updates the stock file writes a record on a work file of the following form.

PART	SUPP	DESC

These records are used to update the supplier file. Since the supplier file is sorted by supplier code and the work file is sorted by supplier code, the work file has first to be sorted. The overall system flow chart is shown in Figure 7–10. Notice that it consists of two almost identical sections, with the results of one being input to the other.

This example shows several programs which are designed to work in harmony to perform a single task. This is an example of a suite of programs. In this case the suite consists of an update program for each of the main files and two sort programs. A commercial system would almost certainly include a separate print program to print the orders on order forms and a program to check the input data. Checking data is discussed in the next section.

Update Programs

The system flow chart in Figure 7–10 indicates that the first update program uses four files, two for input and two for output. Thus the following instruction misses two important details.

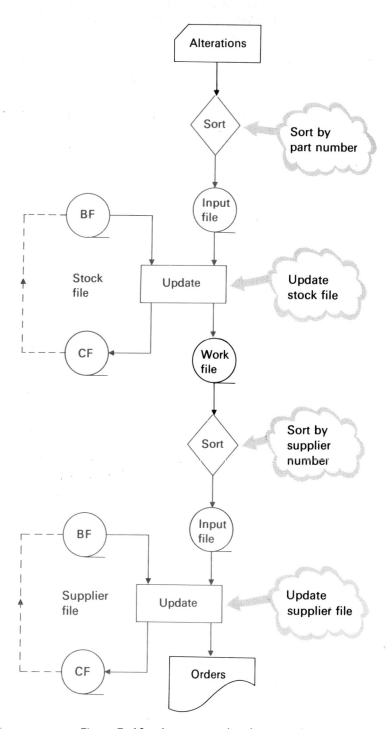

Figure 7–10   A two stage batch processing system

The two missing details are

(i) the name of the file from which the record is to be input,
(ii) where in store the record is to be copied.

We shall adopt the convention that

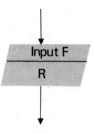

means

read the next record on file F and assign it to the area in store called R.

A similar convention will be used for output.

A first attempt at a flow chart for the stock file update program is given in Figure 7–11.

The flow chart uses the following notation.

Glossary

ID—input file
ALTER—an input
alterations record
QTY (ALTER)—quantity
removed from stock
BF—brought forward
stock file
CF—carried forward
stock file
SPARES—see page 153
RES—results file

This flow chart is drawn from the viewpoint of a programmer who is writing in a high level language such as COBOL and therefore makes no mention of tape header and tailer labels nor of the method of finding an individual record within a block. However

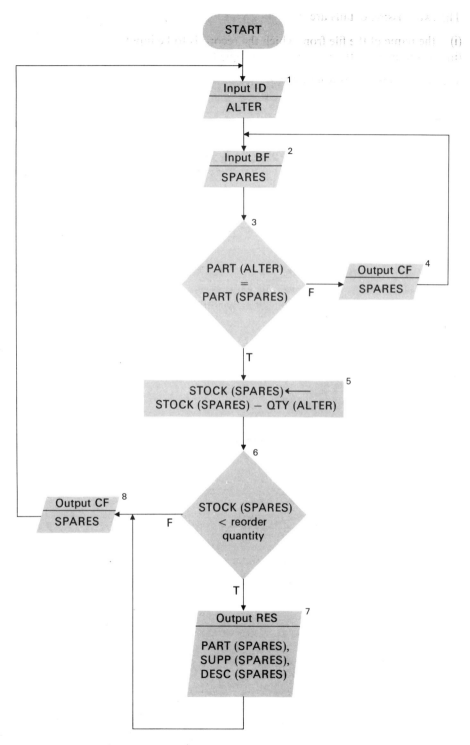

Figure 7–11   First attempt at update program for stock file

167

the programmer cannot ignore what happens when the end of an input file is reached. The standard procedure is that before first using an input file a special high level instruction is inserted specifying where the program should branch to at the end of the file. Although this may sound strange it does in fact simplify programming. In our flow charts we use the following notation.

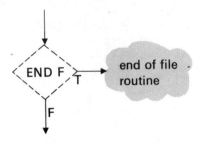

If subsequently an attempt is made to read beyond the last data record of file F, the program will branch to the end of file routine. We can use this notation to complete the program to update the stock file, by inserting at the beginning of the program the extra boxes shown in Figure 7–12.

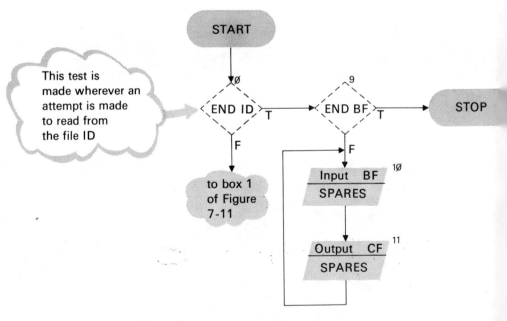

Figure 7–12 End of the file tests

Questions 7.2

1. This exercise refers to the library file described on page 158. When books are returned to the library the corresponding records are deleted from the file. Draw the system flow chart and an outline flow chart of the update program.

2. Each record on a student file contains the following fields. *Student number, sex, name, initials, address, date of birth, marital status, telephone number, faculty code, courses previously taken or presently being taken, results of assignments for courses currently being taken.*

The records are sorted by student number and are held on magnetic tape as a serial file which currently contains over 40,000 records. Draw a system flow chart for preparing a list by faculty of all students taking course XYZ123 and printing the name, address and number of each of these students. Assume that the computer store is too small to hold simultaneously all the records for course XYZ123. The only backing store available is four magnetic tape units.

3. Records on a brought forward serial file contain a sort key and a data field

KEY	DATA

Records on an input data file contain a key, an indicator and a data field.

KEY	INDICATOR	DATA

The indicator has the following significance.

    1—insert a new record with the given key and data field,
    2—delete the corresponding brought forward record.

The input data file and brought forward file are both sorted in the sequence of the keys. A program reads the two files and creates a carried forward file. Draw a detailed flow chart for this program.

7.3 ERRORS

The operation of matching input data to records in the brought forward file is fundamental to batch processing. This is easy with the stock file since each part is identified by a unique part number, but let us look again at the library example. One of the fields in each record gives the title of the book. Identifying books by title and author is so troublesome that the book trade has a numbering system. On the back of the title page of this book the following appears.

    ISBN 0 471 03324 3

This is the International Standard Book Number. Not only does it identify the book unambiguously; it is also shorter than the title. Computer systems in libraries almost invariably use numbers to refer to books. Sometimes International Standard Book Numbers are used, but as these are not printed in all books, many libraries allocate numbers for their own use. For similar reasons borrowers are usually given identification numbers and a more practical form of record would be as follows.

LOAN

ISBN	BORROWER CODE	DATE

When books are returned to the library the corresponding records are deleted from the library file. Difficulties arise if the input data contains errors. If, by mistake, data is input about a book for which there is no record on the brought forward file, the program will search the entire brought forward file looking for the record and when the end is reached something nasty will happen. You might say that it is the responsibility of the library staff not to make mistakes like this, but if the input data consists of many thousands of records the chances are that some mistakes will not be noticed. With most types of input peripheral, data has to be copied by hand before it is fed in on punched cards or paper tape. If data has to be copied mistakes are difficult to avoid. With punched cards or paper tape data is normally verified by punching it twice and comparing the two versions mechanically, but some mistakes still slip through, even when the original data is correct, which is not always the case. Computer systems must therefore be designed to trap errors. Before sorting, input data goes

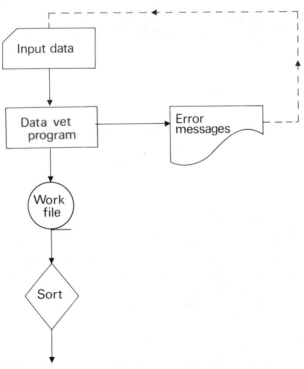

Figure 7–13   Data vet program

170

through a special program, called a data vet, to look for all identifiable errors. This is shown in Figure 7–13. The data vet program looks at each record and at each field within each record to see if any mistakes can be found. Typical checks are as follows.

(i)   Each record has the correct number of fields.
(ii) All fields have the required number of characters.
(iii) Each field has the correct format. That is, each character is valid; numbers are found where numbers are expected; letters are found where letters are expected; numbers are within permitted ranges.

If errors are found the record is rejected and an error message is printed. The broken line on Figure 7–13 indicates that somebody reads the error messages and resubmits the record, usually with the next batch of data. If no errors are found, the record is copied on to a temporary work file. This is sorted and the input file prepared.

Check Digits

With data for the library file what happens if a mistake is made in punching the book number? If, in normal writing, a spelling mistake is made a reader will usually be able to guess what is intended. This is because the English language contains much redundancy, and the words have a meaning which comes through even if mistakes are made. International Standard Book Numbers also contain redundant information and have a structure specially designed for a computer to be able to recognize errors. Look again at the International Standard Book Number of this book, 0 471 03324 3. The last digit is called a modulus eleven check digit. To see the purpose of this number, take the right-hand digit (3) and multiply it by 1, multiply the next digit (4) by 2, and so on, then add the results obtained as shown in Figure 7–14. The check digit has been

$\emptyset \times 1\emptyset$	$\emptyset$
4 x 9	36
7 x 8	56
1 x 7	7
$\emptyset$ x 6	$\emptyset$
3 x 5	15
3 x 4	12
2 x 3	6
4 x 2	8
3 x 1	3
	143

Figure 7–14   A modulus eleven check digit

$\emptyset \times 1\emptyset$	$\emptyset$
4 x 9	36
7 x 8	56
1 x 7	7
$\emptyset$ x 6	$\emptyset$
3 x 5	15
2 x 4	8
3 x 3	9
4 x 2	8
3 x 1	3
	142

Figure 7–15   A transposition error

chosen so that this total (143) is exactly divisible by 11. All valid International Standard Book Numbers have this property. The two commonest types of error which are made when copying numbers are to copy one digit wrongly (0 471 034 24 3 instead of 0 471 033 24 3) or to transpose two digits (0 471 0323 4 3 instead of 0 471 0324 3). Figure 7–15 shows what happens if the last calculation is repeated with the second of these two incorrect numbers. Since 142 is not divisible by 11, a mistake has clearly been made and will be spotted by the data vet program.

Reconciliation Failures

A check digit of this type will pick up errors which consist of a single wrong digit or a simple transposition, but will not pick up all errors. Errors get through even the most carefully controlled input procedures, and some of these errors will be found by the main program. For example, when updating the stock file because parts have been issued from stock, we might find that

(i) the part number on an input record does not correspond to any record on the brought forward file,
(ii) the number of parts issued from stock according to the input data is greater than the number in stock according to the brought forward file.

Errors such as these, where the input data is not compatible with the brought forward file, are called reconciliation failures.. If the main program finds such an error it produces an error report. To round off this chapter Figure 7–16 is the complete system flow chart, which shows reconciliation failures.

Questions 7.3

1. Which of the following are valid International Standard Book Numbers?

    1 471 26778 7
    2 471 26677 8
    Ø 412 76678 7

2. This question refers to the stock file. A program is required to print the quantity in stock of a number of specified parts. The part numbers are punched on cards, one number per card. Draw the system flow chart and the outline flow chart of the main program. Allow for some of the parts not appearing on the brought forward file.

3. A large department store operates a credit system by issuing customers with credit cards against which purchases can be charged. The store maintains a file of credit card holders on magnetic tape and uses a batch system to process transactions. The following information is held in each customer's record on the file.

    Customer Account Number
    Customer Name and Address
    Current Balance

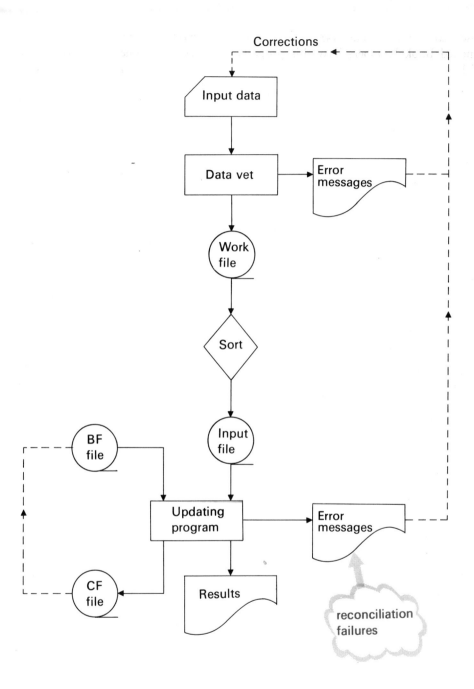

Figure 7–16   The complete system flow chart

The following transactions involve the master file.

    1 Open a new account.
    2 Credit an account.
    3 Debit an account.
    4 Close an existing account.

The transactions are batched each day and are processed each evening. Draw a flow chart for a main program, which makes the transactions for a day and write the carried forward file. Assume that the input data file is sorted by transaction type within account number.

4. In a library, every time a book is issued, a fixed length record is created of the form shown in Figure 7–17. These records are held on magnetic tape in the

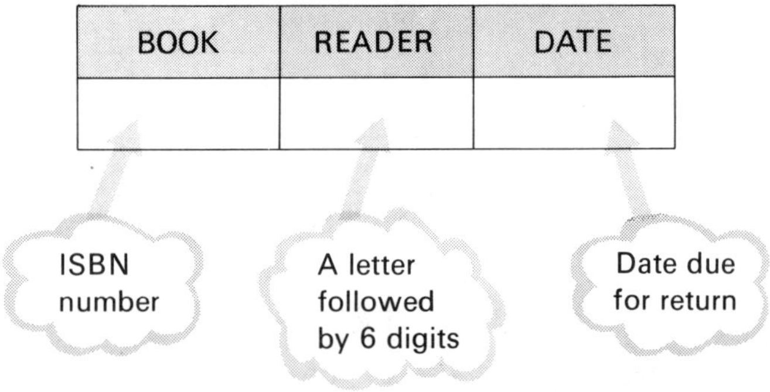

Figure 7–17   An issue record

sequence of ascending book numbers. For each book returned to the library an input record consisting of the following fields

is created. At the end of each day the input records are batched and the library file is updated. The update program deletes records for returned books and lists all books on the file that are overdue.

(i)   Draw a system flow chart for a system to update the library file.
(ii)   What errors are likely to arise and how does your system handle them?
(iii) Construct a detailed flow chart for the update program.

5. An estate agent keeps a computer file of prospective house buyers, by means records with the following fields.

REF	CODE

The REF field contains the customer reference number; it is sufficient to identify the customer and his address. It is also the sort key by which the customer file is ordered. The CODE field contains a code that details the kind of house in which the customer is interested. For each house that comes on the market a punched card is prepared. By comparing the CODE field of a customer record with the data on the card a computer program can tell whether full particulars of the house should be sent to the customer. Each day customer amendment records are prepared with the following fields.

REF	CODE	FLAG

The REF and CODE fields are as above; the FLAG field is set to

     1—this is a new customer to be added to the file,
     2—this is an old customer to be deleted from the file.

Each day a computer run is made. The new records are batched, vetted, sorted and written onto an input file. The data about new houses can always be accommodated within store and is hence not transferred to backing store. The customer file is processed and a list made of which particulars are to be sent to which customers.

  (i)   Draw a system flow chart of this process.
 (ii) What errors are likely to occur and how does your system handle them?
(iii) Draw an outline flow chart of the update program.

CHAPTER EIGHT

MAGNETIC TAPE SORTING

External Sorting

The Classical Four Tape Sort

A Polyphase Sort

Selection Sorting

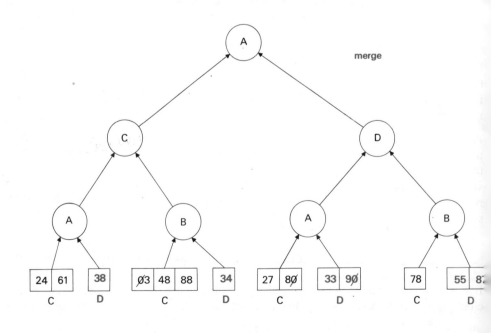

8.1 EXTERNAL SORTING

Sorting is based upon a sort key which may be one or more fields in the records under consideration. Often the fields chosen as a sort key contain letters as well as numbers. To be able to sort them you need to specify an order for all types of characters. You know the order of digits,

Ø 1 2 3 4 5 6 7 8 9,

and the letters of the alphabet,

A B C D E F G H I J K L M N O P Q R S T U V W X Y Z,

but does a number come before a letter? What about a space, or a comma? If the sort keys are numbers, the assertion

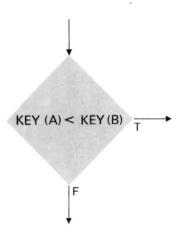

has a well defined meaning. If the sort keys are made up of letters, we can introduce the convention that this assertion is true if KEY(A) would be listed before KEY(B) in a dictionary; but a further convention is needed for combinations of letters, numbers and other symbols.

Actually, if you consider why files are sorted, the order of characters is more or less arbitrary. The important thing is that the order should be clearly defined, since files to be processed together must be sorted in exactly the same way. The usual convention is to order the individual characters according to the binary patterns used to represent them in store. This is known as the collating sequence. Part of the collating sequence for the EBCDIC code, discussed in Section 2.1, is

∇ . (+ *) − / , = A B C D E F G H I J K L M

N O P Q R S T U V W X Y Z Ø 1 2 3 4 5 6 7 8 9

By convention, to compare two character fields they have to be the same length and characters are compared one by one from the left.

Merge Sorting

Algorithms for sorting files are of two types.

(i) Internal sorts, which are used when store is large enough to hold the entire file that is to be sorted.

(ii) External sorts, which are used when the file to be sorted is too large to be held in store and is held on backing store instead.

In Section 5.2 we discussed the tree sort; you have probably come across other methods of internal sorting. For sorting files, these methods require that all records be read into store. This clearly cannot be done if the file is very large. At first glance it may seem improbable that a large file can be sorted while still being held on magnetic tape, which we have emphasized has to be used serially, but it can be done if more than two tapes are used. The basis of the procedure for doing this is as follows. Several records already in collating sequence order form a sequence. If two such sequences are held on different magnetic tapes, they can be merged and written as a single sequence on another tape as shown in Figure 8–1. Sorted sequences on two tapes

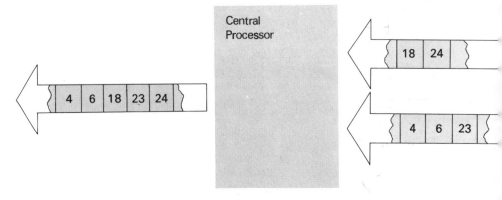

Figure 8–1   Merging two sequences

are read into the computer, one record from each at a time, and merged into a single sequence. Figure 8–2 is a flow chart of this process.

External sort algorithms for magnetic tape repeatedly merge sequences by copying records from two or more tapes to another. Since peripherals are much slower than the central processor, external sorting algorithms concentrate on minimizing input and output, as opposed to internal sorts which try to minimize the number of instructions actually executed.

Most records usually consist of more than one field. However, for ease of reading, the examples in this chapter show just the sort key and

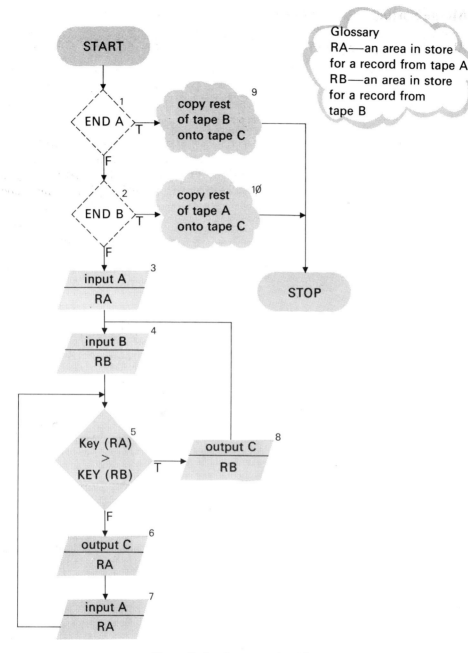

Figure 8–2   A merge algorithm

is to be interpreted as the record whose sort key is 47. As we have said, keys need not be numerical but again for easy reading, all the examples that we discuss have numerical sort keys. By now you will probably have appreciated that we tend to choose simple examples to illustrate abstract concepts. In the next three sections, we shall discuss three external sorting algorithms in terms of the following short, simplified and unrealistic sequence of sort keys.

Try to bear in mind the simplification that we are making by choosing such an example as you read the next sections. We shall always be concerned with sorting this sequence into ascending order.

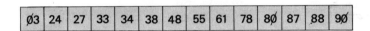

To do this, we shall in some cases divide the original sequence into eight initial subsequences as follows.

Most computer manufacturers provide software routines for sorting data and so there may not appear to be practical reasons for writing a sort program. In fact we shall only attempt to describe these methods in outline with a view to giving you a feel for the processes involved.

Questions 8.1

1. Using the EBCDIC collating sequence arrange the following fields in ascending sequence.

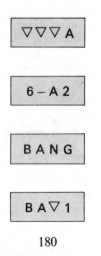

Test whether this is the same sequence as the one obtained from your computer.

2. Expand steps 9 and 1∅ of the flow chart of Figure 8–2.

8.2 THE CLASSICAL FOUR TAPE SORT

The classical four tape sort is the basic method of sorting serial files. Although rarely used nowadays because of the superiority of the polyphase sort (described in the next section), it is well worth studying since the basic concepts of external sorting are demonstrated without the sophistications that tend to complicate more efficient routines. The method uses four magnetic tapes which we label A, B, C and D. Initially we have the unsorted records on tape A in random order. The fourteen records can be divided into eight sequences.

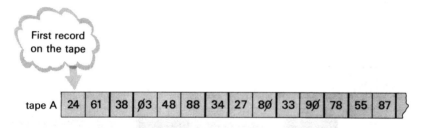

1. Tape A is read and the eight sequences are copied onto tapes C and D alternately. These two tapes will then have the same number of sequences but need not have the same number of records

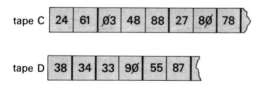

2. The first sequence on tape C is merged with the first on D and the result is written onto tape A. The next sequence on tape C is merged with the next on D and written onto tape B. This is repeated until all sequences on tapes C and D have been merged.

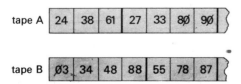

3. Stage 2 is repeated but with tapes A and B being used as input and C and D as output tapes.

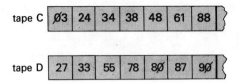

tape C | Ø3 | 24 | 34 | 38 | 48 | 61 | 88 |

tape D | 27 | 33 | 55 | 78 | 8Ø | 87 | 9Ø |

4. Stage 2 is repeated. Since after stage 3 there is only one sequence on tape C and one on tape D these are merged and written onto tape A which then holds the fully sorted file.

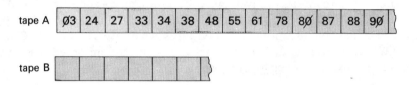

tape A | Ø3 | 24 | 27 | 33 | 34 | 38 | 48 | 55 | 61 | 78 | 8Ø | 87 | 88 | 9Ø |

tape B | | | | | | | |

We now want to draw a flow chart for stage 1, in which the file is split and sequences are written alternatively onto tapes C and D. Space is required in store for only one record, the record just read in. If we label this area R and keep a note of the key of the previous record in a variable P, then the test

$$KEY(R) < P$$

determines whether the end of a sequence has been reached and a new one must be started on the other tape (true) or whether to continue copying to the same tape (false). A simple switching variable S can be used to remember which tape is currently in use.

> If $S = \emptyset$, copy the record to tape C,
> if $S = 1$, copy the record to tape D.

To switch to the other tape, we use the following assignment.

$$S \longleftarrow 1 - S.$$

The flow chart for stage 1 is given in Figure 8–3.

The core of the classical four tape sort lies in stages 2 and 3 which can be repeated alternately until all the records form a single sequence. They involve repeatedly merging sequences from two input tapes onto alternate output tapes. In the previous section we gave a flow chart to merge two sequences onto a single tape. This algorithm forms the backbone of stages 2 and 3 but there are additional complications that arise from using two output tapes rather than one and having several sequences on each tape.

However efficient the details of the merging routine, the total execution time of the program must ultimately depend on the number of records that are written and not on the speed with which they are processed. Suppose that at some stage we have a total of m sequences distributed between tapes A and B. If m is even, half the sequences will be on tape A and half on tape B. After merging there will be $\frac{1}{2}$m sequences distributed between tapes C and D. If m is odd, one tape, perhaps tape A, will have

182

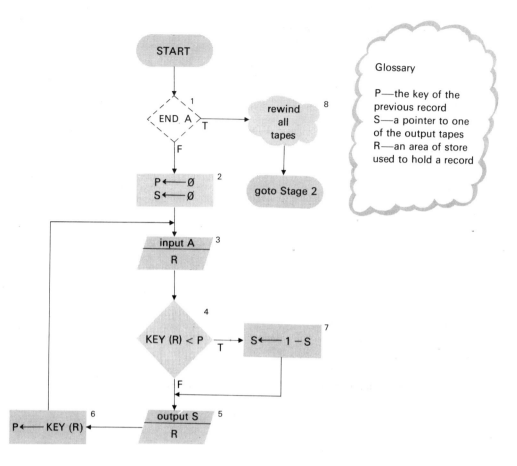

Figure 8–3   First stage of the classical four tape sort

one sequence more than the other. When the sequences are merged the odd sequence
on tape A will be copied onto either C or D without being merged with another. Thus
the total number of sequences distributed between tapes C and D will be $\frac{1}{2}(m + 1)$.
With two input tapes, the best that can be done is to halve the number of sequences
each time the complete file is copied. Therefore the largest number of sequences that
can be merged while copying the file n times is 2^n.

The stages of the four tape sort can be represented on a tree which shows how the
sequences are merged and on what tapes they are held (Figure 8–4). Each record has
been copied as many times as there are levels of the tree. To sort these fourteen records,
which initially formed eight sequences, fifty six records have to be copied.

Questions 8.2

1. (i)   With tape A initially having records with the following keys,

tape A	2Ø	74	94	22	93	45	44	16	Ø4	32	Ø3	62	61	89

write down the contents of the tapes at each stage of the classical four tape
sort.

(ii) Construct a tree which shows how the initial sequences are merged.

2. How would you alter the classical four tape sort to make use of six tape units?
What is the greatest number of sequences that can be merged with the changed
algorithm if the file is copied n times?

3. Draw a flow chart of the classical four tape sort.

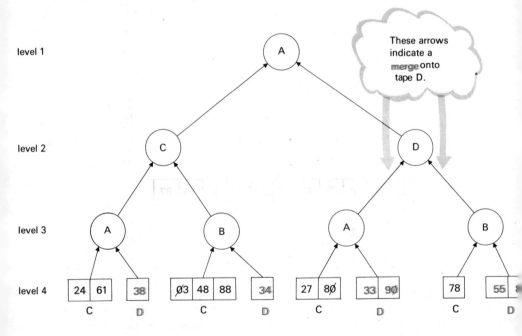

Figure 8-4   Tree representation of sorting

8.3   A POLYPHASE SORT

The time taken to sort a file by successively merging sequences depends on the number
of times that each record is copied. Merging proceeds fastest if

(i)   the files being merged are similar in length,
(ii) as many input tapes as possible are used for each merge.

The classical four tape sort fulfils the first criterion reasonably well but fails on the
second. At any given moment two tapes are being used for input, one tape for output
and the fourth is idle. Polyphase sorting is a method which uses as many input tapes

184

as possible at the expense of merging files of different lengths. The method can be used with any number of tape units from three upwards, but in this section we discuss the stages of a polyphase sort using three magnetic tapes, called A, B and C, to sort the same file as before.

Initially the records are on tape A.

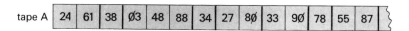

1. The eight sequences are copied from tape A to tapes B and C; five sequences are copied onto tape B and three are copied onto tape C. We shall see later why the original eight sequences are split five to three and not four to four.

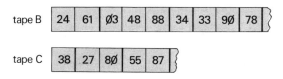

2. The first sequence on tape B is merged with the first on tape C and written onto tape A. This is repeated until all the sequences on tape C have been read. There are now three sequences on tape A and two remaining unread on tape B.

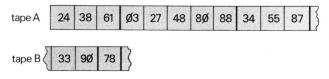

3. Stage 2 is repeated with tapes A and B used for input and merged sequences written onto tape C. At the end of the stage there is one sequence left unread on tape A and two new sequences on tape C.

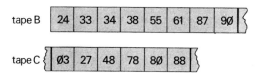

4. Stage 2 is repeated with tapes A and C used for input and merged sequences written onto tape B. There is now one sequence on each of tapes B and C.

tape B | 24 | 33 | 34 | 38 | 55 | 61 | 87 | 9Ø |

tape C | Ø3 | 27 | 48 | 78 | 8Ø | 88 |

5. The two sequences on tapes B and C are merged into the final sequence which is written onto tape A.

185

tape A	Ø3	24	27	33	34	38	48	55	61	78	8Ø	87	88	9Ø

A polyphase sort depends on the number of sequences on each tape at each stage. For the final stage we have the following.

tape	A	B	C
number of sequences	1	Ø	Ø

This can be reached only if at the stage before we had this situation.

tape	A	B	C
number of sequences	Ø	1	1

The single sequence on tape B came from merging a sequence on tape A with a sequence on tape C. Thus at the stage before this was the situation

tape	A	B	C
number of sequences	1	Ø	2

Working backwards in this way, we can build up Figure 8–5. At first sight, this table does not tell us very much, but a pattern emerges if we redraw it as shown in Figure

	Tape		
	A	B	C
Final stage	1	Ø	Ø
Stage 4	Ø	1	1
Stage 3	1	Ø	2
Stage 2	3	2	Ø
Stage 1	Ø	5	3
Initial situation	8		

Figure 8–5   Distribution of sequences

186

	Tape						
	A	B	C	A	B	C	A
Final stage	1	∅	∅				
Stage 4		1	1	∅			
Stage 3			2	1	∅		
Stage 2				3	2	∅	
Stage 1					5	3	∅
Initial situation							8

Figure 8–6   The Fibonnacci numbers

8–6. Each of the numbers on the diagonal is the sum of the two previous ones. These are the Fibonnacci numbers.. If at stage 1 the number of sequences on tapes B and C are successive Fibonnacci numbers, the numbers at each later stage are guaranteed correct. Thus the distribution at stage 1 must be

A	B	C
0	F_n	F_{n-1}

where F_n denotes the nth Fibonnacci number. To obtain this distribution at stage 1 it appears that the file to be sorted must have exactly

$$F_n + F_{n-1}$$

sequences, that is F_{n+1} sequences. However, if the number of sequences on tape A initially is not an exact Fibonnacci number, dummy sequences can be added to tapes B and C. The flow chart fragment in Figure 8–7 is an outline of stage 1. Once the initial distribution of sequences has been completed, the polyphase sort is similar to the classical four tape sort but a bit simpler, since sequences are not copied onto alternate tapes.

As with the classical four tape sort, we can depict the various stages of the polyphase sort on a tree. This is shown in Figure 8–8. Each record is copied as many times as it passes through levels of the tree. To sort these fourteen records, which initially formed eight sequences, fifty eight records have to be copied. Despite using only three magnetic tape units this sort has taken hardly any more input and output than the classical four tape sort. If four tape units had been available a very great saving could have been made and the larger the file the greater the saving.

187

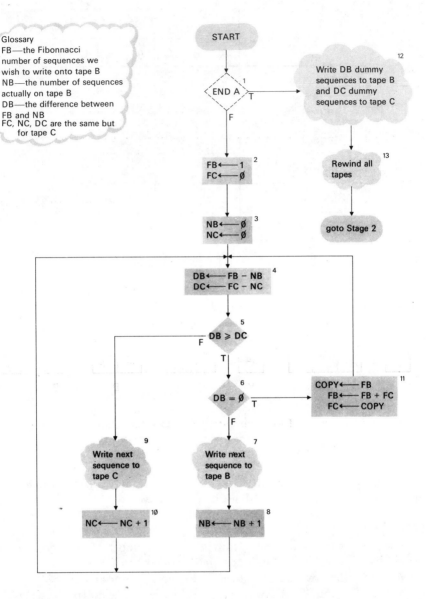

Glossary
FB—the Fibonnacci number of sequences we wish to write onto tape B
NB—the number of sequences actually on tape B
DB—the difference between FB and NB
FC, NC, DC are the same but for tape C

START

END A
T → Write DB dummy sequences to tape B and DC dummy sequences to tape C

F

FB ← 1
FC ← Ø

NB ← Ø
NC ← Ø

DB ← FB − NB
DC ← FC − NC

DB ≥ DC
F
T

DB = Ø
T → COPY ← FB
FB ← FB + FC
FC ← COPY

F

Write next sequence to tape C
Write next sequence to tape B

NC ← NC + 1
NB ← NB + 1

Rewind all tapes

goto Stage 2

Figure 8–7   First stage of the polyphase sort

188

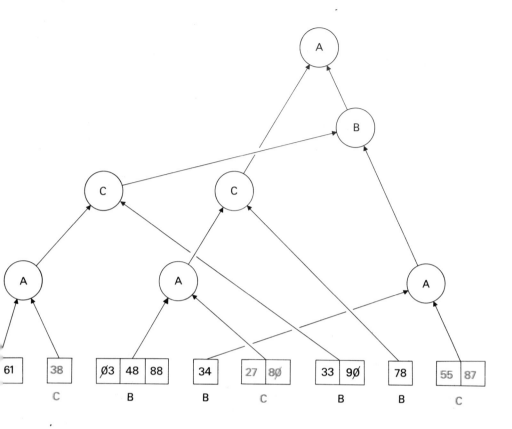

Figure 8–8 Tree representation of polyphase sort

Questions 8.3

. (i) With tape A initially having records with the following keys,

tape A | 2Ø | 74 | 94 | 22 | 93 | 45 | 44 | 16 | Ø4 | 32 | Ø3 | 62 | 61 | 89 |

write down the content of the tapes at each stage of a polyphase three tape sort.

(ii) Construct a tree which shows how these initial sequences are merged.

. In a polyphase sort with four tape units, at each stage sequences are read from three of the tapes and the merged sequence is written to the fourth. If there are originally seventeen sequences on tape A, how many should be allocated to each of tapes B, C and D before the first merge?

3. Draw the tree for a polyphase sort using four tapes and the fourteen records of the examples in this section. How many records are copied?

4. Draw a flow chart for the three tape polyphase sort.

8.4 SELECTION SORTING

In the external sorts that we have described, the first stage is to copy the file from one tape to several others. This can be improved by using the opportunity to set up longer initial sequences. The easiest way to do this is to read into store as many records as can be fitted in, sort them using an internal sort and to write them as a single sequence on one of the output tapes. The sorting can be done by scanning through the records in store, finding the record with the lowest key and writing it to the tape; then finding the record with the next lowest key and writing that out, continuing until all records have been written as a single sequence. This is called a selection sort.

The remarkable thing about a selection sort is that with a simple modification sequences can be built up which are longer than the number of records which can be held simultaneously in store. Once a record has been selected and copied out, the area where it was held in store is no longer required. Another record can be read in and held there. If this new record has a key which is greater than the key of the record just written out, it can then be included in the sequence being built up. This method is called replacement selection. To see how it works suppose that our records are so large that only four can be held in store at once and let us see what happens to the fourteen records whose keys were used for our previous examples. The keys were as follows.

tape A | 24 | 61 | 38 | Ø3 | 48 | 88 | 34 | 27 | 8Ø | 33 | 9Ø | 78 | 55 | 87 |

As many records as possible are read into store.

24
61
38
Ø3

The record with the lowest key, Ø3, is written out and the next record is read into its place.

190

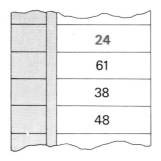

The record with the lowest key, 24, is written out and the next record is read into its place.

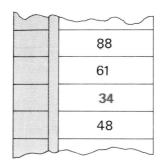

After writing out the record with key **38** and reading in the next record the position is as follows.

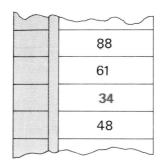

This new record has a key which is smaller than the last one. It cannot be included in the sequence and must wait until another sequence is begun. Meanwhile building up the current sequence can continue using records from the other locations in store. Eventually the following two sequences are set up.

tape B	Ø3	24	38	48	61	8Ø	88	9Ø

tape C	27	33	34	55	78	87

The flow chart for replacement selection is based on repeatedly searching the list of records held in store for the one to be written out next. If the key of the last record to be written is held in a variable LAST, the search is for the next highest record. Suppose that a variable NEXT is initialized as a high number. If

$$LAST < KEY(R_J)$$

and

$$KEY(R_J) < NEXT$$

are true, the Jth record in the list is a candidate for being the next record to be written. Thus the loop to select the next record is as given in Figure 8–9.

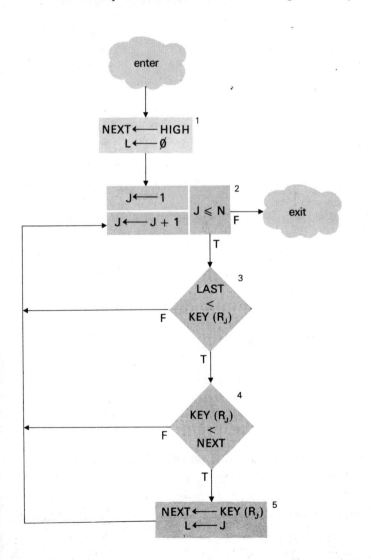

Glossary

NEXT—the key of the next record to be writte[n]
L—the index of the next record to be writte[n]
N—the number of rec[ord]s that can be held in stor[e] simultaneously
LAST—the key of the [last] record to be written

Figure 8–9   The selection loop

192

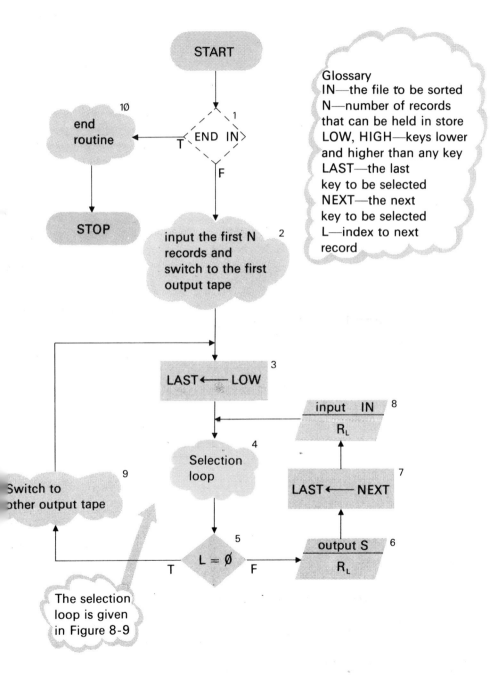

Figure 8–10   Replacement selection

If LAST is greater than all the keys in store the loop will not find a record to be written out and the end of a subsequence has been reached. Under these circumstances box 5 of this fragment will not have been executed and so L will still have the value Ø. This can be used to test whether a record is to be written or the next subsequence is to be started. These ideas are combined in Figure 8–10.

This flow chart can be used with both the classical four tape sort and the polyphase sort. In the former, it is easy to expand clouds 9 and 1Ø of the flow chart; in the latter their details are much more complicated. In whatever context it is used, the purpose of replacement selection is to set up longer initial sequences. If the records are initially in random order and all keys are different, the average length of sequence set up by replacement selection is roughly twice the number of records that can be held in store at one time.

Questions 8.4

1. What sequences will be built up by replacement selection if there is room in store for only three records and the initial tape is as follows?

tape A | 2Ø | 74 | 94 | 22 | 93 | 45 | 44 | 16 | Ø4 | 32 | Ø3 | 62 | 61 | 89

2. What length of subsequence will be built up by replacement selection if

   (i)   the file is originally sorted in the reverse order to what is required,
   (ii) the file is in fact already sorted?

3. What are the details of cloud 1Ø of the flow chart of Figure 8–10 if replacement selection is being used in the classical four tape sort?

4. What alterations must be made to the flow chart of Figure 8–10 to make the process a routine that could be used in the polyphase sort?

CHAPTER NINE

RANDOM ACCESS

Random Access Devices

Computed Entry Addressing

Indexes

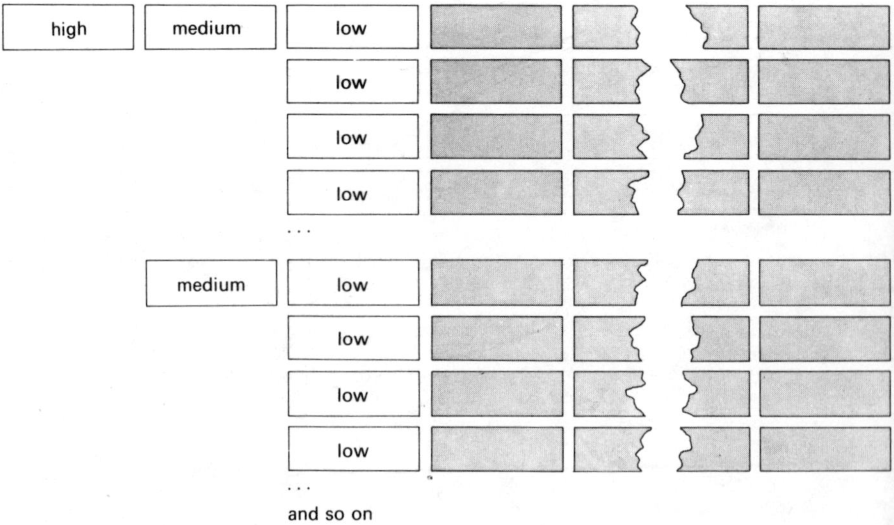

high	medium	low				
		low				
		low				
		low				
	. . .					
	medium	low				
		low				
		low				
		low				
	. . .					
	and so on					

9.1 RANDOM ACCESS DEVICES

Although serial files are surprisingly flexible, they are too restricting in some circumstances. For instance, batch processing can waste one of the great assets of a computer: its speed. Each record may be handled in a few milliseconds once it reaches the central processor, but the delays of gathering data into batches, preparing it for input and correcting errors may mean that hours or even days elapse before results reach the person who wants them. When updating, serial files are inefficient if only a few of the records are changed; this is referred to as a low hit rate. In this case, even records for which there is no relevant input data are copied onto the carried forward file and the updating program wastes time merely copying records from one file to another. Further, serial processing is awkward for files which cannot be sorted conveniently. Batch processing relies on files being sorted into a well-defined order, and cannot be used when no clear cut sorting order exists. In short, serial file processing is not suitable when

(i)   results are wanted quickly,
(ii) the hit rate is low,
(iii) no suitable sorting order exists.

These disadvantages arise from the constraints of serial devices that records have to be processed in the order in which they appear on the file and that at any time a file is used for input or for output, but not for both. These restrictions prevent the use of many of the techniques for handling data that we discussed in Chapters 3, 4 and 5 such as access vectors and pointers. There are other backing store devices which are not constrained in these ways; they are called random access devices. Locations on a random access device are given addresses and when reading or writing a block it is necessary to specify which location is to be used.

Because both use addressed locations, it is sometimes useful to think of a random access backing store in terms of store itself. It is important however to be aware of the difference between the two kinds of store. Each addressed location in store holds a small binary pattern which can be interpreted as, say, a single instruction. On a random access device each addressed location holds a block of data which may contain several thousand characters.

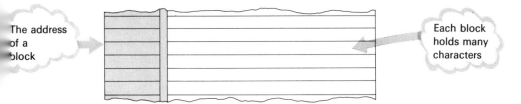

The address of a block

Each block holds many characters

Since data is transferred into store in blocks, there is nothing to be gained from addressing data in smaller chunks than one address per block. However, it is useful to be able to choose the block size rather than be restricted to one fixed size by the design of the peripheral and a choice is normally given to the programmer.

Unlike serial files, where magnetic tape has been standard for a number of years, manufacturers offer many types of random access devices. We shall describe two popular types, magnetic drums and moving head discs.

Drums

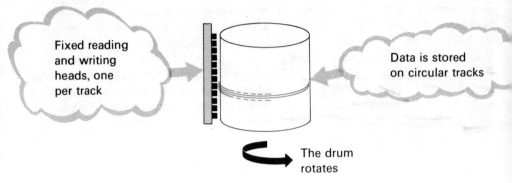

Fixed reading and writing heads, one per track

Data is stored on circular tracks

The drum rotates

Figure 9–1   A magnetic drum

Figure 9–1 shows a magnetic drum. The drum, which rotates at high speed, has a magnetic surface. Data is stored on several circular tracks on this surface, each track having its own reading and writing heads. The time taken to read or write a block consists of

(i)   selecting the track,
(ii) rotating the drum until the beginning of the block is under the head,
(iii) transferring the data to or from store.

Steps (i) and (ii) have to be carried out before any data is transferred. The time taken to perform these two steps is called the latency. The time taken for step (iii) is called the transfer time and the total time taken to complete all steps is called the access time. As you might expect, for a drum, step (i) is entirely electronic and involves a negligible fraction of the access time. Thus the latency and the transfer rate are almost wholly dependent on the speed of the mechanical parts.

Drums come in all shapes and sizes, but a typical small drum might have a storage capacity of two million characters with an average access time of ten milliseconds.

Moving Head Discs

Figure 9–2 is a photograph of a typical moving head disc. It consists of several parallel plates, each rather like a gramophone record but without grooves. When the disc unit is in use the plates are rotating at high speed. Each surface, apart from the top and bottom ones, is coated with a thin layer of magnetic oxide and data is accessed by a head which moves just above the surface, rather like a gramophone pick-up, but

Figure 9–2   A moving head disc unit

with one head per magnetic surface. A typical disc has 20 magnetic surfaces and 400 tracks of data on each. The total storage capacity is about sixty million characters and the average access time is about a twentieth of a second. Figure 9–3 shows a typical way of arranging the data blocks on a surface. Transferring data to or from store requires the following.

(i)   The head is moved until it is over the required track.
(ii) The disc rotates until the correct block passes under the head.
(iii) Data flows via the head to or from store.

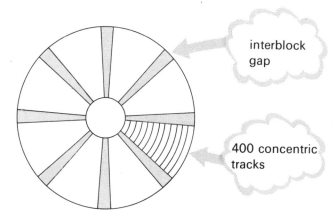

interblock gap

400 concentric tracks

Figure 9–3   Arrangement of data on a disc

As with all types of backing store, discs have mechanical parts and cannot operate as quickly as the electronic central processor. Most of the access time is taken up with

199

the time taken to position the head over a given track which on a typical disc unit varies from 0 to 75 milliseconds. Once a track has been found, a given block can be located in an average time of 12·5 milliseconds.

Notice that with most random access devices the access time is not constant for all blocks. For instance, with a moving head disc, the access time varies with the distance that the head has to move, and the time taken to read the data into store plays a very small part in the final figure for the effective transfer rate. It may be possible to organize the file so that little head movement is required.

For example, in the special but important case of processing a random access file sequentially, the average access time achieved can be very much faster than the average access time for processing the file randomly. Considerable ingenuity goes into arranging data on discs to cut down head movement but the methods depend on the exact equipment used and therefore are beyond the scope of this book. We shall concentrate on the broader aspects of random access devices and outline some of the general methods that are used to process files stored on them.

Question 9.1

1. A moving head disc has 20 magnetic surfaces with 400 tracks of data on each. The time taken to position the moving heads varies from nothing, if the heads are already in position, to 75 millisecs to move across the whole disc, with an average of 35 millisecs. The rotation time is 25 millisecs. The actual transfer rate is 400,000 characters per second. What is the average time taken to read a block of 2,000 characters,

   (i) with serial processing when the next block is on the same or next track to the last,

   (ii) with random processing when the next block can be anywhere on the disc?

9.2 COMPUTED ENTRY ADDRESSING

The machine instructions to handle data stored on magnetic drums and discs make for such complicated programs that a programmer rarely addresses the peripheral directly but uses software routines and special hardware facilities, both provided by the manufacturer, as an intermediary. Having specified the block size, the programmer is usually able to refer to the blocks by means of integers.

$$\emptyset, 1, 2, 3, \ldots$$

The software routines then generate the necessary machine instructions, thus converting a block number into the detailed specification of track, surface and position where the required block is stored.

Unlike serial devices, random access devices can be used for both input and output by the same program and blocks within the file can be accessed in any order. This flexibility is very useful but adds to the burden of writing programs, since every access must specify a block number and whether reading or writing is required. When using a serial file, data is read from an input file in the order in which it appears, and is stored on an output file in the order in which it is written by the program. With random access files, part of any program must be a routine to compute the address at which the file is to be accessed, hence the term computed entry addressing. The address must be included in every input or output instruction. We shall use the following input and output boxes in our flow charts.

(i)   To read a block of data from location N of file F to a location A in store.

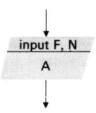

(ii)   To write a block of data from location A in store to location N of file F.

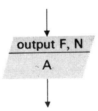

Be careful not to confuse what is meant by these instructions. To copy data from a file to store is input to a program; to copy data from store to the file is output.

For a random access file each record must have a key which can be used to determine where on the file the record is stored. Routines are needed which, given a key, determine where to store the corresponding record, or find the record in the file. These routines have much in common with the techniques used for handling data within store. Indexing, hash coding and linked lists all have counterparts used with random access devices. Indexing is the simplest method for handling data in store mainly because it gives direct access to the required data. The equivalent method on a random access file is for the address to be either the key or a number that can be easily calculated from the key. Such calculations are called key to address transformations.

Example

A file consists of 100,000 records, numbered 0, 1, 2, 3 etc. up to 99,999, each 100 characters long. With a block size of 1000 characters, the address rule might be that if the key is k, divide k by 10. Ordinary division gives

$$k = 1\emptyset q + r.$$

The record will be the rth in block q.

In practice few files have records with such convenient keys as were given in the example and, despite its desirability, a suitable key to address transformation can rarely be found for large files. Hash coding, however, does not require such a well behaved key and is often used with random access files. Within store, the most time consuming factor in using hash coding is the sequential searching required, but with a random access file in which several successive records are held in a block quite long sequential searches can be made while reading only one or two blocks. Thus the average time to access a given record using hash coding may be little greater than the time to read a single block.

Example

In a random access file, records are stored using hash coding. There are 1000 blocks, numbered $\emptyset, 1, 2, \ldots, 999$. The records are 100 characters long and are held 5 to a block. If the key is k where

$$k = 1\emptyset\emptyset\emptyset q + r$$

then the first record tried is the first in block r. We want to construct a flow chart to read the unsorted file from magnetic tape and set up the file on the disc. The central part of the flow chart is given in Figure 9–4. This calculates r, the remainder after division by $1\emptyset\emptyset\emptyset$, reads block r and sees if it is full. Figure 9–5 shows this core embedded in a loop to read successive records from magnetic tape and to write the records to the disc. Figure 9–6 expands the step which assigns to L the address of the next block. It tests both for the end of the disc file and for the file being full.

Not all data structures are suitable for use with random access devices. Differences between the methods used within store and the random access methods arise partly from the sheer size of many files (literally millions of records), but mainly from a desire to minimize the number of blocks accessed at each stage of processing. Within the central processor, the time to access an item of data does not depend upon where it is stored, but if several records have to be read from a file much time is saved if they are all stored in the same block. For instance with variable length data in store an access vector can be used. This is an indirect method of addressing in which data is stored in one area and a vector, stored in another area, points to the record we require. There are two differences between store and backing store that make an access vector inefficient for backing store.

(i) When reading from backing store the exact location in which a record is stored is not important. What is needed is the address of the block which contains the record in question. An indirect method of referring to data in a random access file will give the address of a block rather than a record.

(ii) With a large file there will be so many records that an access vector will be too large to hold in store, and will itself have to be on backing store. The vector will occupy a large number of blocks, many of which may have to be read before the

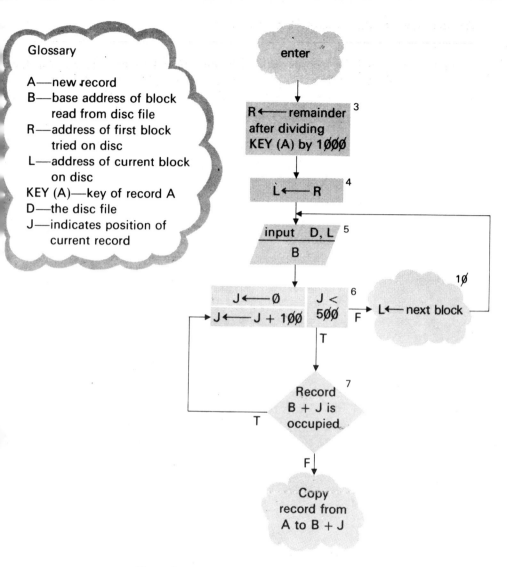

Glossary

A—new record
B—base address of block read from disc file
R—address of first block tried on disc
L—address of current block on disc
KEY (A)—key of record A
D—the disc file
J—indicates position of current record

enter

R ⟵ remainder after dividing KEY (A) by 1ØØØ   3

L ⟵ R   4

input   D, L   5
B

J ⟵ Ø   J ⟵ J + 1ØØ   J < 5ØØ   6   F   L ⟵ next block   1Ø

T

Record B + J is occupied   7

T

F

Copy record from A to B + J

Figure 9—4   Core of hash coding routine

required record can be found. In fact the access vector itself will constitute a fair sized file.

Questions 9.2

1. Suppose that 250 market research interviewers each carry out 100 interviews. Each interview produces a record which is 500 characters long. How would you organize these records on a random access file using a block size of 2,000 characters?

203

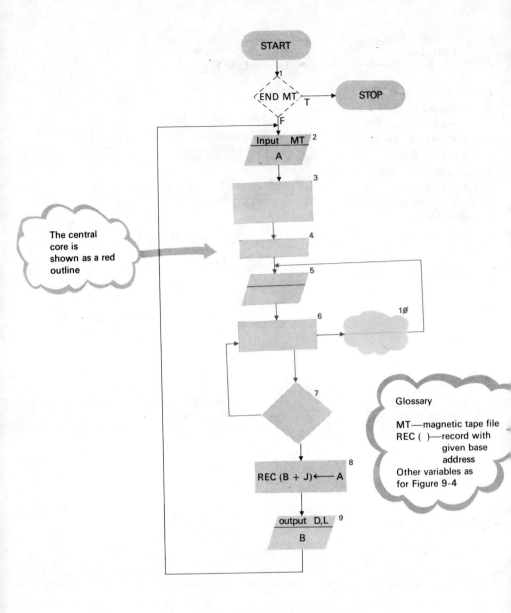

The central core is shown as a red outline

Glossary

MT—magnetic tape file
REC ( )—record with
given base
address
Other variables as
for Figure 9-4

Figure 9–5 The complete hash coding routine

2. Draw a flow chart to find a record given its key, in a file in which records are
organized by a hash coding routine as described in the example worked in this
section. That is, the records are held 5 to a block and if the key is k where

$$k = 1000q + r$$

the first record to try is the first in block r.

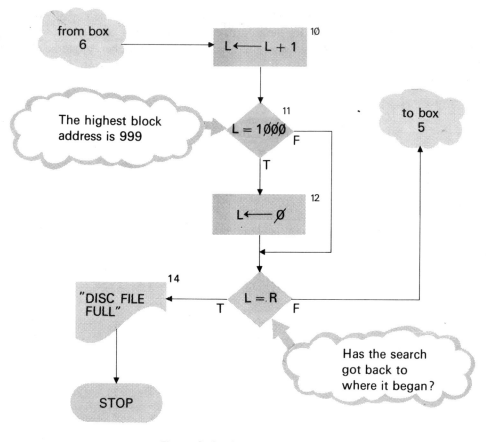

from box 6

L ← L + 1   10

The highest block address is 999

L = 1ØØØ   11
T
F

to box 5

L ← Ø   12

"DISC FILE FULL"   14

L = R
T
F

Has the search got back to where it began?

STOP

Figure 9–6   L ← next block

9.3   INDEXES

In practice most random access files are stored with some sort of index. Indexes are so called because in some ways they are similar to the index at the back of a book. This is the third use of the word *index* that you have seen in this book and is not the same as the meanings of the word that we have seen so far; namely for an array subscript and in the index register. In this section we consider indexes for random access files which are static, that is neither deletions nor insertions are made after the file has been created. Chapter 10 looks at more complicated situations.

A static file with an index consists of two parts, the blocks containing data records and index blocks. To set up the data part of the file the records must be sorted. They are then divided into blocks with as many records per block as will fit. This is a straightforward way to hold the data. The only wasted space occurs with variable length records when there may be unused space at the end of a block. A typical block might hold all records with sort keys between JOHNS and JOHNSON, and, since

205

the file is sorted, all that is required to find a record is to know the key of the first record in each block. An index for the records consists of a list of keys, each key being the means of identifying a block. A pointer, such as a block number, might be added to each key, but if the keys are stored in order the index would have entries such as in Figure 9–7.

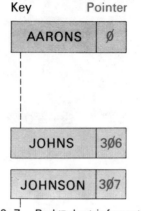

Figure 9–7   Redundant information

The pointer is redundant since the 3Ø6th entry in the index refers to block number 3Ø6. In practice the index would consist of just the keys, which must be fixed length and stored sequentially. The SEEK subroutine in Figure 9–8 uses this index to find the block in which a record with a given key is stored.

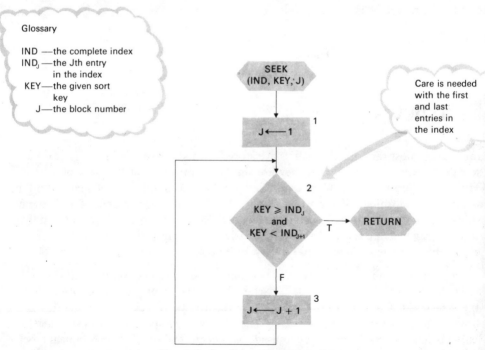

Figure 9–8   Searching the index

206

If the block size were large enough a special block could contain all the keys in the entire index. This kind of index would be easy to work with, but indexes are rarely small enough to be held in a single block. Instead a hierarchy of indexes is used. Here is a typical example. A file consists of 625,000 records each 200 characters long, including a 20 character sort key. How do we organize an index for this file given that the block size is 1,000 characters? With the given block size five records can be held in each block.

| record 1 | record 2 | record 3 | record 4 | record 5 |

There will be $625,000 \div 5 = 125,000$ data blocks.

The key of the first record in each block has to be recorded in a index. This index will contain

$125,000 \times 20 = 2,500,000$ characters.

This is far too many to hold in store simultaneously and so the index itself has to be held on the random access device. With the block size of 1,000 characters each index block can hold 50 keys. Therefore the entire index requires

$125,000 \div 50 = 2,500$ blocks.

It would be inefficient if the whole index had to be searched to find a record with a given key. Therefore an index to the index is created by taking the first key of each block of the first index, which is called a low level index. There are 2,500 such keys and these are held in

$2,500 \div 50 = 50$ blocks.

This index to the low level index is called a medium level index. Since the medium level index itself occupies 50 blocks, there is a final high level index which records the first key in each block of the medium level index.

Figure 9–9 shows how these indexes are used. To find the record with a given key requires the following operations.

(i)   Read the high level index and search it to find which medium level index applies to the specified record.

(ii) Read the medium level index and search it to find which low level index applies to the specified record.

(iii) Read the low level index and search it to find which block contains the specified record.

(iv) Read the block and search it to find the record.

By using this arrangement of indexes any record in this large file can be found by reading only four blocks, yet the indexes use relatively little space on backing store.

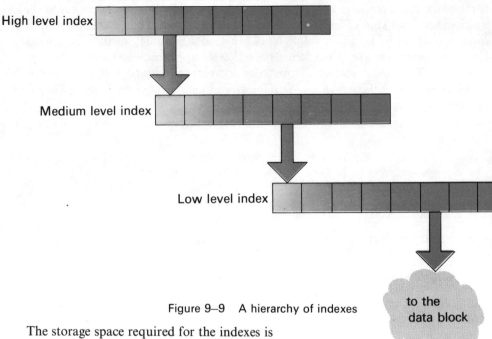

High level index

Medium level index

Low level index

to the
data block

Figure 9–9   A hierarchy of indexes

The storage space required for the indexes is

   2,500 blocks for the low level indexes
     50 blocks for the medium level indexes
      1 block for the high level index

For this file, 2,551 blocks are used for indexes and 125,000 blocks are used for data. That is, of a file of 127,551 blocks about 98 per cent are used for data.

Notice the importance of having a large block size. If the block size were 200 characters, that is, one record per block, each index would hold only 10 keys. There would be

   625,000 blocks of data (one record per block),
    62,500 low level index (ten keys per block),
     6,250 medium level indexes,
       625 high level indexes,
        63 extra high level indexes,
         7 extra extra high level indexes,
         1 extra extra extra high level index.

To find each record seven blocks would have to be read and only 90 per cent of the storage space would be used for data. Thus large block sizes are important with random access files and the larger the file the larger the block size should be to get as many keys as possible to fit into one block.

On a moving head disc, these blocks are stored in such a way as to minimize head movement. This can sometimes be achieved by storing the index blocks close to the data blocks to which they refer. Figure 9–10 shows one way in which the various blocks of data and index can be arranged.

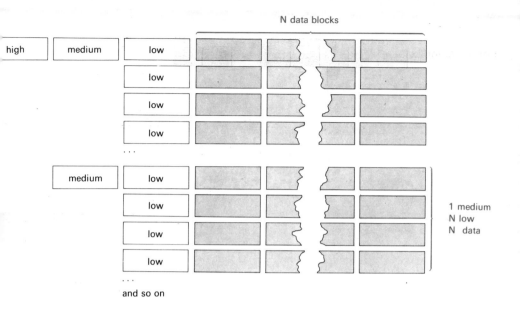

Figure 9–10   An indexed file

Example

The problem is to construct a subroutine which, given a key, finds the block in which the record is stored. With the arrangement shown in Figure 9–10 suppose that the high level index is stored in block $\emptyset$. Suppose that a given key lies between the Jth and the $(J + 1)$th keys in the high level index. The following equation gives M, the address of the medium level index that is needed.

$$M = (J - 1)(N^2 + N + 1) + 1$$

number of blocks
between each
medium level index

address of
the first medium
level index

If the given key lies between the Jth and the $(J + 1)$th keys of the medium level index, the next equation gives L, the address of the low level index that is needed.

$$L = (J - 1)(N + 1) + (M + 1)$$

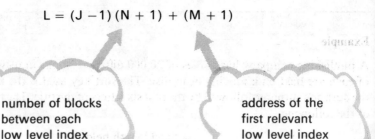

number of blocks
between each
low level index

address of the
first relevant
low level index

As shown in Figure 9–11, the subroutine falls into three similar sections which search respectively the high, medium and low level indexes. Each section makes use of the SEEK subroutine in Figure 9–8.

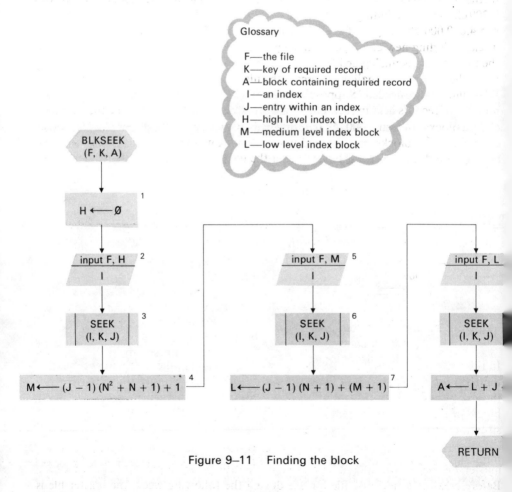

Glossary

F—the file
K—key of required record
A—block containing required record
I—an index
J—entry within an index
H—high level index block
M—medium level index block
L—low level index block

BLKSEEK
(F, K, A)

1 $H \leftarrow \emptyset$

2 input F, H
I

3 SEEK
(I, K, J)

4 $M \leftarrow (J - 1)(N^2 + N + 1) + 1$

5 input F, M
I

6 SEEK
(I, K, J)

7 $L \leftarrow (J - 1)(N + 1) + (M + 1)$

input F, L
I

SEEK
(I, K, J)

$A \leftarrow L + J$

RETURN

Figure 9–11 Finding the block

Example

A publishing company has copies of 20,000 different books in its warehouse; details of each are held on a moving head disc. The sort key used is the first four letters of the author's surname followed by the first six letters of the title. The full record consists of the following.

Sort key	—a fixed length field
Description of book	—a variable length field
Quantity in stock	—a fixed length field

Orders received from bookshops are processed individually. For each title an operator types on a terminal the sort key which consists of the first four letters of the author's surname and the first six letters of the title. A computer program searches the file to find all records with the specified sort key and prints the description of each onto the terminal. The operator decides which is required and indicates this by typing in further characters. Here are some details of the file. The average length of a record is 200 characters including a sort key of 10 characters. The file of 20,000 titles therefore has 4,000,000 characters of data. The publisher publishes about 20 new books, per week, including new editions. With such a small number of insertions and deletions the file is taken as unchanged for a period of a week and not altered during that time. Since the file is quite small, to re-create the file every weekend is not too extravagant. What indexes are needed? Suppose we try a block size of 1,000 characters. The average number of records held in each block will probably be at least four. The total number of data blocks is about 5,000. As the sort key is 10 characters long, each low level index can refer to 100 blocks and one medium level index would refer to 10,000 blocks. No high level index is needed. The lay out of the file is shown in Figure 9–12.

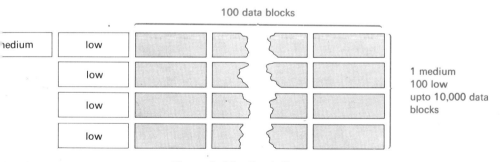

Figure 9–12   Book file

In this example a slightly smaller block size could probably be used without creating the need for a high level index, but search time would not be improved. Also, since the records are of variable length, there is definitely a waste of space by using a small block size. In this case wastage is not a problem but it certainly can be in other situations.

Let us consider the problem of setting up the file every weekend. Suppose that a master file is held on magnetic tape and alterations are input on punched cards. Before creating a new disc file for use during the following week, the master file is updated and a carried forward file is written on magnetic tape. The disc file is then created. Figure 9–13 shows the system flow chart. The file creation program builds up each block in store before writing it onto the disc file. Three areas are reserved in store for the current data and low level index blocks and the medium level index. The outline flow chart is shown in Figure 9–14.

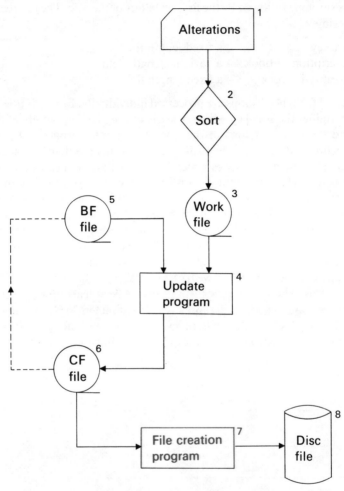

Figure 9–13   System flow chart for re-creating book file

By using indexes and searching them within store very little time is spent reading or writing a record given its key, but it is important to remember that the files discussed in this section are static. That is to say insertion, deletion, or amendment to the length of records are not allowed. In the next chapter we shall discuss the problems of dynamic files.

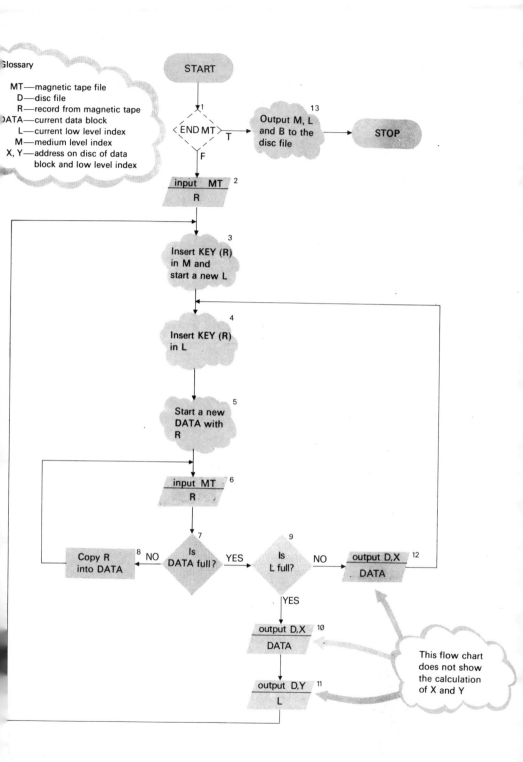

Glossary

MT—magnetic tape file
D—disc file
R—record from magnetic tape
DATA—current data block
L—current low level index
M—medium level index
X, Y—address on disc of data
    block and low level index

START

1 ⟨ END MT ⟩ T → 13 Output M, L and B to the disc file → STOP

F

2 input MT
R

3 Insert KEY (R) in M and start a new L

4 Insert KEY (R) in L

5 Start a new DATA with R

6 input MT
R

7 Is DATA full?

8 Copy R into DATA   NO

YES → 9 Is L full?

NO → 12 output D,X
DATA

YES

10 output D,X
DATA

11 output D,Y
L

This flow chart does not show the calculation of X and Y

Figure 9–14   File creation program

213

Questions 9.3

1. An index is to be set up for a static random access file consisting of 768,000 records, each 100 characters long and including a 15 character sort key.

   (i) How many blocks of file storage are required for the low level and medium level indexes if the block size is 600 characters?

   (ii) If the block size is doubled to 1200 characters how many medium level indexes are then required?

2. Expand Figure 9–14 into a detailed flow chart.

3. A mail order firm has a file of customer records stored on a magnetic disc. The records are of variable length and sorted into alphabetical sequence of customers' names. (The name is used as a sort key.)

The average length of each record is	200 characters
The block size is	1000 characters
The name field is fixed at	25 characters
The firm has	64,000 customers

   Within each block the records are arranged by the fourth method on page 157 with unused space at the end of each block being wasted. The blocks are held on the disc as an indexed file.

   (i) Approximately how many blocks will the file use? Of these how many are
   data blocks,
   low level index blocks,
   medium level index blocks,
   high level index blocks?

   (ii) Construct a flow chart of an algorithm which reads a sequence of names and prints the records corresponding to those names. You can assume that no name is duplicated, but some names may have no record on the file.

CHAPTER TEN

DYNAMIC FILE STRUCTURES

Indexed Sequential Files

Inverted Files and Multilists

A Data Base

File Security

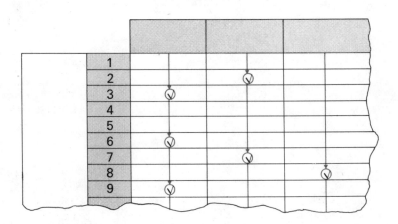

10.1 INDEXED SEQUENTIAL FILES

Data structures and files storage techniques can be classified by whether they are suitable for

(i) random or sequential processing,
(ii) static or dynamic files,
(iii) fixed or variable length records.

No method of storing data that we have mentioned covers the most difficult case, that is random processing of dynamic files of variable length records, yet many practical situations demand just this. In Chapter 9 you saw that random access files with indexes do not have the constraints of serial files. They are not restricted to sequential processing and both reading or writing to the same file is allowed. However, indexes with data stored in the manner described in Section 9.3 require a static file. In this section we discuss a different method of storing data within blocks which allows the insertion and deletion of individual records, that is, a dynamic rather than a static file structure. As you will see, the arrangement allows for insertion or deletion of records in an ordered file without changing the indexes. The resulting file can be processed randomly using the indexes or sequentially without them; it is called an indexed sequential file.

The problem of processing a dynamic file randomly is not peculiar to computing; in fact, exactly the same difficulty arises with many manual filing systems. Figure 10–1 shows part of a library card catalogue, divided among many drawers, with labels to

Figure 10–1   A library catalogue

specify which records are held in each drawer. If all the drawers were kept full, a new record could not be added in sequence without extensive movements of cards and relabelling of drawers. Therefore space is left in each drawer, so that records can be inserted or deleted without altering the contents of more than one drawer. This gets round most of the problems of insertion; deletion is no problem at all. The only difficulty occurs if after a long period one of the drawers becomes full. In this case, the library staff have a choice between either having an overflow drawer for any extra cards, or reorganizing the whole file by moving cards from one drawer to another and relabelling the drawers.

A similar method of storing records can be used with a random access computer file. The storage space available is divided into a number of sections, which are aptly called buckets, and indexes are set up which specify the range of keys of the records held in each bucket. Each entry in an index now refers to a bucket, not to a block as before. By analogy, a bucket corresponds to a drawer of the card catalogue and the index to the labels on the drawers.

Initially the file is sorted and indexes set up, but space is left in each bucket to insert extra records, as shown in Figure 10–2. Reading a record uses the indexes in the manner of the flow chart in Figure 9–11. When a record is inserted into the file the

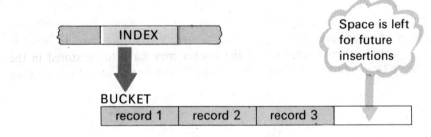

Figure 10–2   Space left in bucket for insertions

indexes are searched to find into which bucket it should go. The record is copied into the bucket without changing the indexes. Since, after several new records have been inserted into a bucket, there may be insufficient room in it for another record to be inserted, overflow areas are provided in which new records can be stored once the bucket is full. Each overflow area is shared by many or all of the data buckets. The file therefore consists of the following,

(i)   index blocks,
(ii)   data buckets,
(iii) overflow areas.

We begin by looking at the buckets associated with a file which has only a single medium level index. In practice a common arrangement is to have each bucket consist of exactly one block and we shall consider only this case. Figure 10–3 shows one way of arranging the indexes, buckets and overflow areas. The overflow area has itself been divided into several blocks. Corresponding to each N data buckets there is

218

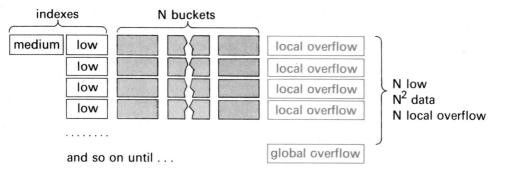

indexes   N buckets

medium	low			local overflow
	low			local overflow
	low			local overflow
	low			local overflow

N low
N² data
N local overflow

. . . .

and so on until . . .   global overflow

Figure 10–3   A common arrangement of overflow areas

a local overflow block and in case the local overflow block should itself overflow there is a global overflow block for the entire file; for the global overflow block to overflow spells trouble. This layout, in which the index and local overflow areas are stored next to the data buckets to which they refer, is good for files on moving head discs, since a fair amount of processing is possible with a minimum of head movement. This reduces the time taken to read from the overflow blocks. Using this file layout, Figure 10–4 shows the procedure for finding and processing a record given the key.

Several different methods are used for storing the individual records within the data buckets and overflow areas. Many records will be stored within each bucket but records that would otherwise belong to the bucket may have to be stored in the overflow areas. Usually the records will be variable length but we start by describing a method of storing fixed length records.

Fixed Length Records

With fixed length records a convenient way to store data in a bucket is to use a linked list, since the pointers can point to records in an overflow area just as easily as they can point to records within the same bucket. Each record in a bucket has the following fields.

| BUCK | REC | DATA |
| | | |

A two part pointer to the next record in sequence

The data part of the record which includes the key

219

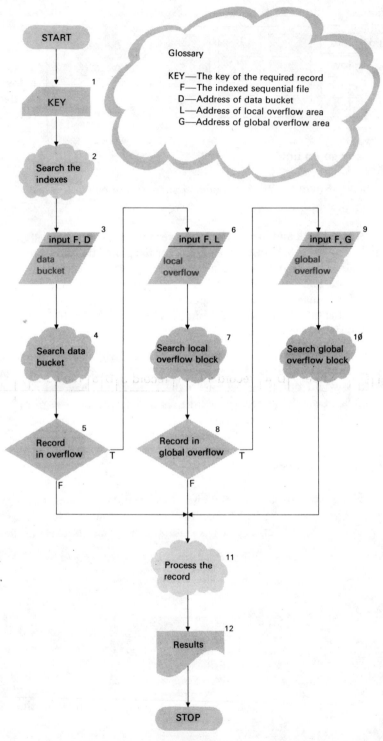

Figure 10−4 Processing a record with a specified key

220

The pointer to the next record in sequence is in two parts; BUCK which indicates which bucket holds the next record, and REC which points to the record within that bucket. The BUCK field might take the following values.

D—the next record is in a data bucket,
L—the next record is in a local overflow bucket,
G—the next record is in the global overflow bucket.

The first three fields of a bucket are also pointers.

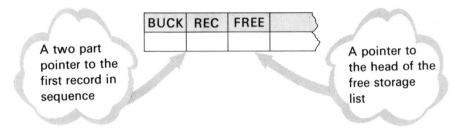

At some stage of processing a bucket might contain the following records.

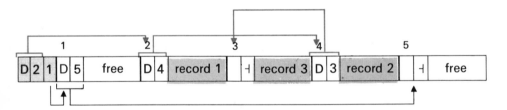

Part of the bucket is occupied by records (red shading); the other parts are free (unshaded) and at the beginning of the bucket are the pointers to the lists of records and free storage (grey shading). Overflow buckets are arranged in the same way except that, since the records in an overflow bucket may be the overflow from several data buckets, the first two pointers are left blank. Thus the list of records which are referred to by a single entry in a low level index may be scattered between data, local overflow and global overflow buckets as shown in Figure 10–5. Follow the red lines on this figure and you will see how the two part pointers link the records into sequence.

Variable Length Records

This first method for arranging the records within blocks cannot be used for variable length records. One method for variable length records is to sort the records within each bucket and to use length fields (denoted RL in the figure).

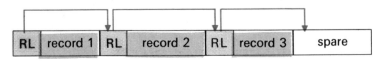

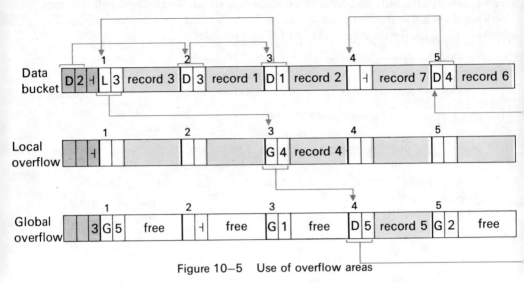

Figure 10–5   Use of overflow areas

Records within the local and global overflow areas are held in exactly the same manner, that is they are sorted into the sequence of keys and stored with length fields. In each block, all spare space is at the end. This arrangement allows relatively simple insertions, but deletion is difficult since a great deal of repositioning may be involved.

Bucket Indexes

To cut down the time spent repositioning data within buckets, one alternative is to divide each bucket into two parts, with space for a bucket index and space for data records. The bucket index is essentially an access vector to the records in that bucket, the only unusual feature being that as well as referring to records within the bucket it may refer to records in the overflow areas. Figure 10–6 shows part of a typical bucket

KEY	ADDRESS
MORGAN, DA	992
MORGAN, DM	88Ø
MORGAN, DT	16Ø2
MORGAN, EA	L
MORGAN, EJ	484

local overflow

Figure 10–6   A bucket index

index. This is not complicated, but there are difficulties with insertion and deletion. In brief, these are as follows.

(i) The bucket index is not static. Because it grows as more records are added to the bucket, the approach shown in Figure 10–7 is sometimes adopted.

(ii) The index might run out of space. In this case the most recent record to be inserted would be copied into the nearest overflow area.

(iii) If a record is deleted, both the gap it leaves in the bucket index and the gap it leaves amongst the records have to be closed up.

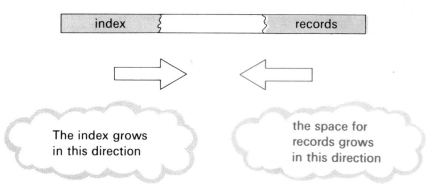

Figure 10–7   A possible arrangement of a block with index

Processing Indexed Sequential Files

Once a bucket has been read into store, processing the records is, in many ways, a problem that you have seen before. A number of records are held in store and it is required to search for, insert or delete a record with a given key. However, there is always the possibility of overflow. This simple difference, combined with a wish to avoid reading or writing blocks unnecessarily adds so much to the complexity of the algorithms that routines to handle them are usually part of the manufacturer's software and the programmer does not need to bother about the details. What he does need to know is how they work in outline.

We have already given in Section 9.3 the steps for processing any indexed file randomly by using the indexes. As well as being used for random processing, an indexed sequential file can be used for sequential processing. Figure 10–8 shows in outline the steps involved in going to the next record in sequence. Note that this procedure makes no use of the indexes.

Setting up an indexed sequential file is similar to setting up a static indexed file. The main differences are that the data buckets are left partly empty to allow for insertion, and the overflow areas have to be made available. The presence of the overflow area means that searching the file for a record with a given key is a bit more complicated than before, but this is a small price to pay for the distinctive feature of indexed sequential files, that they allow for insertion and deletion of variable length records.

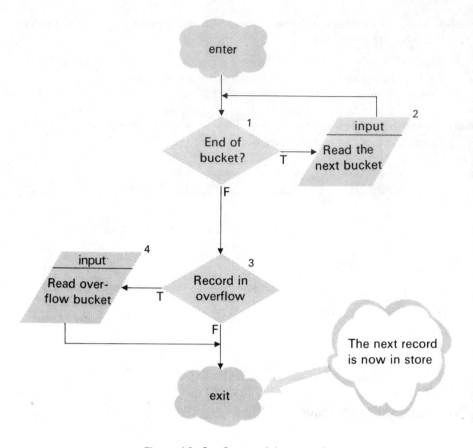

Figure 10–8   Sequential processing

Figure 10–9 is a subroutine to insert a new record into a file which is organized in this way.

Figure 10–10 compares sequential and random processing of indexed sequential files. The figures in this table depend on the way the buckets are organized, on whether sufficient space is available in store to hold more than one bucket at a time and on the number of levels of index; we have assumed that there are high, medium and low level indexes. You can see that sequential processing is very much faster than random processing and unless the hit rate is very low sequential processing should be used.

Questions 10.1

1. (i)   A wholesaler has over 20,000 different items in stock. On average he sells 100 different types of item each day. To maintain a satisfactory service to his customers he needs to update the main file daily. What advantage does an indexed sequential file have over a serial file for processing these transactions?

   (ii)   A mail order company supplies prospective customers with a special Christmas catalogue and keeps a file of customers to whom the catalogue has been

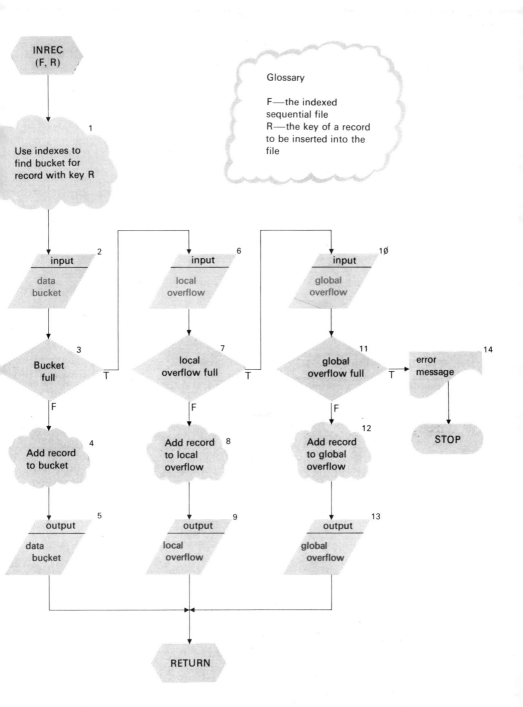

Figure 10–9   Inserting a record into an indexed sequential file

225

Process	Minimum number of transfers	Maximum number of transfers
Sequential read only	Ø	—
Sequential update	Ø	3
Random read only	4	6
Random update	5	7
Insertion or deletion	5	11

Figure 10–10   Processing an indexed sequential file.

sent. During the six months before Christmas the company is adding about 5,000 records to the file every week, with a single updating of the file. The file is sorted in alphabetical sequence of customers' names. Why is a serial file more suitable than a random access file?

2. Expand box 4 of Figure 10–9, for each of the three different bucket layouts described in this section.

3. An indexed sequential file consists of records of average length 250 characters which includes a 40 character key. The bucket size is 2,000 characters. There is a local overflow bucket for every 50 data buckets and a global overflow bucket for every 50 local overflow buckets. The file has a single high level index. When initially established approximately 30 per cent of the space in each data bucket is left blank to allow for insertion.

(i)   What is the total storage space required for the file?
(ii)   What proportion of this space is used for data?

10.2   INVERTED FILES AND MULTILISTS

So far we have looked at files which have a well-defined order into which they can be sorted and used for processing. Not all files have this convenient property and in commercial applications it is rare to find data that is always processed by the same sort key. With serial file processing a common practice is to have several main files sorted in different sequences often with much data in common. Batches of transactions are used to update one file, then resorted into a different sequence and used to update another file. An example of this is on Figure 7–10 where the stock file and supplier file are updated in succession with an intermediate sort. With random access devices an alternative arrangement is often possible. All the data is put into a single file, often called a data base, and a complex of indexes, links and pointers is set up which allows the file to be processed in a variety of sequences.

Here is a typical example involving information retrieval. Because of the enormous numbers of books, journal articles and research reports which are written any research worker has great difficulty knowing where to look for information on a given topic and computer systems are used to help. Although the exact forms taken by these services vary, they all centre on a file of references to which subject information has been added, perhaps in the form of keywords. The form of a record might be the following.

| Article Reference | Keyword | Keyword | ⟩ ⟨ | Keyword |

For instance, two papers on BASIC would appear as follows.

BULL, GM DYNAMIC DEBUGGING IN BASIC COMP J 5.1. FEB 1972 21–24

| BASIC | COMPILER | DEBUGGING | TIME-SHARING |

and

E, JAN FORMAL DEFINITION OF THE BASIC LANGUAGE COMP J 15.1.FEB 1972 37–41

| BSTRACT SYNTAX | BASIC | CONCRETE SYNTAX | LANGUAGE DEFINITION | SYNTAX |

More keywords are usually given than in these examples. Somebody who wants information on a specific topic describes his interests by a list of keywords and relations between them. A person interested in *testing programs on a time sharing computer* might say that he wants references to program testing or debugging with time sharing compilers but does not want anything on BASIC. In terms of keywords he wants

(DEBUGGING or PROGRAM TESTING) and TIME SHARING and COMPILER and (not BASIC).

The input to the search program will be a request record containing a specification such as this for every enquiry.

When very precise and detailed terms are used to describe each item a large number of keywords are needed. This has two potential dangers: the file will be large and therefore slow to search, and an inquiry couched in slightly different terminology may miss an important reference. The opposite arrangement is to use fairly general keywords. This means fewer keywords on the file but each will occur in more records and the individual records will be bigger. The risk is that a person with a very specific inquiry may have to use unnecessarily vague keywords and be offered a large number of references which are of no use to him even though they satisfy the inquiry as he phrased it.

Since, when the file is set up, it is not known which searches will be made, none of the file arrangements seen so far is suitable for this situation. For an alternative approach, the file of article references and keywords can be imagined as a giant array, part of which is shown in Figure 10–11. In this array, a tick indicates that the keyword

Article Reference	Keyword A	Keyword B	Keyword C	Keyword D	Keyword E	Keyword F	Keyword G	Keyword H
Article 1		✓	✓				✓	
Article 2	✓	✓					✓	
Article 3			✓		✓			✓
Article 4		✓				✓		
Article 5				✓		✓	✓	
Article 6	✓			✓				✓

Figure 10–11   A giant array

applies to the corresponding record. Suppose you wanted to know which records, if any, have keyword B and either F or G, but not keyword A. This can be written

(not A) and B and (F or G).

The entire reference file can be searched merely by looking at the columns of this array which correspond to the keywords A, B, F and G. If the array has many thousand columns this is a tremendous saving over searching the entire file. This is an efficient method of searching but an array as large as this one would be difficult to store as it stands. A file of 100,000 records with 1,000 different keywords would be considered small, but the array would have 100,000,000 different positions in it. Fortunately, as each record is likely to use only about 10 of the 1,000 keywords, the array will have few ticks and many spaces and so we can close up the gaps. Here are two alternative methods.

An Inverted File

To create an inverted file the array is inverted (that is rows are turned into columns and vice versa) and then gaps in the rows closed up. The information can now be stored as a file of variable length records as shown in Figure 10–12, one record for each keyword. The inverted file is sorted in the sequence of keywords and held on a random access device, probably as an indexed file. To answer a question such as which records have keywords (C and H) only the inverted file is needed. The description part of the reference need not held on a random access device, for it is usually sufficient to refer the reader to the full reference elsewhere, which need not be on a computer file at all.

228

Keyword A	2	6	
Keyword B	1	2	4
Keyword C	1	3	
Keyword D	5	6	
Keyword E	3		
Keyword F	4	5	
Keyword G	1	2	5
Keyword H	3	6	

Figure 10–12   An inverted file

A Multilist

A multilist is an alternative to an inverted file. Imagine the giant array with links between the records as in Figure 10–13. This figure shows all the records with a given

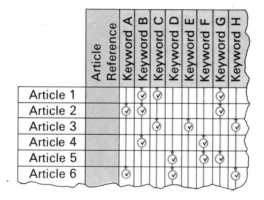

Figure 10–13   A multilist

keyword forming a separate linked list. Unlike an inverted file, to search a multilist the main file has to be used. On the main file each keyword has a pointer to the next record with that keyword. For example the first record would be as follows.

| 1 | Article Reference | B | 2 | C | 3 | G | 2 |

The pointers show that the next record with keyword B is the record for article 2, for keyword C article 3 and for keyword G article 2. To find the first article with a specified keyword a multilist directory is used. This has one entry for each keyword, the first record which contains that keyword.

Suppose that all records are required which have keywords

C and (not H)

229

The entry in the multilist directory for keyword C points to record 1. This record has keyword C with a pointer to record 3 and does not have keyword H. Record 3 has keyword C but also has keyword H. The process continues until the end of the list of records with keyword C is reached.

Questions 10.2

1. What is the multilist directory corresponding to Figure 10–13?

2. Figure 10–12 shows part of an inverted file. Suppose that the inverted file is held on a random access device as an indexed sequential file with a single medium level index. Within each bucket, records are held as described by the first method described on page 221. To make the records fixed length, if there are several articles with a given keyword then there is a separate record for each. Thus the first record for keyword C might be as follows.

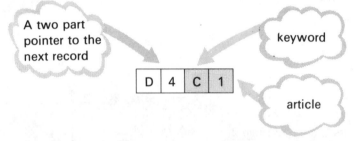

and keyword F has two records which might be as follows.

Draw a flow chart of a program which, given as input a keyword, searches the file for records with that keyword and prints out a list of all articles with that keyword.

3. Draw a flow chart of a program that prints all records with keyword K

   (i) when an inverted file is used,
   (ii) when a multilist is used.

10.3   A DATA BASE

This section consists of an example of a large data base. At a major international airport, cargo handling is controlled by a computer system. Each item entering the cargo depot at the airport has a numbered label stuck on to it. This number together

230

with other data about the item goes to form a record which is held on a large disc file. The record contains a number of fields including the following.

NUM — label number
TIME — time and date of arrival
CUS — indicator set if customs clearance is needed
SHIP — shipper
DEST — destination
IND — indicator whether bound inward, outward or for trans-shipment
AIRIN — airline inwards
AIROUT — airline outwards

This disc file forms a data base for all processing. The requirements of the users of the data base are as follows.

Airport Staff The airport staff need to be able to find details of any item given its label number. They are also responsible for inserting and deleting the records for all cargo as it comes into and leaves the depot.

Customs The customs wish to know what items require customs clearance. By agreement items are cleared in the same chronological sequence as they arrive, which is not the same sequence as the label numbers.

Shippers Each shipper wishes to know what items are ready to be collected.

Airlines Each airline wants to know, for each destination, what items are in the airport.

All these users of the file have terminals connected to a central computer and are liable to interrogate the file at any time. No file structure that you have yet seen is versatile enough to handle all these enquiries, but it can be done by combining several structures.

Indexed Sequential File

Since the file is large and insertions and deletions continual, it is maintained as an indexed sequential file. The label number is an obvious choice for a sort key, but unfortunately the numbers are allocated in batches and this would create a situation in which a few sections of the file were overflowing while others were almost empty. This problem can be got round by transforming the label number before it is used as a sort key. An easy way to do this is to reverse its digits. Thus, if

NUM = 823681,

then

KEY = 186328.

This simple process allows the file to be held as an indexed sequential file with a sort key that is derived from the label number. This satisfies the airport staff.

Linked Queue

Now consider the problem of the customs officers who wish to process the file in chronological sequence. Their need can be met by creating a queue of all records that require customs clearance. The queue can be held as a linked list of records in the order of their arrival. Figure 10–14 shows an extra pointer field added to each such record giving the key of the record that arrived immediately afterwards.

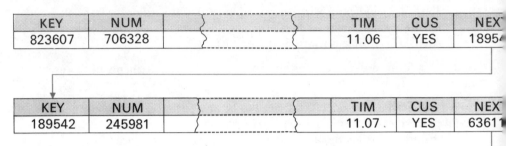

KEY	NUM	}	TIM	CUS	NEX
823607	706328	}	11.06	YES	1895

KEY	NUM	}	TIM	CUS	NEX
189542	245981	}	11.07	YES	6361

Figure 10–14　A linked queue

The main difference between this linked list and the ones discussed in Chapter 5 is that the pointer field does not give the address of the next record but its sort key. Thus the indexes have to be used to find the next record, which may appear to be inefficient, but means that records can be moved within data buckets or overflow areas and even that indexes can be updated without the pointer having to be altered.

Inverted File

Shippers are less concerned with the time of arrival. They merely want to know which items to collect. As in the previous section, you can imagine this information laid out in a giant matrix, with shipper codes along the top and identification numbers down the side. Figure 10–15 shows part of it. As in the keyword example, some method is

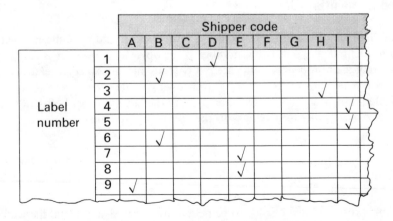

Figure 10–15　Information for shippers

232

needed of closing up the gaps, and an inverted file is one way of doing this. Each record of the inverted file corresponds to a given shipper and has the label numbers of all items ready for that shipper to collect. Figure 10–16 shows the first few records of the inverted file.

	A	9	
	B	2	6
	D	1	
Shipper	E	7	8
code	H	3	
	I	4	5

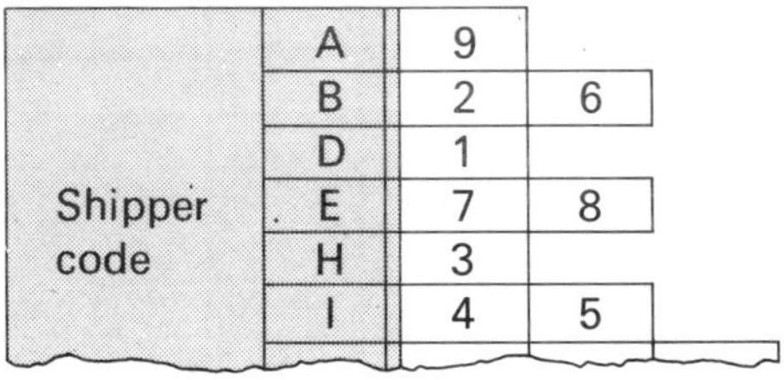

Figure 10–16   An inverted file of information for shippers

In the keyword example the inverted file did not change once it had been set up. In this example the main file is constantly changing and hence the inverted file is itself a dynamic file of variable length records. It would be held as a separate indexed sequential file. A shipper can use the indexes of the inverted file to find the label numbers of the records which are ready for collection. He can then use the indexes of the main file to read the full record. Notice that alterations to the main file now involve the inverted file as well. For example, when the airport staff dispatch an item from the depot the corresponding record in the main file is deleted. The SHIP field of this record is used to enter the inverted file and the corresponding shipper record is updated.

Multilists

If the airlines want to know what items to dispatch to which destination, on the face of it they could find this information from an inverted file similar to the one used for the shippers. This inverted file would have a record for each airline and destination. But consider the amount of freight that TWA or British Airways carry between New York and London. The corresponding records of the inverted file would be unmanageable. Instead of using an inverted file, another pointer is added to each record of the main file. These pointers link all records for a given airline and destination. This sets up a multilist as shown in Figure 10–17. An added advantage of the multilist is that, if all new records are inserted at the end of the list, they will be processed on a first come first served basis. To do this, the multilist directory gives the key of the first and last record of each list. The directory might begin as in Figure 10–18.

The file now has sufficient structure for all required processing. Each stage of processing may involve several parts of the structure. For example, consider an inward bound item which requires customs clearance. After clearance, the customs program must go through the steps shown in Figure 10–19. This flow chart indicates some of the steps but, to give you an idea of the scale of work involved in a large system, the

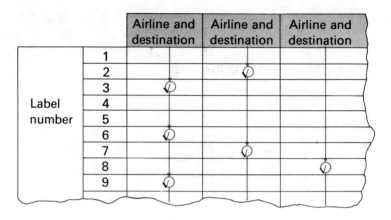

Figure 10–17 A multilist

Name of list	First label number	Last label number
AF ATHENS	662481	362121
AF BRUSSELS	830421	219850
AF CHICAGO	689981	116252

Air line   destination

Figure 10–18 The multilist directory

cargo handling computer system at one major airport required one hundred man years of systems design and programming and the hardware cost five million pounds. However, we hope that this section suggests to you the basic simplicity of the ideas behind large data bases.

Questions 10.3

1. Draw an outline flow chart of the processing involved when the airport staff dispatch an item from the depot.

2. TWA are loading freight for a flight to Miami. Draw a flow chart of the routine to find what items are ready to be dispatched.

3. A shipper wishes to know whether a specified item has yet received customs clearance. Why is this difficult with the data base described? What is the best that can be done?

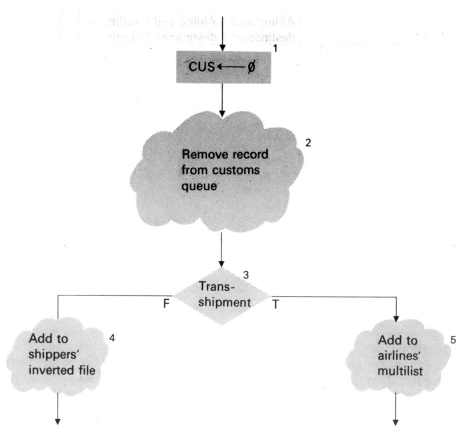

Figure 10–19   Updating the file

10.4   FILE SECURITY

If file processing runs into trouble, there is an ever present risk of destroying data on a file. Even if all programs that use the file are bug free, the data can be lost in a wide variety of ways.

Equipment failure.   This can be as minor as damage to the magnetic surface of a tape, or as major as the computer installation being burnt down.

Data errors.   No data vet or check for reconciliation failures, will pick up all data errors. Most undetected errors concern only a single record, but incorrect input data can also cause major trouble, such as by deleting large portions of a file. Many programs require running instructions, perhaps read as parameters from cards. An error in one of these cards can make nonsense of a program.

Operator mistakes.   The computer operator has an opportunity to make a mistake every time that he runs a program or deals with a peripheral. Some of these errors can result in incorrect files being written or destruction of existing ones.

Malicious damage.   Every large organization has some discontented employees; such people can cause havoc in a computer room.

You can see the importance of file security if you consider the type of data held on computer files: taxation, accounts, criminal records, stock holdings, pay roll, and so on. Such data held on computer files is fundamental to the running of many organizations. It has cost much money to set up and often is irreplaceable if lost. The designer of any computer system will strive to minimize the number of occasions when data on files is lost or in error, but inevitably file corruption will occur sooner or later. Therefore the system must also include arrangements to retrieve the situation when things go wrong. .

Serial Files

Most methods of file security rely on making several copies of each file, and, if one copy is lost or corrupted, to have a procedure for making do with one of the others. This is particularly straightforward with serial file updating. For instance consider the updating of the stock file described on page 165. If all goes well, once the carried forward file is written the brought forward file could be discarded. The reel of magnetic tape could be used for another purpose. However it is an elementary precaution to save the brought forward file, in case the carried forward file is lost, or the new tape proves to be unreadable, or the wrong data was written on to it. So long as the input data cards have also been saved, the computer operator has the chance to rerun the suite of programs, correcting any mistakes. In practice it is usual to save several generations of any file held on magnetic tape. With the stock file, a four tape cycle might be decided upon. The picturesque language used to describe the different generations is to refer to them as father, son, etc. (See Figure 10–20.)

With this arrangement, a mistake can be retrieved even after it has been perpetuated through several generations. As an added precaution, although most tapes will be held in racks near the computer, one generation is often stored in a fire proof safe, perhaps in a different building.

One of the easiest mistakes for an operator to make when running a suite of programs, is to load the wrong magnetic tape, particularly when there are many generations of the same file. The routine that opens the file, therefore, checks the file name as written on the tape header label. Part of the file name is a generation number which is used in file updating where the carried forward and brought forward files have the same name. When the file is opened the generation number is checked. A further precaution against operator mistakes is a simple hardware check. No tape can be written on unless a plastic write permit ring is put in a groove on the tape reel as shown in Figure 10–21.

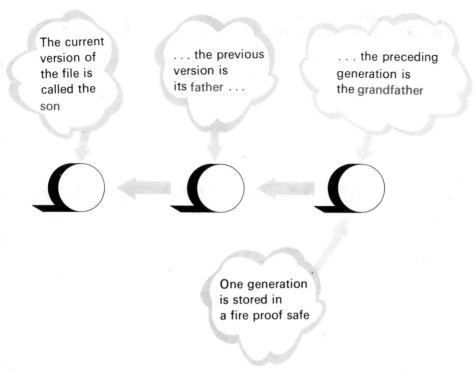

Figure 10-20   Tape security

Random Access Files

File security is a major problem with random access files. When used sequentially the same procedures can be used as for serial files, but when alterations are made continually to a random access file some other method is necessary. On page 211 we looked at a book publisher who inputs orders to a random access file from terminals. Every order results in an alteration to the file and, unless some precautions are taken, the old values are lost for ever. The basic precaution is to copy the entire disc file onto a magnetic tape once an hour. The incoming order forms are divided into batches corresponding to each hour's work. If the computer system fails in any way it can be restarted by reloading the most recent copy of the disc file from tape. Up to one hour's work will have been lost, but the restart procedure is simple and the cost is not great if breakdowns are infrequent.

An alternative procedure that the publisher might have chosen is to log all transactions, by writing a copy of every input and output record onto a serial file. As before, the disc file is dumped onto magnetic tape at regular intervals. If a breakdown occurs the disc file at the moment of breakdown can be re-created by a special program which, starting from the previous dump, reads the log and makes any alterations to the file. This procedure sounds almost ideal, since no data has to be resubmitted, but in fact should be avoided wherever possible, because of the complexities of the retrieval

Figure 10-21   The write permit ring

program. This program is likely to be very difficult to write and the cost of writing and testing it, together with the computer time used to log every transaction, could easily outweigh the savings it produces. Also a bug in the program or an unexpected type of breakdown could easily make restarting from the previous dump necessary after all.

Large Terminal Systems

Section 10–3 looked at a terminal system for cargo handling at an airport. With this system the loss of a file could be very serious. Dumps can be taken at frequent intervals but more is required. The method sometimes used is to have two complete computers, two central processors linked together updating two identical disc files. If one breaks down, processing continues with the other. This is an expensive solution and the programming required to arrange that two computers work in parallel is not easy. However if a large organization cannot function without its computer system the cost may well be justified.

Privacy

Particularly with terminal systems, privacy of data on files may be important, either because data is confidential or because of the danger that an unauthorized user could corrupt a file. Three methods are in general use for protecting files on terminal systems.

Passwords. Before a user can read or write to a file he is required by the program to type a password on the terminal. Only if this is correct can he use the file.

Identity badges. Each user is issued with a magnetic card or badge. The terminal has a special slot into which the badge can be inserted. The file can be used only while a valid badge is in the slot.

Read only terminals. Although users at any terminal are allowed to read a file, only users at specified terminals are allowed to alter it.

In this section we have done little more than point out some areas where file security is important. In practical situations it is a constant problem to which there may be no ultimate solution.

Question 10.4

1. What methods of file security would you recommend for

   (i)   the batch processing system described in Figure 7–10,

  (ii)   the data base system described in Section 10–3?

CHAPTER ELEVEN

MAKING EFFICIENT USE OF A COMPUTER

The Concurrent Operation of Peripherals

Buffering

Multiprogramming

Time Sharing

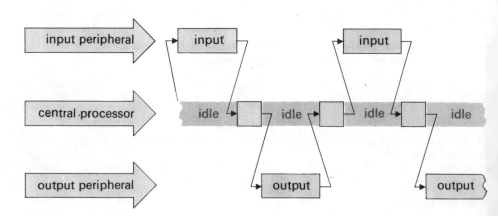

11.1 THE CONCURRENT OPERATIONS OF PERIPHERALS

As soon as you start using computers you find that at every stage of running a program there is some software interface between you and the machine. For example, every computer system uses software routines to translate high level programs into machine instructions, to load programs into store and to handle input and output. These routines are part of the system software. Their purpose is to make the use of a computer system convenient and efficient.

You may remember that in Chapter 2 we said that the input and output instructions described there were greatly simplified. We now want to discuss some of the simplifications that we think are important. The first thing to realize is that peripherals are much slower than the central processor. Figure 11–1 gives some typical speeds. The difference between the time taken to read a block and the speed of the arithmetic unit is clear. In most data processing the time taken to process each record is much less than the time taken to read in data and output results. Rather than have the central processor wait whenever any input or output is required, computers are designed so that several peripherals and the central processor can operate at the same time. To leave the control unit free to continue executing instructions, each peripheral has a peripheral control unit which is responsible for the actual transfer of data. The peripheral control unit for each input peripheral has the following registers, as shown in Figure 11–2.

(i)   A DATA register into which each word of data is read before being copied into store.
(ii) A COUNT register showing how many words of data are yet to be transferred.
(iii) An ADDRESS register showing where in store the next word of data is to be stored.

Peripherals	Speed
card reader (80 characters per card)	300 to 2,000 cards per minute
line printer (120 characters per line)	600 to 1,500 lines per minute
typewriter terminal	600 to 900 characters per minute
magnetic tape (1,000 characters per block)	1,600 blocks per minute
moving head disc (1,000 characters per	
block—sequential processing	2,400 blocks per minute
—random processing	600 blocks per minute
Central processor (medium sized computer)	
add instruction	40,000,000 instructions per minute
access store	75,000,000 words per minute

Figure 11–1   Typical peripheral speeds

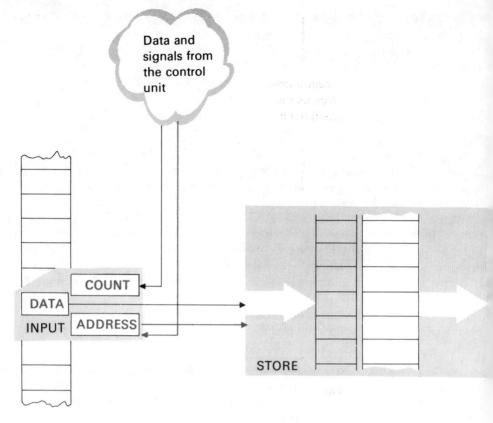

Figure 11–2   Registers in the peripheral control unit

With input, as soon as a word of data has been read by the peripheral control unit, it is copied from the DATA register into the location in store given by ADDRESS, COUNT is decreased by one and ADDRESS is increased by one. The arrangement for an output peripheral is similar. Since the store is connected to each peripheral control unit as well as to the central processor, there will be occasions when two or more parts of the computer system wish to access the store at the same instant. In this event the hardware allows one access to take place first and delays the others. This delay is known as hesitation and is so short that to all intents and purposes all parts of the computer work simultaneously.

The first simplification that was made in Chapter 2 is now clear. To execute an input instruction the control unit signals to the peripheral control unit the number of words to transfer, and an address in store. Having initiated the transfer, the control unit does not have to wait until it has been completed, but can go on to execute another instruction. This is shown in Figure 11–3.

Suppose a program reads a record from a punched card, processes it and prints a result, repeating the sequence for every record of input data. If all operations take place consecutively, the processing of two records can be represented as shown in

242

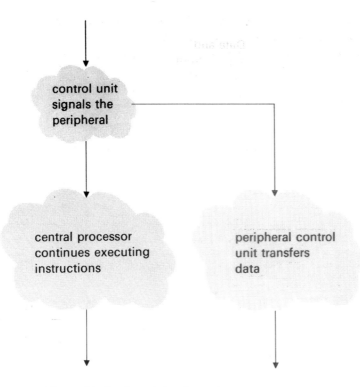

Figure 11–3   A peripheral transfer

Figure 11–4. The diagram shows that execution of the program is constantly being delayed. Once input has been initiated, the program has to wait until the record has been read into store before it can be processed. The program also waits until the processed record has been output. The flow chart in Figure 11–5 shows this waiting. While the program waits, the computer must idle. Essentially all idling consists of

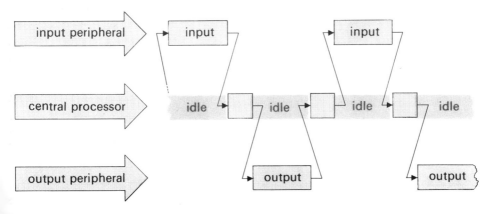

Figure 11–4   A typical sequence of input and output

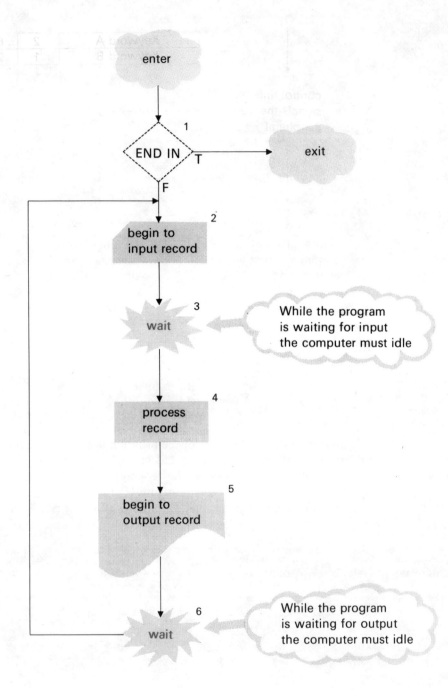

Figure 11–5   Waiting for peripherals

244

executing an endless loop until interrupted. The program could keep repeating the following test.

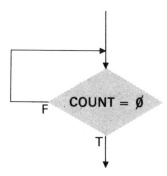

This seems simple, but does not work if several peripherals are in operation, and in practice all idling is done within a special software routine called the supervisor. The supervisor maintains a table which indicates what processing is waiting for each peripheral. This table is consulted and updated at the beginning and end of every peripheral transfer. Also, since the detailed routines for initiating a transfer of data are common to every program, these routines are also part of the supervisor. This is our first mention of the supervisor; as you will see later it is the key to the efficient operation of any computer system.

Figure 11–4 shows each of the activities of input, processing and output being completed before the next is started. Only one part of the computer system is in action at any one time and the central processor is idle almost all the time. Since peripherals can operate concurrently with the central processor and with each other, more efficient use can be made of all parts of the computer. For instance, as shown in Figure 11–6, there is no need to wait until the output of one record is completed before beginning to read the next punched card. If the input and output records occupy different areas in store, having set the printer to write out the result of one calculation, the control unit can go on to the instructions which initiate the input of another record. Oddly enough the main loop of the program is almost exactly as before (see Figure 11–7). As soon as the program has initiated the output of one record it begins to read the next. It then waits until both input and output are complete. In

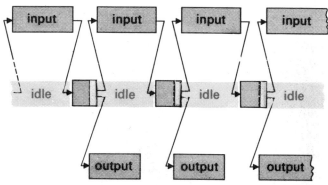

Figure 11–6   Concurrent input and output

245

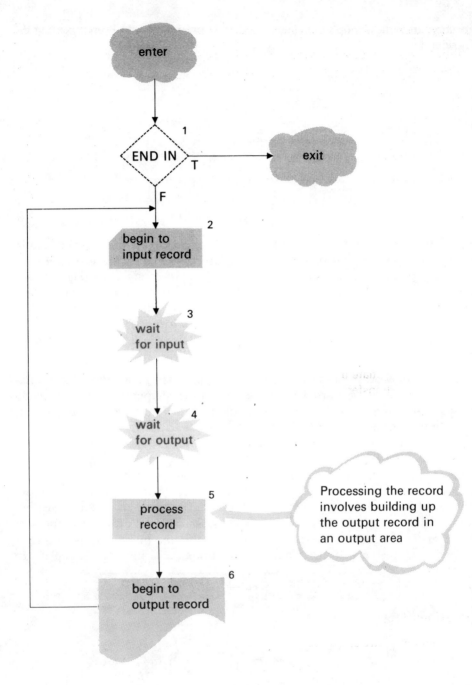

Figure 11—7   Concurrent input and output

this way the two peripherals are able to operate concurrently and the execution of
the program is faster than before.

There are three dangers in concurrent operation of peripherals that must be avoided. These are

(i)   starting transfer to a peripheral that is already in action,
(ii) using data before it has been input,
(iii) altering the contents of an area of store which is being output.

To play safe you could always use the sequence of instructions shown in Figure 11–8. However, this prevents the concurrent operation of peripherals. In the next section we discuss methods of avoiding the dangers, while still allowing concurrent operation.

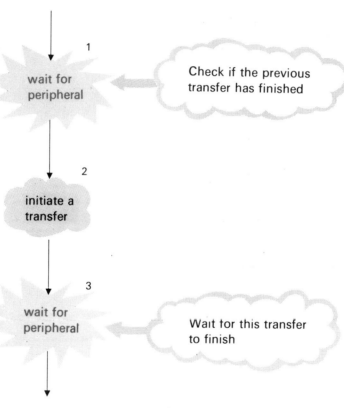

Figure 11–8   A safe procedure

Questions 11.1

1. In the flow chart of Figure 11–7 how much time is spent over the execution of step 4 if

   (i) input takes 20 milliseconds and output takes 10 milliseconds,
   (ii) input takes 10 milliseconds and output takes 20 milliseconds?

2. Why is the diagram of Figure 11–4 essentially independent of the time taken for input and output?

3. Try to draw up a table similar to Figure 11–1 for the computer that you use.

11.2 BUFFERING

In the last section we looked at a program loop to read a record from a punched card, process it and print a result. With concurrent operation of peripherals, it is possible in theory for this program to be executed as fast as the slowest part of it will allow. Organizing the program to do this creates a problem of where to hold data in store. For instance, many programs read each record in turn into the same area in store, overwriting the previous one. This is only possible if processing each record finishes before reading the next begins, otherwise there is a danger of overwriting data before it has been processed. For maximum speed, however, as soon as one record has been read, reading the next should begin so that the card reader can run nearly continuously. As shown in Figure 11–9, this can be achieved by reading each record into one area in store called a buffer, and at the very first stage of processing, copying it from the buffer into another area in store called a work area where there is no danger of it being overwritten. If a record is not read into the buffer until the previous record has been copied into the work area the card reader cannot run absolutely continuously but the delay is very, very small, as shown in Figure 11–10.

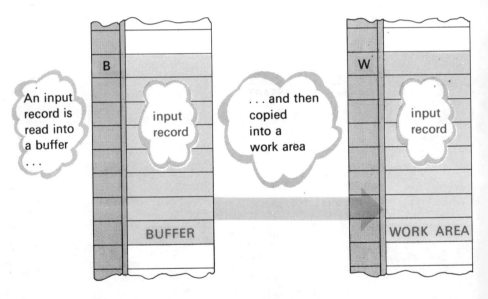

Figure 11–9 Buffering

This use of a buffer is so standard that it is usual to use software routines for buffered input and output. Remember that the object of such routines is to take the difficulties out of writing a program yet to make the execution of programs as efficient as possible. For example, consider the effect of buffering in a program based on the flow chart in Figure 11–11. Although the programmer thinks that the effect of the input instruction is to read a record from the card reader into his program, in fact, the software tries to be one record ahead of the program. If, at step 1, there is already a record in the input buffer, this is copied into the work area and the peripheral begins reading the

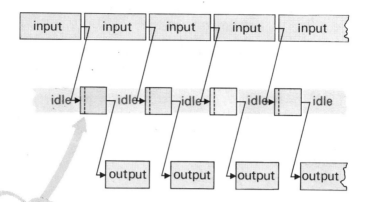

The first stage of processing is to copy the input record from the buffer into the work area

Figure 11–10   Input buffering

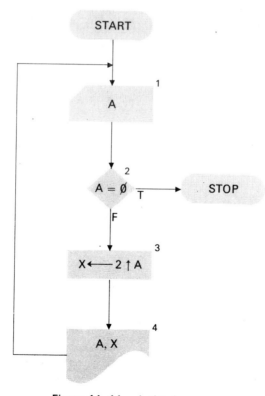

Figure 11–11   A simple program

next record into the buffer. The program uses the record in the work area while the next record is being read into the buffer.

Since this buffering technique is the same for every program instruction that uses a card reader, an input instruction in a program is compiled into a call to a housekeeping routine. The routine, which we shall call INCR, is based on the two steps of copying a record from the buffer into the work area and initiating the input of the next record. There are two problems. First, when the routine is called the program will have to wait if reading the previous card into the buffer is incomplete. Second, there may be no more cards to be read from the card reader. For this reason, before trying to read a card, INCR checks whether there is a card available to be read. If not, an error flag called END is set. The next time INCR is called, there is a branch to an out of data routine. Figure 11–12 shows these features added to the core of INCR.

We now want to look at the problem of data held on magnetic tape. Since transfers from magnetic tape are much faster than from a card reader, a different method of buffering is used. The form of buffering described so far in this section is called single buffering. If the input peripheral is a slow one, such as a card reader, the time taken to copy each record from the buffer to the work area is negligible compared with the time taken to read each card. However the time is not negligible with faster peripherals such as a magnetic tape unit. For a magnetic tape unit to run non-stop two buffers are used, each the size of the largest block. As shown in Figure 11–13, blocks are read into them alternately. This saves copying each block from a buffer into a work area, since, while records in one buffer are being processed, the next block is being read into the other buffer, hence the term double buffering

Here is a typical program instruction.

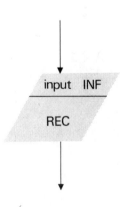

input INF

REC

250

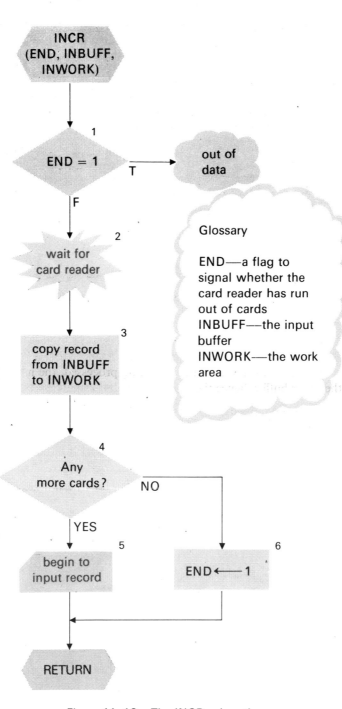

Figure 11–12   The INCR subroutine

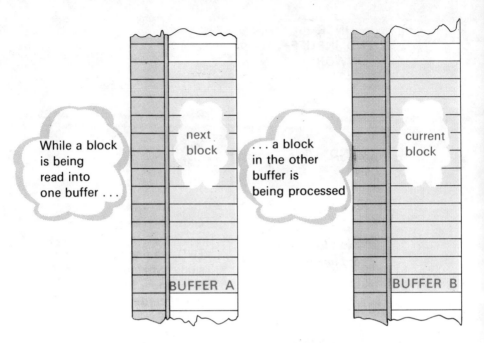

Figure 11–13   Double buffering

This is compiled into a call of a routine **INMT** which assigns to **REC** the address of the next record to be processed. The details of **INMT** depend on how many records are held in each block. Figure 11–14 shows the simplest case, one record per block. Before A is set to the address of the record that has been copied into the current buffer, the record is tested to see if the tape trailer block has been reached. If it is, there is a branch to the end of file routine. This is equivalent to the flow chart box.

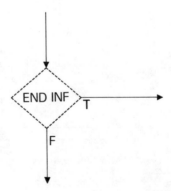

If several records are stored in each block, the subroutine must divide into two paths depending on whether all records in the current block have been processed. Figure 11–15 is a flow chart of a routine for the case of fixed length records stored **N** to a block.

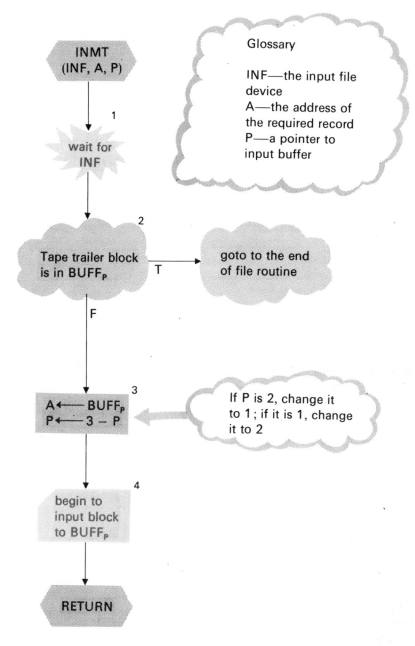

Figure 11–14   INMT with one record per block

Matters are further complicated by the fact that every file, whether for input or output, must be opened when first used. This is carried out by a housekeeping routine which checks that the peripheral is available for the program and reads the first block into a buffer. After all records have been read and before execution of the program is

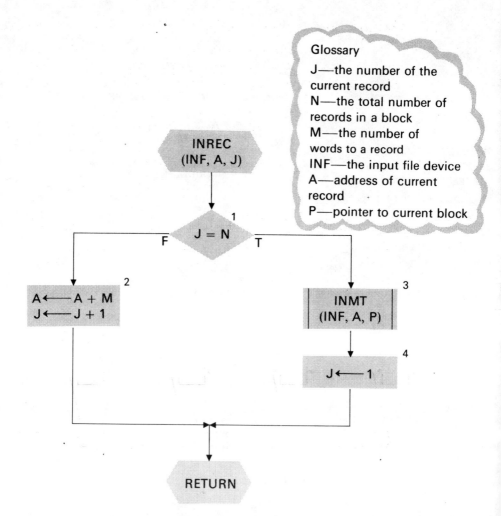

Figure 11–15   INREC for N records per block

finished, all the files must be closed. The routines for opening and closing files are tied closely to the hardware for which they are designed and we shall not discuss them.

When an input instruction in a high level programming language is translated into machine instructions they make the next record in sequence available to the program. However, we have only just scratched the surface of all the complications that arise in practice. These complications are of little interest to you if you are writing in a high level language. You must, of course, specify your files but you can rely on the software to cope with other details.

Questions 11.2

1. Draw a flow chart for a housekeeping routine, OUTLP, which arranges for a record to be printed using single buffering.

2. Draw a flow chart for a housekeeping routine, **OUTTAPE**, which arranges for a record to be added to an output buffer, the whole buffer being written onto magnetic tape once it contains **N** records.

11.3   MULTIPROGRAMMING

As illustrated in Figure 11–10, the concurrent operation of peripherals speeds up the execution of many programs but, even so, the central processor may be idle much of the time. The problem is that only one program is being executed, and this program can go no faster than the slowest peripheral will allow. Matters can be improved by multiprogramming. This is a technique whereby several programs share the central processor. Imagine two programs, one of which repeatedly reads a record, processes it and prints a result, while the other is a big calculation which uses the central processor for a long period of time without input or output. Figure 11–16 shows how, with

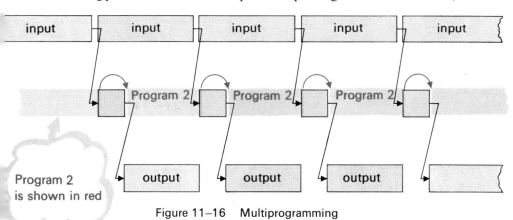

Figure 11–16   Multiprogramming

multiprogramming, the second program can use the central processor while the other is waiting for input or output. If you compare this with Figure 11–10, you will see that the first program is running as fast as if the second did not exist and the second program is only held up a small amount of time. The central processor is now working continuously. The control and arithmetic units are shared but each program has its own area within store and its own peripherals. Multiprogramming differs from other methods of sharing the central processor in that each program has a priority, and a program will never be executed if any program with higher priority is able to use the central processor. Efficient multiprogramming depends on correct allocation of these priorities.

Example

Program A reads an input number, does a calculation lasting one hour and prints the result. Program B reads 60,000 cards each containing a single number, adds the

255

numbers together and prints the result. The card reader has a maximum speed of 1,000 cards per minute. Two card readers and two line printers are available. If program A were to have priority over program B we would have the situation shown in Figure 11–17. After reading its input record, program A will have sole use of the

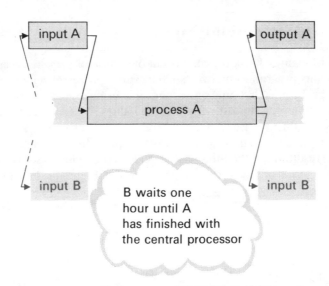

Figure 11–17   Program A has priority

central processor until its calculation is complete. Since program B can use the central processor only while A is waiting, B will have to wait for an hour until A has finished its calculation. If program B were given priority we have the situation shown in Figure 11–18. Whenever a card has been read for program B to process the central processor is allocated to B which performs a brief calculation and initiates the reading of the next card. Program B now has to wait for the next card and program A can continue,

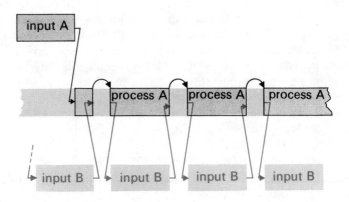

Figure 11–18   Program B has priority

having been briefly delayed. Since program B spends most of its time waiting for input, program A runs almost as fast as if it had sole use of the computer, yet program B has highest priority and is executed as fast as possible.

The example leads to the following rather surprising generalization. If several programs are multiprogrammed, the programs which, given sole use of the computer, would spend the highest proportion of time waiting should be given highest priority. If high priority is given to programs which spend most of their time waiting, the low priority programs will have plenty of opportunity to use the central processor.

Off Line Input and Output

Off line input and output is a simple but very effective use of multiprogramming. Consider a typical update program as shown in Figure 11–19. This program uses three magnetic tapes and a line printer. Since the printer is much slower than the tape units, much more efficient use of the various parts of the computer can be made by dividing the process into two separate programs as shown in Figure 11–20. The results from the update program are written onto another file on magnetic tape. This speeds up execution of the update program. A separate print program is used to print the results. In a similar manner it is often efficient if a program which has input from punched cards uses a special input program to read the cards onto a serial file and to use this file as input to the main program.

Because serial files on disc or tapes are so much faster than card readers or line printers a main program will be very much quicker if all input and output is from serial files. The disadvantage is that extra programs are needed for input and output, but these

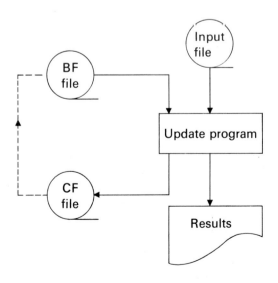

Figure 11–19   An update program

257

are small programs which take little space in store and use the central processor very lightly. They are therefore suitable for multiprogramming with a high priority.

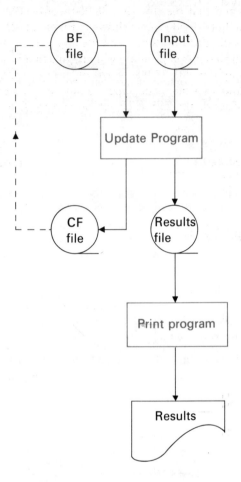

Figure 11–20   Off line output

Job Streaming

Off line input and output is so simple and effective that it is almost standard with large computer systems and common on smaller ones. It is often used with a technique called job streaming. To understand job streaming turn back to the system flow chart of Figure 7–16, page 173. In this figure you see the system flow chart of a typical batch processing system. If all printing is off line the work load might be divided into three types of program.

(i)   Print programs. These read from a serial file and require a line printer for output.
(ii) Input programs involving a data vet. These require a card reader for input and two serial files for output.

258

(iii) **Main programs and sorts.** These require three or four serial files.

Suppose now that the computer system has one card reader, a line printer and seven magnetic tape units and that the store has 48,000 words (192,000 characters). With job streaming this might be divided up as shown in Figure 11–21. In effect the computer can be thought of as divided into three separate computers, running independently. A programmer writing a data vet program will imagine that he is writing a program to be executed on a computer with 12,000 words of store and that the only peripherals are a card reader and two magnetic tapes. Similarly the computer operator will schedule the flow of work through each job stream as if he were operating three separate computers.

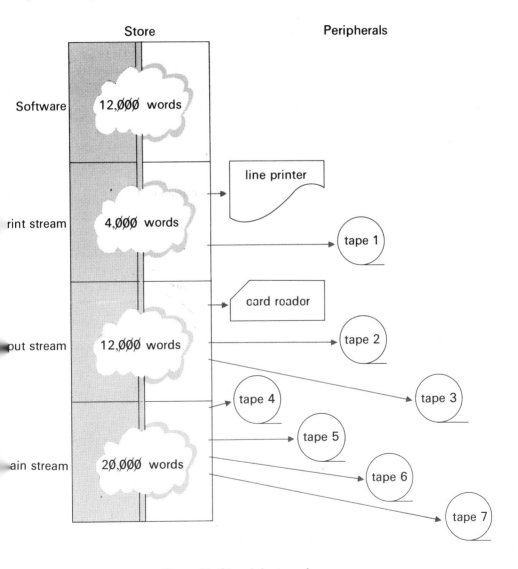

Figure 11–21   Job streaming

An advantage of job streaming is the discipline it imposes on the designers and writers of programs. A typical computer installation will have many hundreds of programs. If each programmer were to work without regard to the others, efficient operation of the computer would be impossible. On the other hand, if every program is designed to fit into one of these three streams, when it comes to be executed it can be put in the correct stream with confidence that sufficient space in store, and the right peripherals will be available. Because the same peripherals are always allocated to each stream, the computer operator can allocate multiprogramming priorities to the stream and need not change them for every program.

Job streaming also has an advantage for the software writer. With multiprogramming, suppose that three programs are in store and that job streaming is not being used. Figure 11–22 shows the store layout. If program B finishes, the area in store that it occupies becomes free. Some computer systems immediately move all other programs up in store so that all the spare space is after the last program. This is efficient in its use of space but time consuming since a very large number of words may have to be copied and in that some means is needed to adjust the addresses in all machine

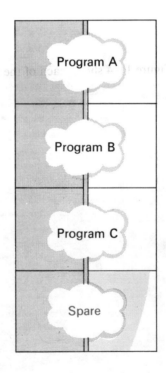

Figure 11–22 Store layout without job streaming

instructions. With job streaming each program is stored within the area allocated to its stream, as shown in Figure 11–23. There is no need to move up other programs when one finishes, since the next program of the stream has been written to fit into the area allocated.

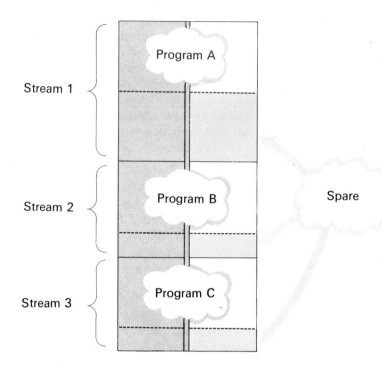

Figure 11–23   Store layout with job streaming

Questions 11.3

1. Two programs are to be multiprogrammed together. Program A reads, in sequence, the records of an indexed sequential file from a magnetic disc and, without processing them, copies them onto a magnetic tape. Program B reads a single punched card, carries out a long mathematical calculation and prints the result.

   Outline briefly the consequences of giving program A priority over program B, and the consequences of giving program B priority over program A. Which program should be given priority?

2. Redraw the system flow chart of Figure 7–16, page 173, to include off line input and output. How would you use job streaming?

11.4 TIME SHARING

To work well multiprogramming requires certain conditions to be fulfilled. Most of the programs must be peripheral dominated, that is, they must be the kind of program that could not make full use of the central processor. Moreover the computer operator must know in some detail the characteristics of each program so that he can allocate priorities. These conditions are fulfilled in many commercial computer systems and multiprogramming is used in the most commercial data processing. When the conditions are not met, an alternative approach can sometimes be provided by time sharing. This is an entirely different method of several programs sharing a computer system. In its simplest form it consists of a number of users each with his own terminal connected to a central computer as shown in Figure 11–24. A typical time sharing system might have thirty two terminals. These could be local terminals, close to the computer and permanently wired to it, or remote terminals which are usually connected by telephone lines.

A user of a terminal might type in a program, compile and run it. Typing in a program or receiving output on a terminal are slow processes dominated by the typing speed of the user, the design of the terminal and the speed of the transmission line. Many terminals have a maximum working speed of ten or fifteen characters per second, yet even this is fast compared with the rate at which most people type to say nothing of the time that the user spends thinking about his program. As a result, input and output use the central processor hardly at all. However, when the user instructs the computer to run his program the situation changes completely. Time sharing systems are often used by scientific departments or universities and many programs run on them will be calculations any one of which, if given the chance, would take over the central processor and never let any other program take a turn. Since the operator in the computer room will usually not know what work is being done on each terminal he

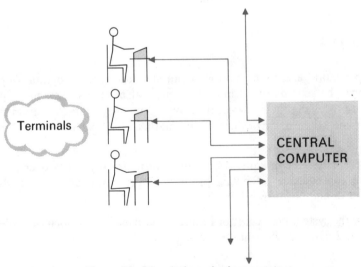

Figure 11–24   A time sharing system

262

does not know which program should have priority. Time sharing fails to meet the criteria for successful multiprogramming and some other method is necessary to share the central processor among the programs wanting to use it.

The method used is called time slicing. The basic idea is very simple; the programs in turn are given sole use of the central processor for a short period of time which might be one tenth of a second. A clock is built into the control unit of the central processor. When the central processor is allocated to a program the clock is set to a given value. When the time limit is up, the clock interrupts the program and the next program is offered the use of the central processor. The mechanism by which this interruption is carried out is discussed in the next chapter. Even though the central processor is his for only a fraction of the time a user of a terminal in a time sharing system hardly suspects that he does not have sole use of the entire computer system. This is in part due to the fact that at any given time most users of the system will be involved in input or output, which can run concurrently with other processing. As a consequence, a program will frequently not wish to use the central processor when its turn comes round, or during its turn it will come to an input, output or stop instruction. In each case its turn comes to an end and the central processor is offered to the next program. When choosing the next program, the simplest arrangement is to number the programs and to offer the central processor to each in strict rotation. With thirty two terminals, the logic of the scheduling algorithm is based on the infinite loop shown in Figure 11–25.

One problem with time sharing systems is how to share the store among several programs. A solution would be to have a very large store and for each program to have its own private area, but this would be wasteful since at any given time only one program is being executed. With small time sharing systems an arrangement sometimes used is to divide the store into two sections as shown in Figure 11–26. The software area contains the software used by all the programs and routines to pass input and output to the terminals. The user area is allocated to the program that has current use of the central processor. When the time limit is up, the program with its data is dumped onto a high speed peripheral, usually a drum, as one large block. Each program has its own area on the drum and when its turn comes round again, the program is copied back into store. This means that each program can pick up again exactly where it left off. This is called roll in roll out.

Paging

Roll in roll out is simple and effective in many circumstances, but is not suitable for large time sharing systems because the computer can easily find that it spends all its time dumping and retrieving the user area. Also simple time slicing with no priorities gives trouble with big systems. At any given moment the users can be divided into two main types; users who are typing in programs and editing them, and those who have set a program to run and are waiting for the results. Users who are editing programs require a quick response from the computer. Every time that they type in a line of program they will have to wait for that line to be processed. However, the

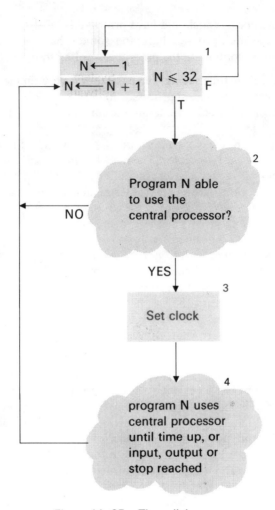

$$N \leftarrow 1$$
$$N \leftarrow N + 1$$
$$N \leqslant 32 \quad F$$

T

Program N able to use the central processor?

NO

YES

Set clock

program N uses central processor until time up, or input, output or stop reached

Figure 11–25   Time slicing

processing that they require is unlikely to take much computer time. Therefore it is reasonable to give editing priority over running programs. One simple way of doing this is to allow every program that requires editing to interrupt the program that is being executed and to carry out the necessary editing (which will take only a few milliseconds).

In their allocation of store most large systems use a compromise between the two extremes of copying every item to and from backing store, or having the store large enough to hold all programs simultaneously. In its simple forms the method used is called paging and in its advanced forms is called virtual memory. The idea behind paging is that over a short period of time most programs do not use all the storage space that they actually occupy. For instance, one program may contain a large number of error routines which are rarely executed, another program may be involved in a small loop of instructions.

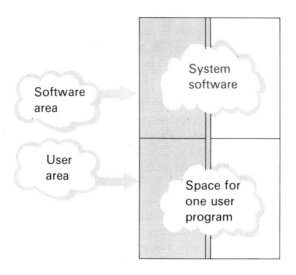

Figure 11–26   Store allocation for roll in roll out

Consider the two programs shown in Figure 11–27. The area in store occupied by each program has been divided into four sections called pages. Program A is a data vet. Except when an error occurs it can be executed with only the first page in store. Program B uses a data matrix, which is held in one page. The other pages read in the matrix, make calculations and output the matrix. Since these phases are independent, only one section of program and the data matrix need to be in store at a given time. Therefore at some moment we could imagine the situation in store to be as shown

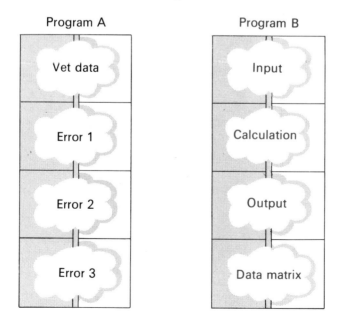

Figure 11–27   Two programs divided into pages

in Figure 11–28. This arrangement allows both programs to be executed until they require one of the pages not currently in store. Copies of these pages are held on a drum. Suppose, for example, that Program A finds an error and branches to an error routine on another page. This page will be copied from the drum into store and execution of program A can continue.

The system software is responsible for bringing in any page that is required for processing. It also has the responsibility of recalculating all store addresses as each instruction is executed, since any part of any program can be anywhere in store at the moment of execution. To make room for the incoming page, a page currently in store must be dumped onto the drum. One simple but surprisingly effective rule for selecting the page to dump is to use a first in first out convention and to dump the page that has been in store longest. For instance, when it wishes to bring in an error routine for program A the software might find the data matrix has been in store longest. The data matrix is copied onto the drum and the error routine read in. During the next time slice the error routine will be executed.

This example is unrealistically small, but it illustrates how, at the cost of repeated transfers to and from the drum, two programs can be executed in harmony despite each being larger than the available user area in store. A large time sharing system might run thirty two terminals with a store divided into one hundred pages. The size of any user program is restricted not by the size of store, but by the amount of space allocated to it on the drum plus the maximum number of pages that the software can handle. This software is inevitably very complex and we shall not attempt to discuss it further.

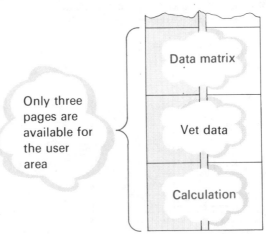

Figure 11–28   Space in store for three pages

CHAPTER TWELVE

THE SUPERVISOR

Interrupts

A Multiprogramming Supervisor

Supervisor Service Routines

Peripheral Handling

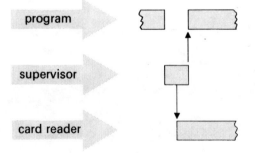

12.1 INTERRUPTS

Chapter 11 looked at concurrent operation of peripherals, multiprogramming and time sharing from the user's point of view without describing how they are carried out. One of the most surprising aspects of computing is that machines which are essentially similar to the one described in Chapter 2 prove to be so versatile in practice. This versatility depends heavily on software which is integrated so closely into the design of the machine that it often appears to be a physical part of the machine. Different manufacturers use different names for this software. Control program, executive, supervisor program, they all mean the same thing; we shall use the term supervisor. The supervisor is held permanently in store and controls all aspects of the execution of programs. It has routines to run programs, look after errors and control the operation of peripherals. The following are examples of when the supervisor is used.

(i)   A peripheral transfer is completed.
(ii) The central processor attempts to execute an impossible instruction such as to divide by zero.
(iii) The computer operator thinks that a program is in an endless loop and wants to stop it.
(iv) With time slicing, the clock shows that it is time to interrupt the current program and run the next.

In Chapter 2, when we looked at the operating cycle, we stressed that the control unit continues to fetch and execute instructions indefinitely (see Figure 12–1).

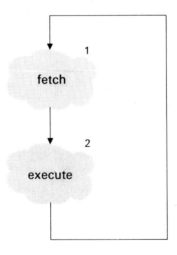

Figure 12–1   The operating cycle

Breaking into the operating cycle is caused by an interrupt. Within the control unit there is a special register, called the interrupt register, which is normally set to zero. Setting the interrupt register to any other value is a signal to interrupt the normal operating cycle. Each bit in the interrupt register has its own significance and indicates the source of the interrupt; Figure 12–2 shows a typical arrangement. The interrupt register can be thought of as having a bit for each peripheral, for each program, for

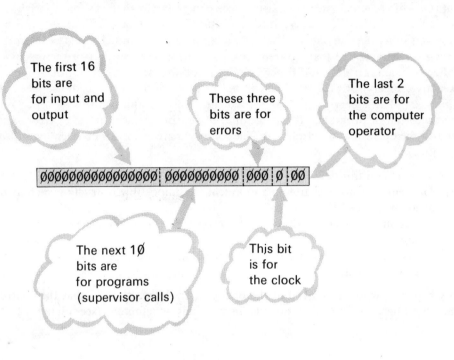

Figure 12–2   The interrupt register

each type of error, for the clock and for special buttons on the operator's console. In fact there is no real reason why the interrupt register should have exactly thirty two bits, as we have shown; its size depends on the number of different interrupts that the computer manufacturer wants to allow for.

As a normal part of the operating cycle, after executing each instruction, the control unit checks that the interrupt register is still Ø. If any bit has been set to 1, it does not fetch the next instruction from the address given by the sequence control register, but branches to the instruction held in location 1, which is the first instruction of the supervisor. So the operating cycle has the additional features shown in Figure 12–3. One feature is missing from this figure. After an interrupt, there would be complications if another interrupt were to occur before the first has been serviced. To avoid confusion there is a special bit in the control unit, called the interrupt inhibit bit. The test for an interrupt is made only if this bit is set to zero. Figure 12–4 shows the complete operating cycle.

The instructions held in store from location 1 onwards form the supervisor. They are the subject of the next section. At this stage we want to look in more detail at how the various types of interrupt arise.

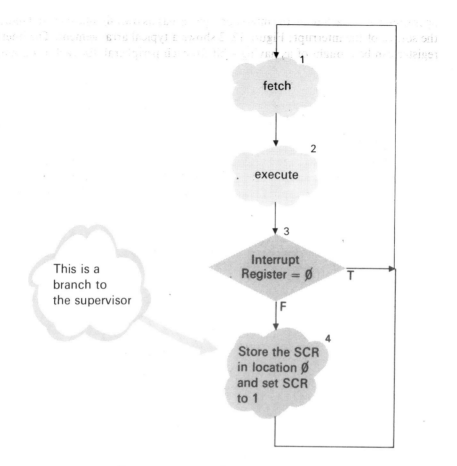

Figure 12-3   Test for an interrupt

The Computer Operator

Figure 12-5 is a picture of a computer operator's console. It is much like an ordinary terminal with some special buttons. The computer operator types messages to the supervisor program on the console and the supervisor prints messages back to the operator. In a typical computer system two of the buttons, labelled INPUT and ACCEPT, correspond to two bits in the interrupt register as shown in Figure 12-6.

Unlike other peripherals, which can be allocated to any program, the console is permanently allocated to the supervisor. If the computer operator wishes to type in a message, he presses the INPUT button which causes an interrupt. When the supervisor is ready to accept a message it sends a signal which unlocks the keyboard and the operator types a message. Pressing ACCEPT causes a second interrupt and informs the supervisor that the message is complete and is to be acted upon.

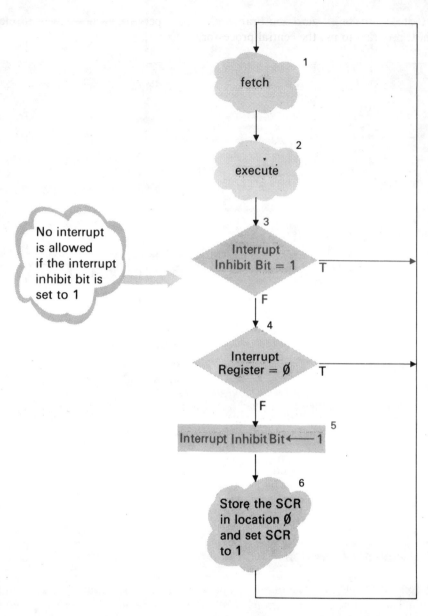

Figure 12–4   The complete operating cycle

Clock Interrupts

With time slicing, each program is allocated to the central processor for a fixed period of time, perhaps one tenth of a second. So that the supervisor knows when to change programs, the clock is connected to a bit of the interrupt register as shown in Figure 12–6. When the time limit is up the clock sets this bit to 1. After execution of the current instruction has been completed, the control unit tests the interrupt register, sees that it is no longer zero and branches to the supervisor, which can then select the next program to use the central processor.

Figure 12–5   The operator's console

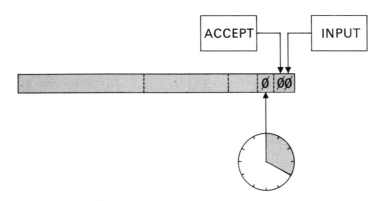

Figure 12–6   Operator and clock interrupts

Execution Errors

Another use of interrupts is to retrieve the situation when the computer tries to execute an impossible instruction. Remember that, in store, machine instructions and data are both stored as binary patterns. Although all machine instructions are binary patterns, not all binary patterns are valid machine instructions. If a program contains a mistake, the computer may try to execute an invalid instruction. These errors fall into three categories,

(i)   invalid operator code,
(ii) invalid operand,
(iii) arithmetic overflow.

You may wonder how the first two errors can occur, since the program that loads the instructions into store can easily check that each is a valid instruction. However, it is perfectly possible for a sequence of apparently valid instructions to result in an error, when taken together. For example consider the following where each location has a valid content, but an attempt to execute the instruction in location **56** creates an invalid operand.

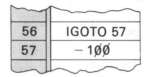

| 56 | IGOTO 57 |
| 57 | − 1ØØ |

Figure 12–7   An invalid operand

If an execution error occurs, the control unit sets a bit in the interrupt register and bypasses the rest of the execute cycle. Figure 12–8 shows three bits in the interrupt register available for signifying errors, one for each type that we mentioned.

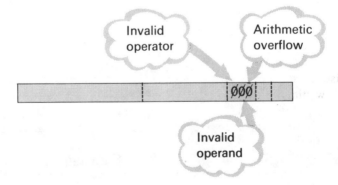

Figure 12–8   Execution errors

Supervisor Calls

A program may call the supervisor by setting a bit in the interrupt register. For instance, in our discussion of peripheral software we used the following.

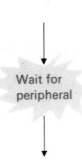

Wait for
peripheral

This is a call to the supervisor to test if the peripheral is busy and if necessary to suspend the program until the transfer is complete. After any supervisor call, the supervisor needs to know exactly why it was called. The interrupt register gives some information but only one bit is allocated to each program and there are many reasons why a program might want to call the supervisor. Therefore, the operator code of the machine instructions used for supervisor calls should specify the action required. Figure 12–9 lists the supervisor calls that we shall look at.

Operator code	Action required	Operand significance
IN	Start peripheral for input	See page 292
OUT	Start peripheral for output	See page 292
MESS	Type message on operator's console	Address of message
SUS	Suspend program until operator restarts	None
BUSY	Test if peripheral busy	Peripheral number
STOP	Stop	None

Figure 12–9   Supervisor calls

Peripheral Interrupts

The supervisor needs to know when a peripheral completes a data transfer, in case a program is waiting for the peripheral. This is done by the peripheral control unit setting a bit in the interrupt register. Figure 12–10 shows each peripheral connected to its own bit in the interrupt register, so that the supervisor can identify what caused the interrupt. In practice, each peripheral control unit controls several peripherals and the input and output channels into store are shared. Each bit in the interrupt register refers to the channel and not to the individual peripheral. We shall ignore this complication and look at the simple case where each bit corresponds to a single peripheral. To see how these interrupts are used, consider the example of reading a punched card. This involves the supervisor at least twice. First the program interrupts with a supervisor call and asks for the peripheral to be started (Figure 12–11). At the end of the transfer the peripheral signals with a second interrupt (Figure 12–12).

So much for how interrupts arise. In the next section we discuss what happens after an interrupt has occurred. Since interrupts cannot be fully appreciated without knowing what happens when they do occur, questions on this chapter have been gathered together at the end of the last section.

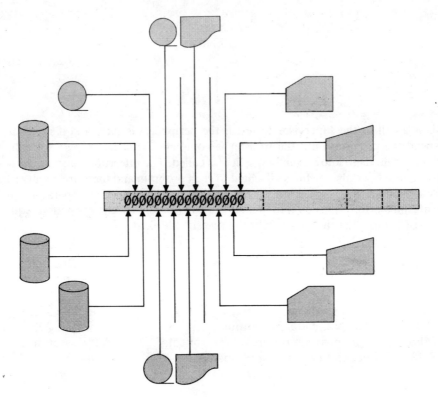

Figure 12–10   Peripheral interrupts

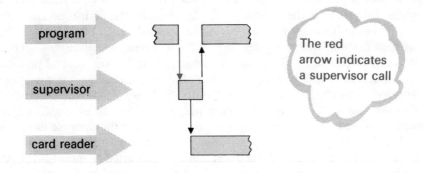

Figure 12–11   A supervisor call

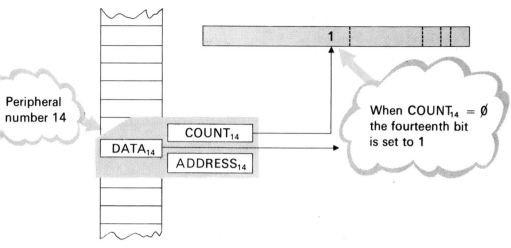

Figure 12–12   A peripheral interrupt

12.2   A MULTIPROGRAMMING SUPERVISOR

The supervisor consists of a number of service routines used for specific purposes, such as interpreting and acting upon a message from the operator, and a control routine In most computers the whole supervisor is held permanently in store. For instance, Figure 12–13 shows a common arrangement. The area of store occupied by the supervisor is not available to user programs. Since it is stored in an area beginning at location 1, the control routine will be entered for every interrupt. The first stage of the control routine is to decide what caused the interrupt, which is equivalent to the loop shown in Figure 12–14. One complication is that sometimes an interrupt occurs before the supervisor has finished processing a previous one. For instance while processing an operator message a peripheral might complete input or output. Because of the interrupt inhibit bit being set, the supervisor cannot be interrupted, but the new interrupt will still set a bit in the interrupt register. This means that after processing one interrupt the supervisor must go back and look at the interrupt register to see if all interrupts have been processed. The supervisor looks at the bits of the interrupt register one by one beginning with the left hand bit. As a consequence, interrupts are processed not in the order in which they occur but in the order of the bits in the interrupt register. In other words some interrupts have priority over others. Figure 12–15 shows the order of priorities. Machine instructions are needed to test individual bits of the interrupt register and, after servicing an interrupt, to restore the corresponding bit to zero. Using these instructions Figure 12–16 shows the first half of the control routine.

When all interrupts have been processed there are two possibilities for the control routine. It can either run a user program, or idle. For an interrupted program to continue processing it is not enough to save the content of the sequence control register when the interrupt occurs and to reload it as in the return from a subroutine. If processing is to continue as though no interrupt had taken place, the contents of

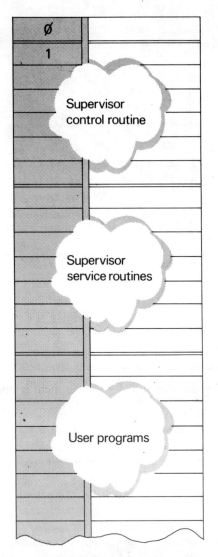

Figure 12–13   The supervisor in store

the accumulator and index register must also be restored to their original values. This involves saving their contents when the program is interrupted and reloading them immediately before returning. It is also necessary to restore the interrupt inhibit bit to Ø to accept further interrupts. Thus the supervisor control routine is based on the outline shown in Figure 12–17.

Multiprogramming

When multiprogramming, the supervisor and several user programs are held in store together, though only one can be executed at a given time. Deciding which program

278

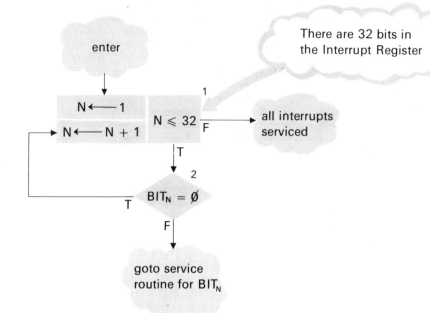

Figure 12–14   The first part of the control routine

should use the central processor at any given moment is one task of the supervisor control routine. The following are the principal events which might cause the central processor to be switched from one program to another.

(i)   One of the programs begins input or output.
(ii)   Input or output of a block is completed.
(iii) A program has been loaded and is ready to be executed.
(iv)   The execution of a program is completed.
(v)   The operator intervenes.
(vi)   An error is detected.

Since each of these events involves an interrupt, the supervisor will be entered. When all interrupts have been serviced the control routine decides which program has use of the central processor until the next interrupt. Figure 12–18 shows how the supervisor control routine is divided into two sections. As you saw in Chapter 11, each user program in store is given a priority. The highest priority program always uses the central processor unless it has no use for it and if all programs are waiting for an

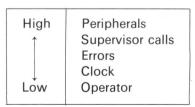

Figure 12–15   Interrupt priorities

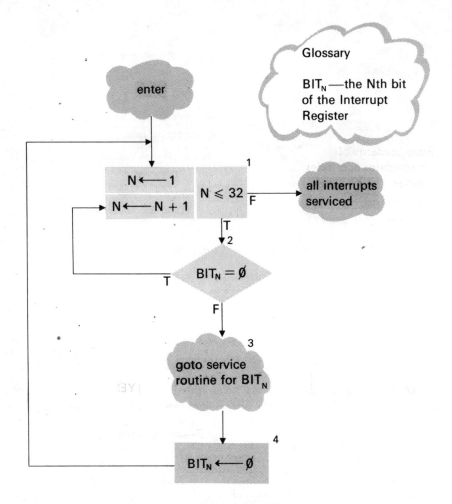

Figure 12–16   Servicing all interrupts

external event such as completion of input or output the supervisor must idle. Therefore, to select the program to use the central processor, the supervisor must know for each program what priority it has and whether it can make use of the central processor.

To go to the selected program the supervisor must restore the correct values to the accumulator, the index register and the sequence control register. This information must be stored for each program either within store or in special hardware registers. We shall discuss the former; logically they are the same. Figure 12–19 shows the information organized in the form of a supervisor table giving information about each program.

Whenever the supervisor is entered the first step is to store the current values of the sequence control register, accumulator and index register in the table. The priority

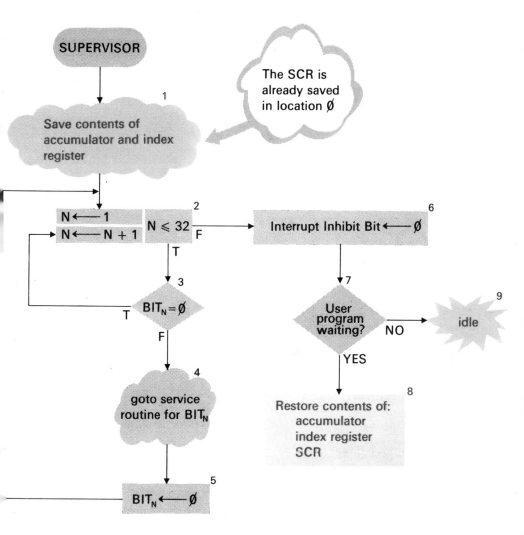

Figure 12-17   The control routine

column in the table is set by the operator as he loads each program. The status indicator might be coded as follows.

$\emptyset$—this row is not in use at present,
1—the program is waiting to use the central processor,
2—the program is waiting for the operator,
3—the program is waiting for a peripheral.

Deciding which program to execute next is simply a question of examining the status indicators to find the highest priority program with status indicator set to 1. If no

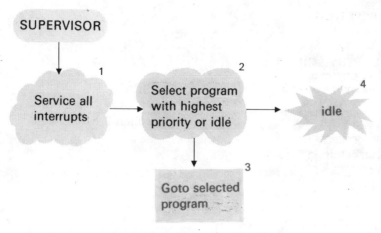

Figure 12–18   Multiprogramming

indicator is set to 1 the supervisor must idle. It does this by executing a small loop of instructions until interrupted, such as the following.

To complete this section, Figure 12–20 gives an outline of the entire multiprogramming supervisor. (Questions on this section can be found at the end of this chapter.)

	PROG	SCR	ACC	IR	PRIORITY	STATUS
	Program name	Sequence control register	Accumulator	Index register	Priority	Status indicator
1						
2						
3						
4						

Figure 12–19   The supervisor table

12.3   SUPERVISOR SERVICE ROUTINES

The control routine identifies the cause of each interrupt and calls appropriate service routines. This section looks at the details of some of these routines. To begin, Figure

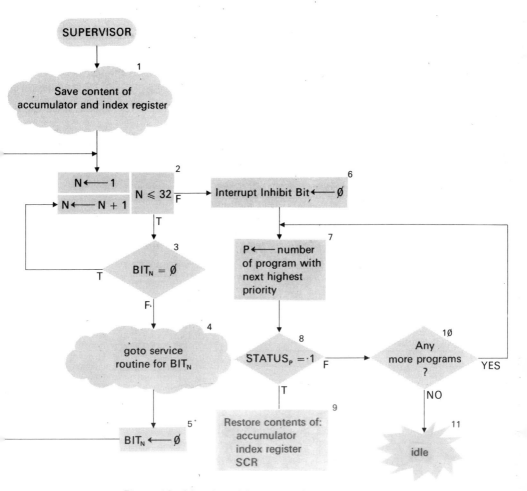

Figure 12–20   A multiprogramming supervisor

12–21 shows an expansion of step 4 of the supervisor flow chart. This fragment shows branches to the principal types of service routine, but within each type a variety of different processes are needed.

Operator Interrupts

The computer operator can cause two types of interrupts. Pressing the INPUT key on his console asks if the supervisor is ready for a message; the ACCEPT key tells the supervisor that the message is now complete. The order in which these interrupts are processed is important. Since the supervisor searches the interrupt register from left to right, ACCEPT has priority over INPUT. This means that, if after submitting one message the operator presses the INPUT button to submit another, the supervisor will process the first message before allowing the operator to type in the next. Thus there is no danger of a second message overwriting the first. Figure 12–22 shows an outline of the service routine corresponding to pressing the INPUT key.

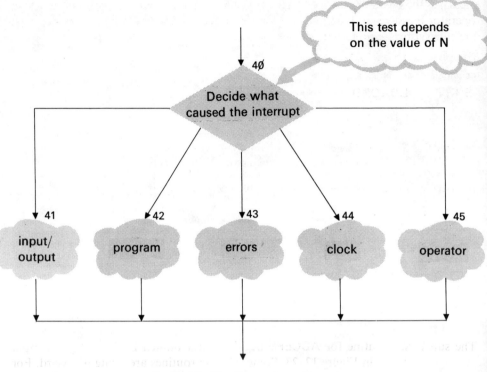

Figure 12–21   Expansion of step 4

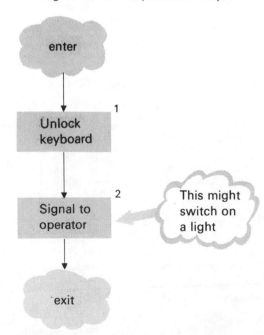

Figure 12–22   The input service routine

To understand the service routine for the **ACCEPT** key, you need to know what messages the operator can send to the supervisor. For example, here is a sequence of operator messages to load and run a program called **SORT** (output messages from the supervisor are printed in red).

LOAD   SORT 4

SORT   LOADED

> load a program called SORT from peripheral number 4

The operator now types

ALLOCATE   SORT 6
ALLOCATE   SORT 7

in order to allocate peripherals **6** and **7** to the program. When he types

GO   SORT

the program is run, beginning at its first instruction. The program will run and, if all goes well, the end of execution will be announced by a message such as

SORT   HALTED OK

The operator can then delete the program from store by typing

DELETE   SORT

The supervisor routine for **ACCEPT** begins with a branch for each type of input message as shown in Figure 12–23. Some of these routines are straightforward. For

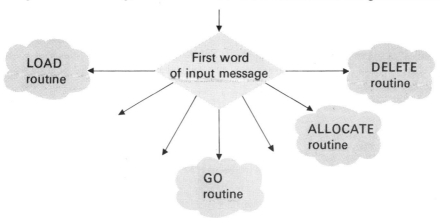

Figure 12–23   The ACCEPT service routine

example, Figure 12–24 shows the **GO** routine, which sets a program to run by simply changing the corresponding status indicator to 1. Figure 12–25 shows the routine for allocating peripheral J to the program named **SORT**.

Other types of operator message are more complicated. For instance, loading a program into store is so time consuming that it would be inefficient to delay all other

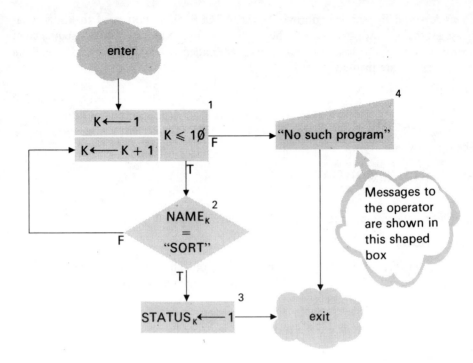

Figure 12–24   The GO routine

programs while it was taking place. Therefore once the service routine has initiated the action and updated the relevant tables the supervisor restarts a user program. The details are complex and we shall omit them.

Clock Interrupts

Clock interrupts are not used with multiprogramming. As described in Section 11–3, they are fundamental to time sharing. At the end of this section we ask you to construct the service routine that corresponds to a clock interrupt.

Execution Errors

The service routines for execution error have to retrieve the situation before the computer grinds to a halt, and to print information to help the operator or programmer discover what went wrong. The error message gives as much diagnostic information to the operator as possible. The type of error can be found from an inspection of the interrupt register, but it often helps the programmer to know the content of the sequence control register and printing the contents of the accumulator and index register is also likely to be useful. Figure 12–26 shows the outline of the error routine.

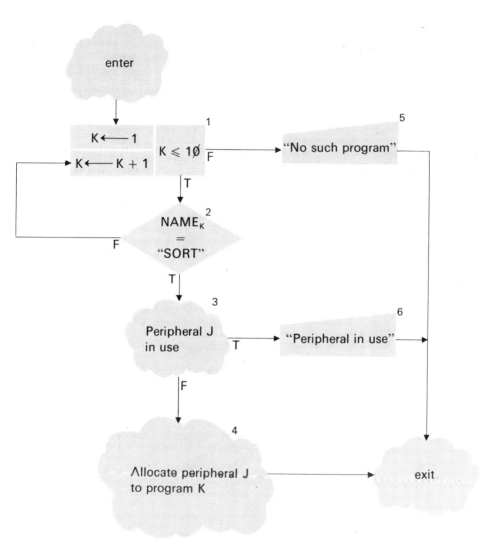

Figure 12–25   The ALLOCATE routine

Supervisor Calls

As Figure 12–9 shows, with a supervisor call, the operator code specifies why the supervisor has been called and the operand gives further information required by the appropriate service routine. Therefore the first stage of the service routine is to inspect the operator code of this instruction, as shown in Figure 12–27. This simple outline hides all the complications of this kind of service routine. One of the easy ones to follow occurs when a stop instruction calls the supervisor (see Figure 12–28). However, peripheral handling is so important that it forms the whole of the next section and

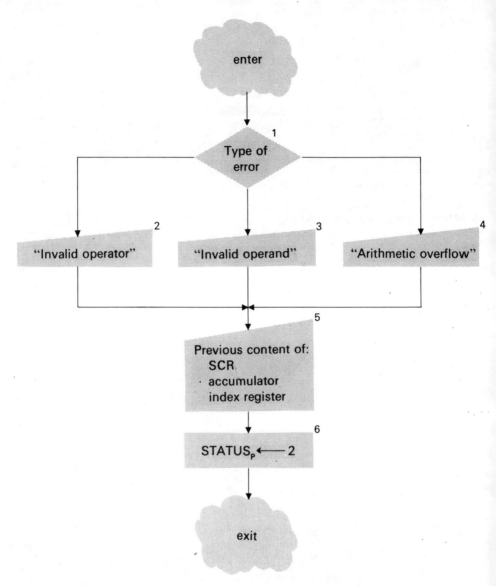

Figure 12–26   The execution error routine

we look there at the two types of supervisor call which involve peripherals. The other two types of supervisor call are used to communicate with the operator. Suppose, for example, that a program is designed to print on special stationery such as order forms. A message

`CHANGE STATIONERY`

is output using a supervisor call with operator code **MESS**. It is followed by a supervisor call with operator code **SUS** which suspends the program.

288

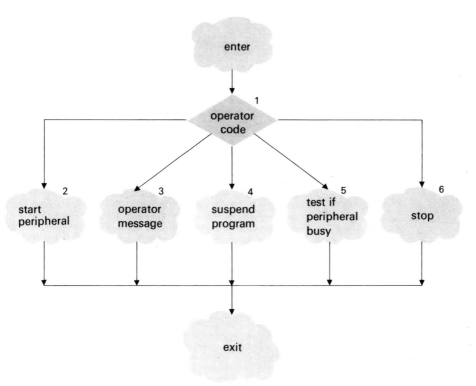

Figure 12−27   Supervisor calls

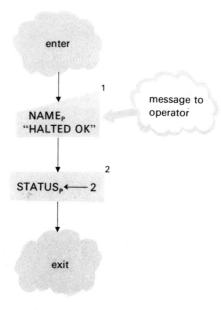

Figure 12−28   The STOP routine

Peripheral Interrupts

The supervisor maintains tables to keep track of the programs and peripherals under its control. You have already seen that it maintains a table with an entry for every program. There is a similar table with a record for every peripheral (see Figure 12–29). This indicates

(i)   to which program the peripheral is allocated,
(ii) whether the peripheral is busy,
(iii) whether the program is held up waiting for that peripheral.

	ALLOC	BUSY	WAIT
	Allocated to program	Busy indicator	Program waiting
1			
2			
3			
4			

Figure 12–29   The peripheral table

A peripheral interrupt occurs when a peripheral finishes input or output and the peripheral control unit signals by setting a bit in the interrupt register. The service routine has to change the corresponding entries in two tables: in the peripheral table to indicate that it is no longer busy, and, if a program has been waiting for the peripheral, to change its status indicator in the supervisor table. This gives the flow chart shown in Figure 12–30.

In this section we have described a number of the supervisor service routines. Although they have different functions, they all depend upon the two tables maintained for programs and peripherals. By keeping these tables correct, the supervisor always knows what is happening throughout the computer system. (Questions on this section can be found at the end of this chapter.)

12.4   PERIPHERAL HANDLING

Now at last we are in a position to fill in the stages that are gone through in executing the simple instruction such as the following.

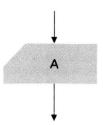

To read the contents of a punched card into a specified area of store involves the program, the supervisor and the peripheral control unit. You have seen that for a program written in a high level language the compiler replaces your input instruction by a call to a housekeeping routine INCR (see Figure 11–12, page 251) and that a copy of the INCR is added to your program. If you are programming in machine instructions you would not use housekeeping routines but would have to program all the details yourself. In either case further software is involved since steps 2 and 5 of the INCR routine are supervisor calls. The first tests whether the peripheral is busy. If a transfer is in progress, the program has to wait until the peripheral becomes

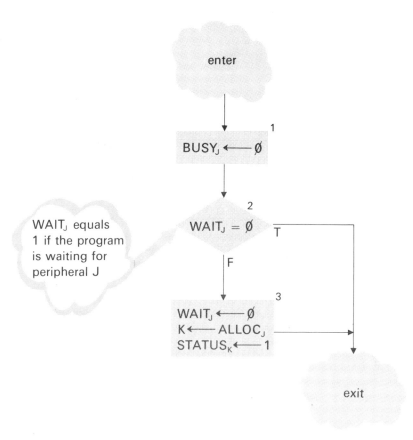

Figure 12–30   End of peripheral transfer

291

free. The second is an instruction to begin a transfer of data. Figure 12–31 shows the three levels involved.

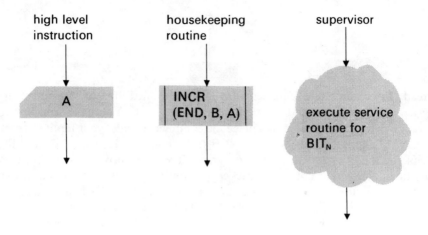

Figure 12–31   Three levels of peripheral transfer

Here is a supervisor call to test if peripheral J is busy.

The supervisor service routine must test BUSY$_J$, the entry in the supervisor table which tells whether the peripheral is busy. If the peripheral is busy the STATUS indicator must be changed to show that execution of the program cannot continue, and the peripheral WAIT indicator must be changed to show that the program allocated to it is waiting. Figure 12–32 shows the service routine. If the peripheral is busy, the program waits until the peripheral interrupt that marks the end of the transfer. We gave the service routine for an end of transfer in Figure 12–30. The indicators that have been set to show that a program has to wait for the peripheral are cancelled by the end of transfer routine.

The second type of supervisor call used in peripheral handling initiates the transfer of data. This requires more information than can be held in a single machine instruction. Therefore the operand of the supervisor call is a pointer to the necessary information (see Figure 12–33). The supervisor service routine signals the values of COUNT and ADDRESS to the peripheral control unit and records that the peripheral is now busy in the supervisor table. Figure 12–34 is a flow chart of the service routine.

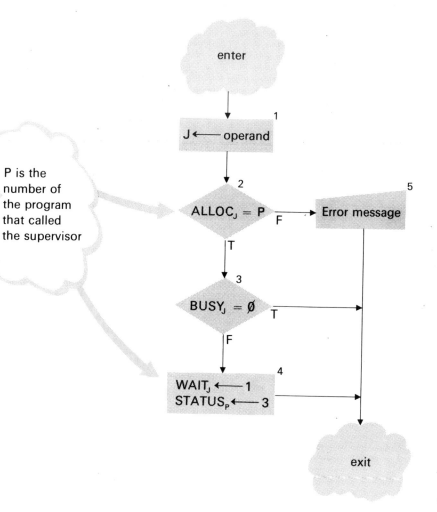

Figure 12-32   Wait if peripheral busy

The operand is this address

PERIPHERAL	6
COUNT	2Ø
ADDRESS	1485

Figure 12-33   Data for a peripheral transfer

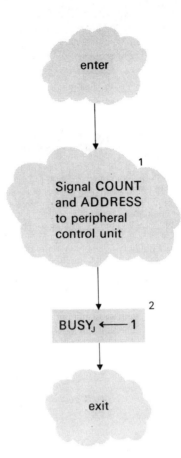

Figure 12—34   Initiate peripheral transfer

Example

To see how these various supervisor calls and peripheral interrupts fit together, suppose that a program is executing the input loop shown in Figure 12–35. Also suppose that this program has highest priority and that execution of the loop is dominated by the card reader. Figure 12–36 shows the sequence of interrupts which is repeated for each card that is read. When the program wants to read the next card, the housekeeping routine is called. First the routine interrupts with a supervisor call to test whether the card reader is busy. The supervisor checks the BUSY status of the card reader and finds that the transfer is not yet complete. Accordingly program A must wait and another program can be started. When the card has been read, the peripheral control unit sets an interrupt. The service routine for the end of transfer finds that program A is waiting for this peripheral and so changes its WAIT status. When the control routine comes to select the next program, program A can be restarted since it is no longer waiting for the end of a transfer. The next few instructions to be executed are those of the housekeeping routine which copy the data just transferred into the buffer into a work area. When the buffer has been cleared, the routine initiates the next transfer by means of a supervisor call. The service routine to initiate

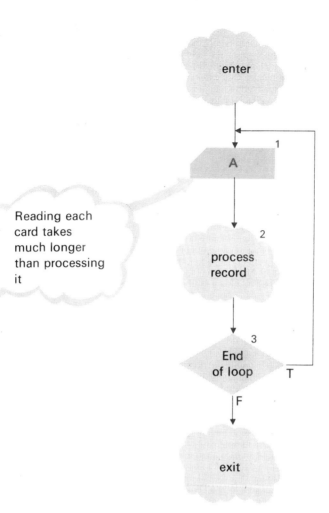

enter

A 1

Reading each card takes much longer than processing it

process record 2

End of loop 3 T

F

exit

Figure 12–35   An input loop

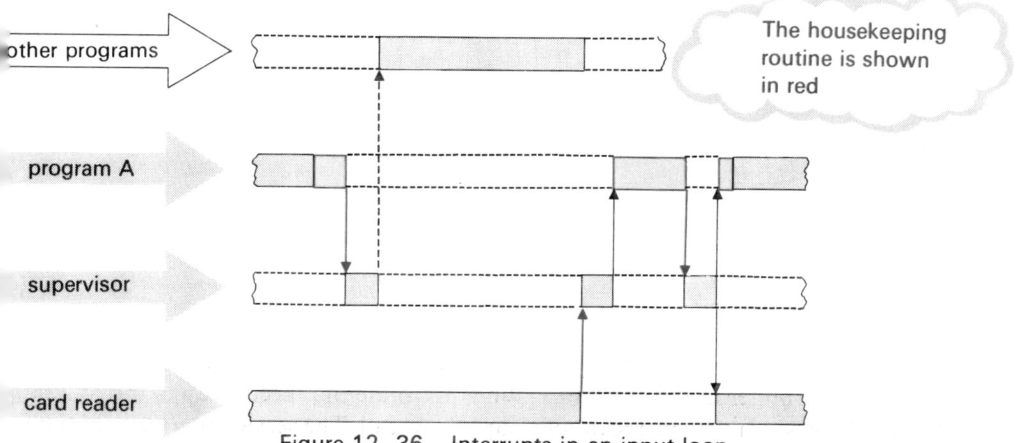

other programs

The housekeeping routine is shown in red

program A

supervisor

card reader

Figure 12–36   Interrupts in an input loop

the transfer is executed and, since program A does not yet need to wait, it can be restarted. At the next call of housekeeping routine, the program will interrupt to test if the card reader is busy and the pattern of events will be repeated.

Although it may at first sight seem rather complicated, the software that we have discussed in this chapter and the previous one all have the same underlying aims, to make efficient use of a computer and to take tricky details out of your hands, leaving you free to write programs in a language that bears some relation to the problem you want to solve. In this chapter we have discussed what happens at machine level. Equally important is the software to translate your high level program into machine instructions. This is the subject of the next two chapters.

Questions 12.4

1. Construct examples of machine instructions that lead to

   (i)   an invalid operator code,
   (ii) an invalid operand,
   (iii) arithmetic overflow.

2. Which of the following statements are true?

   (i) Every time a word of data is transferred into store an interrupt occurs.
   (ii) If the computer attempts to execute the instruction

        LOAD −1

   an invalid operand interrupt occurs.
   (iii) Every time that a user program requires input or output, the supervisor is entered.
   (iv) Interrupts set by the operator have priority over all other interrupts.
   (v) The supervisor cannot be interrupted.

3. Suppose that the computer is idling and that the operator wants to load a program and run it. To do this, the following steps are performed by the operator and the supervisor program.

   (i)   *The operator presses* INPUT *and instructs the supervisor to load a program.*
   (ii) *The supervisor loads the program.*
   (iii) *The supervisor sends a message to the operator that the program has been loaded and the computer idles while waiting for a reply.*
   (iv) *The operator presses* INPUT *and instructs the supervisor to run the program.*
   (v)   *The supervisor branches to the first instruction of the program.*

   How many interrupts occur during each of these steps?

4. A program follows the steps given in the flow chart of Figure 11–7. Suppose that this is the only program being run, and that, as the loop consisting of boxes 2 to 6 is executed,

input takes 100 milliseconds,
output takes 200 milliseconds,
processing takes 50 milliseconds.

(i)   Which peripheral works non-stop?
(ii) Draw a diagram to show when the peripherals are running and when the central processor is idle or executing a program.
(iii) What pattern of interrupts is repeated as the loop is executed?

5. At a given moment an interrupt occurs. The following bits in the interrupt register have been set.

| ∅∅∅∅∅∅1∅∅∅∅∅∅∅∅∅∅ | ∅∅∅∅1∅∅∅∅∅ | ∅∅∅ | ∅ | ∅∅ |

The multiprogramming supervisor has the following table, where priorities run in the order 1, 2, . . . , 1∅ from highest to lowest.

	Program name	Sequence control register	Accumulator	Index register	Priority	Status indicator
1	∅	∅	∅	∅	∅	∅
2	∅	∅	∅	∅	∅	∅
3	SORT	4∅2	8	11	7	1
4	∅	∅	∅	∅	∅	∅
5	FINDX	6∅∅4	∅	1	2	1
6	∅	∅	∅	∅	∅	∅
7	∅	∅	∅	∅	∅	∅
8	LIST	1∅1∅4	1∅∅	9	4	3
9	∅	∅	∅	∅	∅	∅
1∅	∅	∅	∅	∅	∅	∅

Before the supervisor was entered, program 5 was using the central processor. The last instruction executed was the following.

Peripheral number 6 is currently busy. Program 8 is waiting for peripheral 7 to complete a transfer. What happens?

6. Three programs, A, B and C, are run concurrently by a multiprogramming supervisor. The purpose of each program is as follows.

A—to read a file held on magnetic tape and to copy the data onto a magnetic disc.

B—repeatedly to read three items of data from a paper tape, perform a long calculation and print a single result on a teletypewriter.

C—to read data from punched cards and list it on a line printer.

297

(i) In what order of priority should the program be arranged? Give the reasons for your answer.

(ii) Suppose that the programs are given the priorities you selected in part (i) and that

> Program A is waiting for input,
> Program B is using the central processor,
> Program C is waiting for output.

The following events occur in sequence.

(a) Program B comes to an input instruction and has to wait.
(b) A data transfer to the line printer is completed.
(c) A data transfer from magnetic tape is completed.
(d) Program C comes to a stop instruction.
(e) Program A comes to an output instruction.

Describe what happens to the programs as each event occurs by drawing up and filling in a table like the following.

	Program A	Program B	Program C
Initially	Waiting for input	Using Central Processor	Waiting for output
After event (a)			
After event (b)			

(iii) Give a detailed explanation of what happens immediately after event (c).

CHAPTER THIRTEEN

LOADING A PROGRAM

The Translation Process

The Linkage Editor

The Loader

A Bootstrap Routine

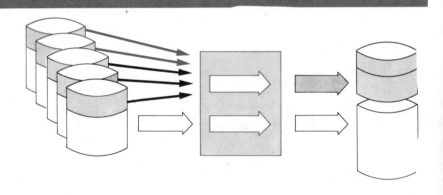

13.1 THE TRANSLATION PROCESS

We can depict the translation of a program into machine instructions by the following diagram.

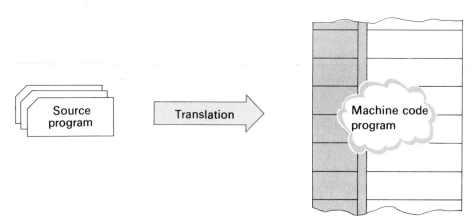

The program is written as a sequence of statements in a suitable programming language. This is known as the source program and is often punched onto punched cards. The program that is executed by the computer is a sequence of binary patterns held in store. In a very simple computer system the entire process of translation may consist of a single step. The statements of the source program are read one at a time by a translation program which generates the equivalent machine code program in store. However, this is a very restrictive situation. It does not allow for a program to be built up from many subroutines (in particular library routines can not be incorporated) and no copy is kept of the program, so that if it is to be run a second time the source statements have to be input again and retranslated. Because of these disadvantages most computer systems use a more complex translation process, which is in three main steps, carried out by three separate software programs. These programs are called the compiler, the linkage editor and the loader.

The Compiler

A compiler is a program that reads statements written in a high level language and outputs a string of machine instructions. If the statements are written in assembly code this conversion is carried out by the assembler, but in all other aspects the process is the same. In either case, the main program is compiled separately from any subroutines that it calls. Compiling each routine separately has many advantages. It means that the same variable names and labels can be used in different routines without danger of confusion; it also makes possible mixed language programs in which each routine is written in the most suitable language. The term segment is used to refer to a sequence of statements which are compiled together, that is to either a subroutine or a main program.

Compiling is the subject of Chapter 14. At present all you need to know is that the compiler reads the source statements of a single segment, and outputs machine instructions and data in a semi-compiled form. It also produces a header label which describes the segment to the linkage editor and loader. The header label and the semi-compiled code are written onto a suitable output file, which is often a disc file, as shown in Figure 13–1.

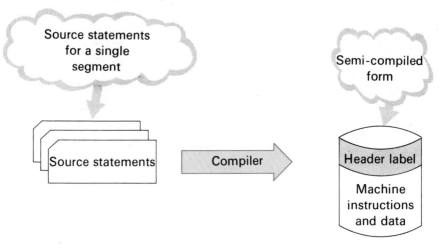

Figure 13–1   Compiling a segment

The compiler does not usually know where a segment will be held in store when it is executed. It therefore cannot allocate absolute addresses to instructions and data, but it can decide where each is to be held relative to the beginning of the segment. In semi-compiled form, the machine instructions for each segment are allocated addresses as though occupying a continuous area of store beginning at location zero. The data and variables used by the segment are sometimes allocated addresses immediately before or after the instructions. Alternatively, they too may be allocated addresses as though stored in an area which begins at location zero. We shall discuss the latter arrangement. One of the tasks of the loader will be to replace these addresses by the values needed when the segment is executed.

Most segments will have some loose ends that the compiler can not handle. The most important category of these are calls of other segments, which are known as external references, and the use of common data areas shared by several segments. Since the compiler handles only one segment at a time, it does not attempt to sort these out, but adds information about them to the header label. The header label must therefore contain the following information.

(i)   The name of the segment and whether it is a main program or a subroutine.
(ii)   The number of locations required for the machine instructions and for the data.
(iii) A list of external references to other segments and of common data.

The Linkage Editor

A machine program is made up of one or more segments. These segments are linked together into a single program by the linkage editor, which has two main functions.

302

First it goes through the header labels reconciling all external references. If any segment contains an instruction to call a subroutine that subroutine must be found, either as another segment of the program or in the library. Library subroutines are added to the program and their header labels checked to see if they contain any external references. When all external references have been satisfied, the second stage is for the linkage editor to prepare a map showing how the different sections of code and data areas would be arranged in store if the whole program were to be loaded beginning at location zero.

The linkage editor works entirely with the header labels of the segments and does not process the actual semi-compiled code. However, it is usual to copy the machine instructions and data of all segments into a single file. The output from the linkage editor is known as a loadable program and consists of a map of the program and the header labels and semi-compiled forms of all program segments (Figure 13–2). Loadable programs are often stored on random access devices.

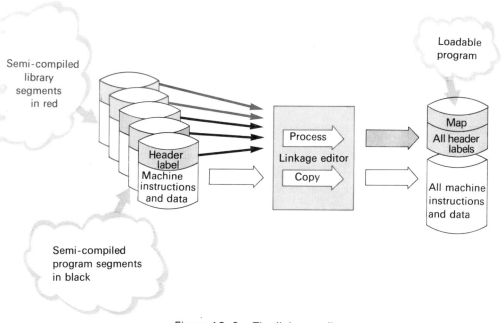

Figure 13–2   The linkage editor

The Loader

The third stage of translation is to load the program into store. This is carried out by the loader, which has two main tasks, apart from copying the machine instructions and pre-set data into store. First it has to tidy up all external references within each segment. These will have been left incomplete by the compiler. Second, it has to adjust the addresses in all machine instructions. These have been compiled as though every segment and its data were each held beginning at location zero in store. Therefore every address in the semi-compiled version of the program must be changed by adding the base address of either the machine instructions or the data area (Figure 13–3).

303

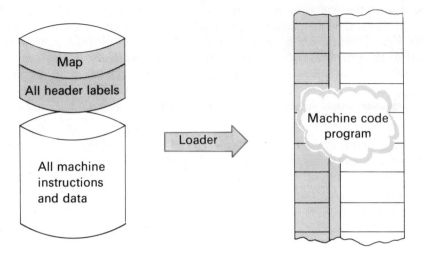

Figure 13–3   The loader

With multiprogramming, every time that a program is loaded it is likely to be held in a different place in store, but the linkage editor map sets up every program as if it were to be stored beginning at location zero. This means that before or during execution every address must be recalculated. Changing the addresses is carried out in one of two ways depending on the design of computer.

(i) **At loading.**   In this method the loader adds to every address in the program the address of the first location in which the program is stored. This is called absolute addressing.

(ii) **On execution.**   The address of the first location of the program is stored in a special register. As part of the execution of each instruction this address is added to every address as the instruction is executed. This technique is known as relative addressing and the register is known as the base register.

Although it seems more complicated, relative addressing has important advantages. Absolute addressing sets an upper limit on the size of store. For example, suppose that the computer has a word length of 32 bits. Using 20 bits for the address of an operand, of which one is for the index register, the store cannot exceed

$$2^{19} = 524,288 \text{ words}$$

This may seem a large number, but stores of many million words are increasingly common and paging allows even larger ranges of addesses. With relative addressing, the largest address that can be held in the base register is

$$2^{32}$$

which is a huge number. Relative addressing allows fewer bits to be used for the operand address and is particularly suitable for any system that involves moving programs around in store, such as a paging system.

Questions 13.1

1. On early computers semi-compiled segments and loadable programs were often stored on magnetic tape. What advantages can you see from storing them in disc files?

2. Some computers use relative addressing of individual segments within a program. Describe how this would work and discuss its advantages and disadvantages?

13.2 THE LINKAGE EDITOR

Figure 13–4 is an outline flow chart for the linkage editor. The input to the linkage editor consists of the header labels of each segment of a program. The header label is a record which might have the following fields.

> NAME—the name of the segment.
> TYPE—whether a main program or a subroutine.
> INST—number of store locations required for machine instructions.
> DATA—number of store location required for data and variables.
> EXREF—a list of subroutines called from this segment (external references).
> COMDAT—a list of common data areas that this segment shares with other segments and their sizes.

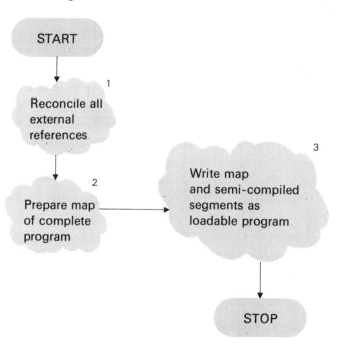

Figure 13–4 The linkage editor

305

External References

The first stage of the linkage editor is to reconcile all external references. For this purpose it holds three lists of names, as shown in Figure 13–5. The first is a list of segments in the program. The second is a list of those external references so far found which are to segments not in the first list, and the third is a list of common data areas, with their sizes. This first stage of the linkage editor is based on a subroutine HEADER, which given the header label of a new segment adjusts the entries in these three tables. Figure 13–6 gives the flow chart of HEADER. This subroutine adds the name of the segment to the list of segments in the program. If there is an external reference in EXTERNAL to the segment it can now be deleted, but any new external references or common data areas must be added to the corresponding lists. Figure 13–7 shows the first part of the linkage editor and how it makes use of the HEADER subroutine to satisfy all external references. This part of the linkage editor also checks for two types of error, that the first segment is a main program and the remainder are all subroutines, and that all external references can, in fact, be satisfied.

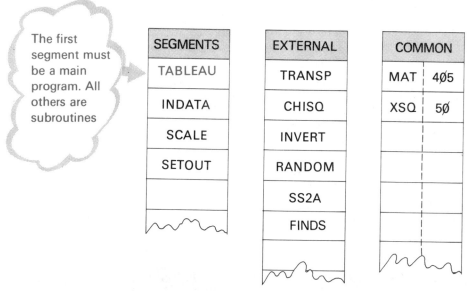

Figure 13–5   Tables held by the linkage editor

The Map

The linkage editor is now ready to prepare the map of how the program and its data will be arranged in store. The usual arrangement is for each segment to have a separate area for its instructions and data. Thus a program consisting of two segments and a common data area would be stored as shown in Figure 13–8. With this arrangement preparing the map is straightforward. The map will consist of a file of records each with three fields.

MAP

NAME	INST	DATA

The three fields are the name of the segment and the addresses of the areas in store in which the instructions and data would be held if the program were to be loaded beginning at location zero. Figure 13–9 is a flow chart of this part of the linkage editor for this arrangement of the segments within store.

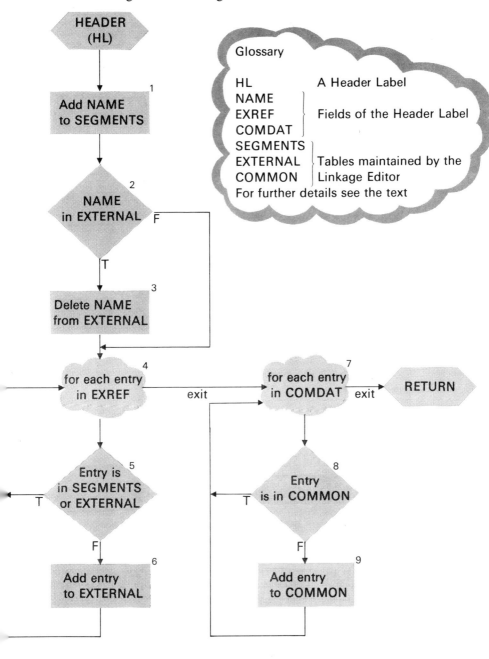

Figure 13–6   HEADER subroutine

307

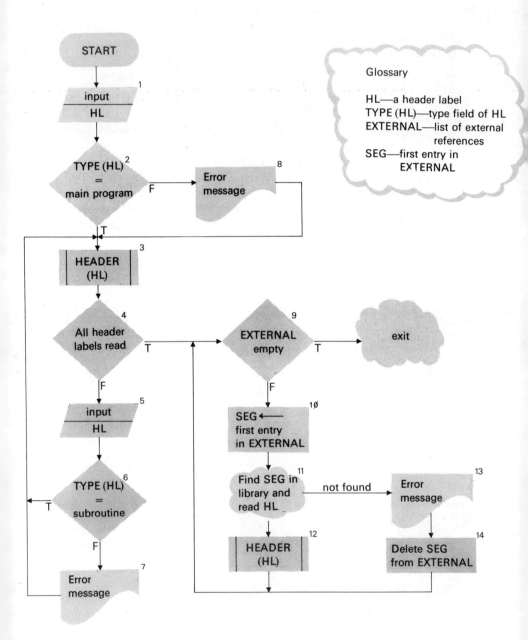

Figure 13–7   The linkage editor—first stage

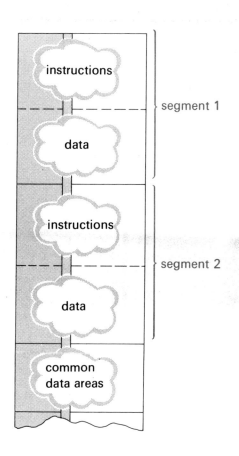

Figure 13–8   Segments stored separately

309

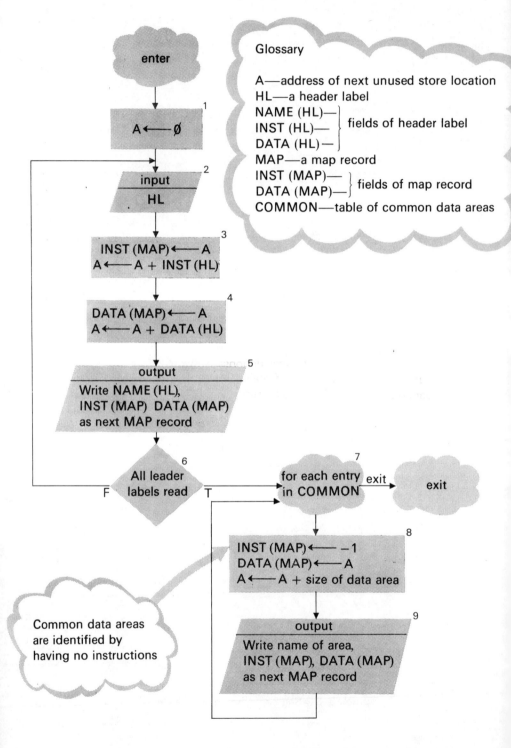

Figure 13-9   Preparing the map

Block Structure

The arrangement shown in Figure 13–8 is used in many programming languages, such as FORTRAN, but advanced programming languages, such as ALGOL, often use a different arrangement in which all segments share the same area of store for their variables. Variables within this area are arranged as a stack. To see how the stack works consider the execution of the fragment of a program shown in Figure 13–10. For the first stage during the execution of part of the main program the stack will contain values of the variables used by that segment only. We have denoted these by a, b, c and d as shown in Figure 13–11. Suppose now that SUB1 is called, which uses variables e and f. These variables are added to the stack as shown in Figure 13–12. Within SUB1 the program has use of all the variables in the stack. This simplifies passing of parameters. On return from SUB1 the variables e and f are deleted from the stack and their values are lost for ever. The next step is to call SUB2. This uses variables called b, e and g. They are added to the stack as in Figure 13–13. Now there is a possible source of confusion, since the stack contains two variables with name b. By convention, confusion is avoided by using the most recent occurrence of b as the variable referred to by any mention of b within SUB2.

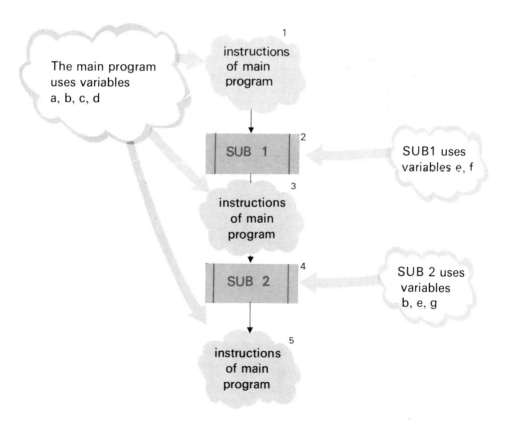

Figure 13–10   A typical program

311

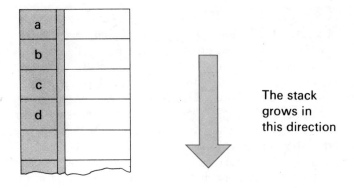

Figure 13–11   Variables used in main program

This arrangement of a program is known as block structure and the routines are known as blocks. One implication of the method of allocating storage space is that variables and labels are local to the block within which they are declared but global to any block which is nested inside their block (unless the same identifier is used within the nested block). For the above example the situation is summed up by Figure 13–14.

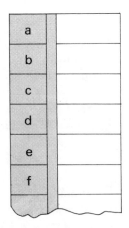

Figure 13–12   Variables for SUB1 added to the stack

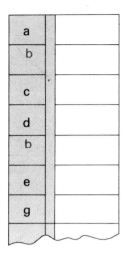

Since the stack contains two variables called b the most recent one is used in all calculations

Figure 13–13   A possible source of confusion

Amongst its other advantages, block structure allows recursion, that is routines that call themselves. Each time that a routine is called space is allocated in the stack for its variables. Thus if a routine is called recursively there will be two copies of the variables in the stack, but confusion is avoided by the convention of always using the most recent.

	Block		
	main program	SUB 1	SUB 2
a	local	global	global
b	local	global	
c	local	global	global
d	local	global	global
e		local	
f		local	
b			local
e			local
g			local

Figure 13–14   Local and global variables

313

Questions 13.2

1. Examine the program described by Figure 1–15 which uses the subroutine shown in Figure 1–14.

   (i) When this program is compiled what are the values in the header label for each segment of the TYPE, EXREF and COMDAT fields?
   (ii) What will the map of this program look like?

2. Figure 13–15 shows a subroutine FACTORIAL which, given a positive integer N, calculates N factorial, F.

$$F = N \times (N - 1) \times (N - 2) \times \ldots \times 3 \times 2 \times 1$$

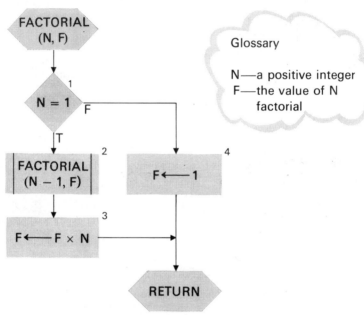

Figure 13–15   A recursive subroutine

This subroutine is recursive in that it calls itself. If this subroutine were written in a programming language that used block structure, what entries would appear in the stack if the following instruction is executed when J = 3?

13.3 THE LOADER

Input to the loader consists of the map of the program supplied by the linkage editor together with header labels and semi-compiled code for each segment prepared by the compiler. The supervisor will pass to the loader the address of the location into which the first instruction is to be loaded. The details of the loader depend on whether the computer uses relative or absolute addressing (see page 304) and, with relative addressing, whether there is a base register for each segment or a single register for the whole program. We shall look at the case of relative addressing of complete programs, that is wherever the program is physically stored the addresses within it will be the same as if the first instruction was stored in location zero.

Figure 13–16 is an outline of the loader. Most of the steps are straightforward, since the map contains all the required information. For example, Figure 13–17 shows the

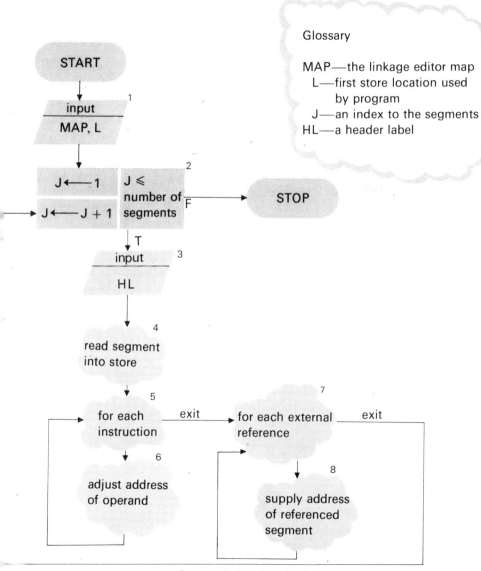

Glossary

MAP—the linkage editor map
L—first store location used
by program
J—an index to the segments
HL—a header label

Figure 13–16 The loader

315

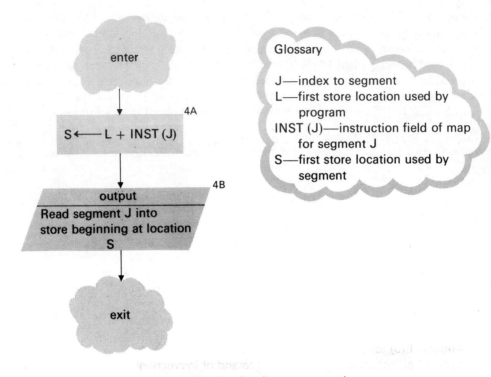

Figure 13–17   Reading a segment into store

expansion of step 4, which reads a segment into store. Adjusting the addresses of
operands within the program is equally simple. In our simple machine code the
operand of every machine instruction or supervisor call is an address. The compiler
creates a semi-compiled form which assumes that the segment is loaded as if the first
instruction and the data both begin at location zero. The correct address can be put
into each instruction as shown in Figure 13–18.

The difficult part of the loader lies in supplying the address of each external reference.
For simplicity suppose first, that segment J has only one external reference. This
consists of one or more calls to a subroutine named SUB. When the segment is
compiled, the compiler does not know the address of SUB. It therefore reserves the
first location allocated to data for an address constant. This will eventually hold the
address of SUB and can be used with indirect addressing to call SUB as in Figure
13–19. The loader knows from the map where SUB will be stored and can therefore
fill in the address constant. The flow chart in Figure 13–20 generalizes this to the case
of several external references.

Questions 13.3

1. What changes would have to be made to the loader for use with absolute addressing, that is the address of every operand is the address of the actual location in
   store in which that operand is held?

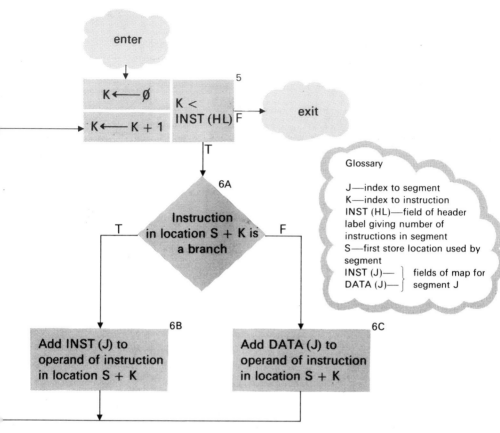

Figure 13–18   Adjusting operand addresses

2. Examine the program described by Figure 1–15. This uses the subroutine SCORE shown in Figure 1–14.

(i)   Write machine instructions for each segment as if each segment and its data were held from location Ø upwards.

(ii) What header labels would go with each segment?

(iii) What will the map of the program be?

(iv) What will the operands of each instruction be if the program is loaded in store beginning at location 5Ø, in a computer which uses relative addressing?

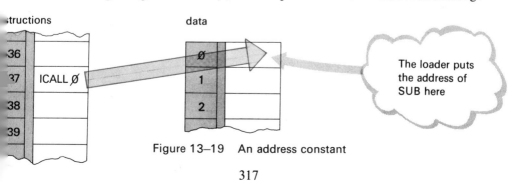

Figure 13–19   An address constant

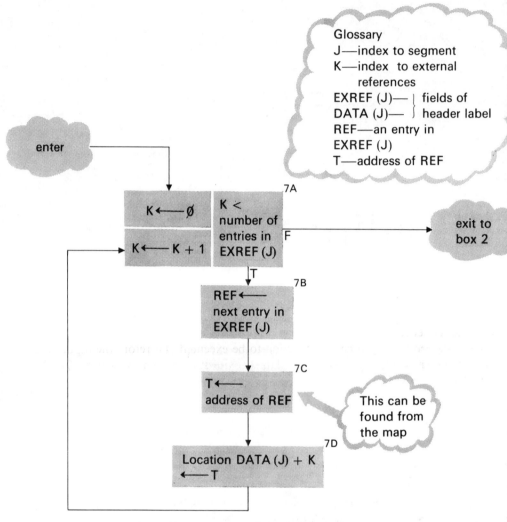

Figure 13–20   External references

13.4 A BOOTSTRAP ROUTINE

All that we have done so far overlooks a basic problem. We have always assumed that the supervisor is already in store and can be used to call in the loader or any other routine. We have not yet considered how to get the supervisor into the computer when it is first switched on. In this section we discuss how to get started. For this we need to see what happens when the computer is switched on and the operator presses the START button.

One method is as follows. On the side of the central processor are two groups of hand switches. On the first group the operator can set up a single machine instruction as a binary pattern. There are as many switches as the computer has bits in each word. If the word length is 32 bits, there will be 32 switches. If a switch is up it corresponds to the binary digit Ø; if down it corresponds to the digit 1 (Figure 13–21). The other group of switches allow the operator to set the initial value of the sequence control register. Suppose that he sets this to zero and on the other group of switches sets the binary pattern for the instruction

     INPUT Ø

When the START button is pressed the central processor executes the special instruction shown in Figure 13–22 and then continues with the usual fetch execute cycle.

Figure 13–21   A machine instruction as a binary pattern set on hand switches

The operator must provide input data. Before deciding on what data to provide, consider what happens next. The control unit will fetch another instruction and, since the sequence control register is set to zero, it will fetch the contents of location Ø which it decodes as the next instruction to be executed. Therefore the input data must be an instruction. If the input data provided is the binary pattern for the instruction

     INPUT 1

at the end of the instruction that is triggered by the START button, the sequence control register will contain the value zero and the store will contain the following.

Ø	INPUT 1
1	

The fetch cycle of the next instruction will read the contents of location Ø into the instruction register and increase the sequence control register to one. This instruction will input a word of data into location 1.

We are now in a position to fill location 1 before its content is required as an instruction. Suppose that the next item of input data is the code for the instruction

     INPUT 2.

When this has been read into location 1, the execution of the second instruction is complete and there will be an instruction in location 2, waiting to be fetched.

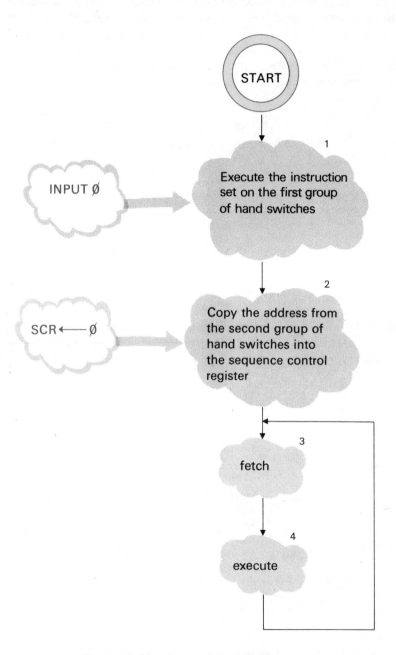

Figure 13-22   Pressing the START button

The computer is certainly executing instructions, but so far not to any very useful purpose. What is wanted is a method of putting instructions elsewhere in store. This can be achieved by the input to location 2 being the instruction

GOTO Ø

A program loop has now been set up. Can you see how to use it to input a program? The following instructions have been input to store.

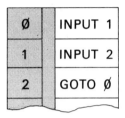

When the instruction in location 2 is executed, the sequence control register will be set to Ø. Thus the next instruction to be executed is in location Ø. This instruction is

INPUT 1.

Before you read any further see if you can answer the following questions.

(i)   What is the next item of input data?
(ii) What further data is required to read a complete program into locations 3 to 5Ø?
(iii) What is required to begin execution of the program?

These questions can be answered as follows.

(i)   The input to location 1 is the instruction

INPUT 3

so that a program instruction can be read into location 3 when the instruction in location 1 is executed.

(ii) Following the execution of the instruction in location Ø, the situation in store is as shown in Figure 13–23. The remaining input data must be as follows.

first program instruction
INPUT 4
second program instruction
INPUT 5
and so on

.
.
.

INPUT 5Ø
last program instruction.

321

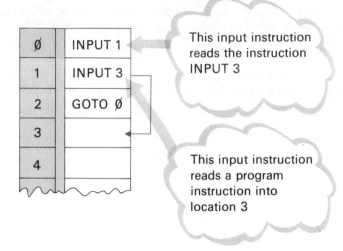

Figure 13–23   The core of the bootstrap

(iii) Execution of the program requires one further item of data.

> GOTO 3

This causes the computer to jump out of the input loop to the first program instruction.

The technique described above enables us to read a program and to store it in the computer. The first three instructions are

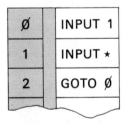

where ⋆ is set each time the instruction

> INPUT 1

is executed. These form a simple routine whose effect is to load a program into store. Because it seems to haul itself into store by its own boot laces it is often called a bootstrap routine.

Under normal circumstances, the program read in by the bootstrap is a special program called the system loader which reads in the supervisor. The last act of the system loader before handing over to the supervisor is to overwrite itself with the last few instructions of the supervisor, thus leaving no trace of itself in store. From this moment on, the supervisor is in control and all new programs are loaded by the supervisor.

Question 13.4

1. The operator sets the instruction

    INPUT 1∅

and the address

    1∅

on the hand switches. He then presses the START button. The following input data is provided.

    INPUT 11
    INPUT 12
    GOTO 1∅
    INPUT 13
    OUTPUT 1∅
    INPUT 14
    OUTPUT 11
    INPUT 15
    STOP
    GOTO 13

What output is produced?

CHAPTER FOURTEEN

COMPILING

Syntax and Semantics

Three Stages of a Compiler

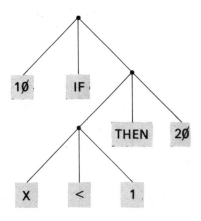

14.1 SYNTAX AND SEMANTICS

In the previous chapter we discussed the way in which a computer program written in a high level language is converted into machine instructions. The key stage in this process is the compiler. Since almost all programs are written in high level languages, the compiler is a fundamental part of software, and worth discussing for no other reason than its importance. However, we feel that there are two fringe benefits that can be gained from an understanding of how a compiler works. First, getting to grips with a compiler will show you the need for a rigorous method of defining a programming language. This is the subject of this section. Second, if you know something of how a compiler works, you will be properly equipped to think about your own high level programs in terms of the machine instructions that the compiler will generate from them. This can often help you to write more efficient high level programs.

We start by looking at the problem of defining a programming language. To use a spoken language it is not enough to know what words are allowed in that language. You also need to know how to construct and interpret meaningful sentences. Consider the following words.

COMPILER, FORTRAN, INSTRUCTIONS, INTO, MACHINE, THIS, TRANSLATES

When arranged in the following order,

MACHINE COMPILER THIS FORTRAN INSTRUCTIONS TRANSLATES INTO

they do not form a meaningful sentence, and could not be translated into an equivalent meaningful sentence in another language, such as French. When arranged in the following order

THIS FORTRAN MACHINE TRANSLATES INSTRUCTIONS INTO COMPILER

they seem to form a sentence correctly in that nouns, verbs etc., are in the correct juxtaposition, that is, the syntax of the sentence is correct, but the sentence still cannot be transformed into a meaningful sentence in French since it has no meaning in English, that is, the semantics is incorrect. These two aspects of a spoken language have important counterparts in programming languages.

Syntax

The method usually adopted for describing the syntax of any language is to give a set of rules forming a grammar. The idea of a grammar for a language such as English or French is one of a set of rules which define how sentences and phrases may be constructed. These rules are expressed, for an English reader at least, in English. To define a programming language a special notation is often used, referred to as Backus Naur Form after J. Backus and P. Naur, who used it to define the syntax of ALGOL 60.

Looked at from the point of view of compiling each source instruction is no more than a string of symbols. This implies that a grammar for a programming language largely defines whether any particular string represents a syntactically correct instruction. To use the grammar a string is broken down into two or more substrings, each of which is either a single symbol or can itself be broken down further. Following this procedure of breaking down the whole into its constituent parts, a stage is reached where each substring is ultimately judged on the basis of whether single symbols are correct.

Here is a rule of grammar expressed in Backus Naur notation.

$$\langle digit \rangle :: = \emptyset|1|2|3|4|5|6|7|8|9$$

This is interpreted as follows.

> *A string of the syntactic class digit is defined as either a $\emptyset$ or a 1 or a 2 or a 3 or a 4 or a 5 or a 6 or a 7 or an 8 or a 9.*

This definition of a digit can be used to define an integer. The rule

$$\langle integer \rangle :: = \langle digit \rangle|\langle integer \rangle\langle digit \rangle$$

is interpreted strictly as

> *a string of the syntactic class integer is defined as a string of the syntactic class digit or a string of the syntactic class integer joined to a string of the syntactic class digit,*

but more loosely (and a bit more comprehensibly) as

> *an integer is defined as a digit or an integer followed by a digit.*

Under these two rules the class $\langle integer \rangle$ consists of all strings of one or more of the digits $\emptyset$ to 9, and there is no limit on the number of digits in an integer. All strings that satisfy this definition are syntactically acceptable as integers, but they may not be semantically acceptable since they may be too large to be stored by the computer. The reason for there being no syntactic limit to the number of digits in an integer defined in this way is because the class $\langle integer \rangle$ appears in the second alternative for $\langle integer \rangle$ itself; that is, given any string in the class $\langle integer \rangle$, we can create another integer by adding another digit to its right hand end.

The following table summarizes the Backus Naur notation.

Notation	Description	Spoken form
$\langle XXX \rangle$	A string of the syntactic class XXX	An XXX
:: =	Connects the syntactic class on its left to the definition of that class given on its right.	is defined as
$\langle XXX \rangle\langle YYY \rangle$	Indicates any string of the syntactic class XXX joined to any string of the syntactic class YYY.	an XXX followed by a YYY

Notation	Description	Spoken form
|	A separator for alternatives in a definition.	or

The symbols

$$\langle \quad \rangle \qquad ::= \qquad |$$

are the only ones that are used in describing a grammar. Any other symbol stands for itself and is joined to what appears next to it.

A set of syntax rules can be used to demonstrate the syntactic class to which a particular string belongs, by showing that its construction satisfies the rules of the class. The general approach is illustrated by the following example.

Example

Using the rules in Backus Naur notation,

$\langle$digit$\rangle ::= \emptyset|1|2|3|4|5|6|7|8|9$

$\langle$integer$\rangle ::= \langle$digit$\rangle|\langle$integer$\rangle\langle$digit$\rangle$

it can be shown that the string **583** belongs to the syntactic class $\langle$integer$\rangle$ by constructing a tree which has the symbols **5, 8, 3** of the given string as its leaves.

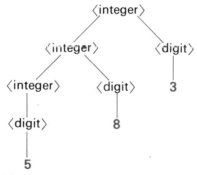

Each node is constructed from its descendants if the juxtaposition of the descendants can be found on the right hand side of one of the syntax rules.

If a string can be analysed in such a way that its individual symbols appear as leaves on a tree which is constructed according to the rules which defined the language, the string is syntactically acceptable in that language and it belongs to the syntactic class which appears at the root of the tree. Analysing a string in this way is called parsing. To parse a sentence written in English, each word is identified as a noun, verb, adjective, article, etc. and their juxtaposition is checked. This is the same process as

327

the one in the above example. A tree constructed for this purpose is called a parse tree, and the set of rules which define a programming language is called the grammar of the language.

One of the questions that has to be asked about a given grammar is whether it assigns a unique parse tree to every string. If not, then a string can have two or more differently structured parse trees associated with it, and the grammar is ambiguous. As an example, consider the following simple grammar for the class ⟨expression⟩.

⟨expression⟩ :: = ⟨variable⟩|⟨expression⟩ + ⟨expression⟩|
⟨expression⟩ × ⟨expression⟩

⟨variable⟩ :: = A|B|C

The following trees satisfy this grammar.

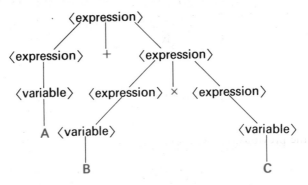

This parse tree shows that A + B × C is a legal expression, but so does the following.

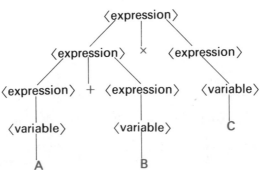

The cause of the ambiguity is that the grammar given by the rules does not specify whether multiplication should take precedence over addition. This can only be done by nesting classes within others. For example, the following rules give a grammar expressing the conventional precedence of multiplication over addition.

⟨expression⟩ :: = ⟨term⟩|⟨expression⟩ + ⟨term⟩

⟨term⟩ :: = ⟨variable⟩|⟨term⟩ × ⟨variable⟩

⟨variable⟩ :: = A|B|C

In these rules the class ⟨term⟩ is nested within the class ⟨expression⟩. Since multiplication takes place within terms and addition within expressions, the grammar gives multiplication precedence over addition.

Using these three rules, the string A + B × C can now be parsed uniquely as follows.

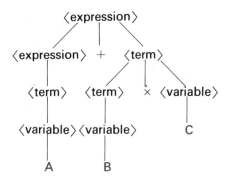

Trees like this one show both the syntax of each expression and which rules were used to create the tree. In compiling, once the tree has been constructed, the rules used to obtain it cease to be of interest. The syntax of a string is adequately represented by a simplified tree which omits the rules and which shows only the symbols. Here, for example, is the previous tree with the rules of grammar omitted.

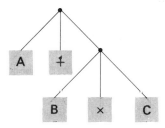

Semantics

If you want to understand a program, recognizing a sequence of symbols as a valid statement with respect to a particular grammar still leaves the problem of deciding what the statement means. Parsing creates a parse tree; the tree is unique if the grammar is unambiguous and trees are only obtained for valid statements. Thus parsing takes care of the syntax of the language. The meaning of a programming language, that is, its semantics, is more difficult to define.

From a theoretical point of view the popular technique is to describe the effect of executing instructions on an abstract machine, such as the model computer that we discussed in Chapter 2. Although of theoretical interest, this approach is too complicated to be of much practical use. The practical solution is to describe the meaning of statements informally in English. Using this approach, each rule of syntax is accompanied by a description of the meaning of this construction. Thus the syntax rules forming a grammar for the class ⟨expression⟩ given earlier,

$$\langle expression \rangle ::= \langle term \rangle | \langle expression \rangle + \langle term \rangle$$

$$\langle term \rangle ::= \langle variable \rangle | \langle term \rangle \times \langle variable \rangle$$

$$\langle variable \rangle ::= A | B | C$$

might be accompanied by a descriptive statement on the following lines.

Variables, denoted by the characters A, B *and* C, *possess numerical values which may be combined by the operations of addition and multiplication. Expressions are used to denote the desired combinations. Each expression is evaluated by summing one or more terms; a term which is a variable takes the value currently assigned to that variable, while a term which is a product of variables takes the value obtained by multiplying their current values.*

Item	Description
Constants	An integer
Variables	A letter of the alphabet or a letter followed by a digit.
Operators (in order of precedence) Arithmetic Relational Assignment	↑ $\times$, / +, − <, >, = , # =
Statement types LET IF ... THEN ... GOTO INPUT PRINT END	Examples are as follows LET X = A + B $\times$ C (assignment statement) IF X > Ø THEN 7Ø GOTO 7Ø INPUT X PRINT X, Y END (The final statement of every program)
Statement labels	An integer which precedes only those statements referred to by branch statements and $1 \leqslant label \leqslant 999$

Figure 14–1   A description of ACE

An informal description like this relies heavily on the reader's interpretation of words like values, assigned, addition and so on. Two different readers may not always make the same interpretation if the English is not sufficiently clear and careful. Further, the reader must have a clear understanding of the meaning of each of the basic terms.

To see the complication involved in defining the syntax and semantics of a language, look at the reference manual of any major programming language. It is likely to be a document at least as big as this book and to understand it thoroughly would take a lot of hard work. To simplify matters we have devised our own programming language, which, for want of a better name, is called ACE (A Compiling Example). In the next section we shall show you what is involved in constructing a compiler to translate ACE programs into the machine code described in Chapters 2 and 6.

If you are familiar with the languages FORTRAN and BASIC, you will realize that ACE is a much simplified cross between the two. For example, we have severely restricted the number of types of allowable statements. Figure 14-1 gives a brief and informal description of ACE. Brackets are used in the normal manner and commas are used to separate variable names in input and output lists. Spaces are optional, in that they have no syntactic significance, but can be used to improve the legibility of the program.

Example

In Figure 14-2, the flow chart to find the smallest item in an input list is repeated from Chapter 2. Here is the corresponding ACE program.

```
      LET  C0  =  0
      INPUT  S
30    LET  C0  =  C0  +  1
      INPUT  X
      IF  X  <  0  THEN  80
      IF  X  <  S  THEN  70
      GOTO  30
70    LET  S  =  X
      GOTO  30
80    PRINT  C0, S
      END
```

No programming language is properly defined until it has been given a completely formal description. In an exercise we ask you to construct a grammar for ACE. Essentially this is straightforward if you are methodical about applying the notation to the informal description. The most difficult part lies in representing the normal precedence of arithmetic operators. This involves nesting some classes within others. You will need to nest ⟨term⟩, for × and /, within ⟨expression⟩, for + and −. Since brackets have precedence above everything, you will need the following class

⟨primary⟩ :: = ⟨constant⟩|⟨variable⟩|(⟨expression⟩)

All these can be nested within ⟨decision expression⟩, for =, < and >.

But this is the only hint. We suggest that you allow plenty of time for the question and that you make sure you understand the solution (given as an appendix) very thoroughly.

Questions 14.1

1. Construct an ACE program for the flow chart of Figure 14–3.

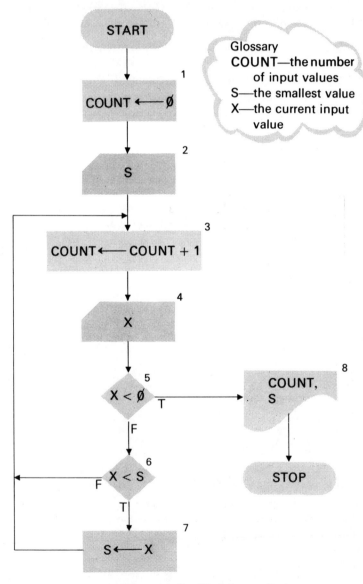

Figure 14–2   Find the smallest

332

2. In an ACE program,

   (i)   what condition must be imposed on right labels, that is labels that occur on the right hand end of a statement,
   (ii) what conditions must be imposed on left labels?

3. Write out the syntax of ACE in Backus Naur notation, and give a semantic description of the language.

   (The solution to this question is given in the Appendix.)

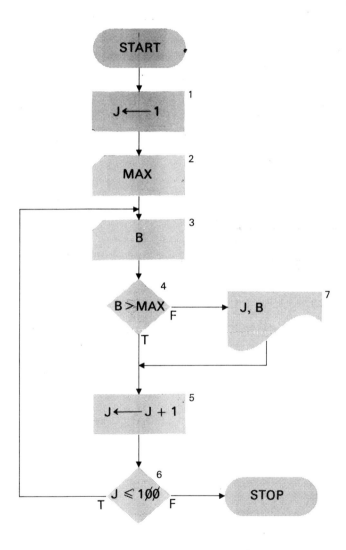

Figure 14–3   A simple flow chart

14.2   THREE STAGES OF A COMPILER

In the last section we described ACE, a simple high level programming language; in earlier chapters, we defined a low level machine language. In this section we want to show you the main steps in constructing a compiler.

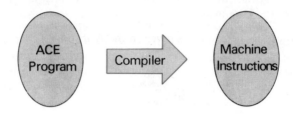

You have seen that an ACE program consists of statements such as the following.

```
   INPUT Y
   LET X = 105
10 IF X < 1 THEN 20
   LET X = Y - X
   GOTO 10
20 PRINT X
   END
```

There are three basic stages in translating this kind of program into machine instructions. These are lexical analysis, parsing and code generation.

Lexical Analysis

The program statements are input to the compiler using a peripheral, such as by typing them on a terminal, or by punching each statement onto a punched card. In either case the source program is input as a string of variable length records which we can imagine as being separated by the symbol ⊣ and from which all spaces have been removed.

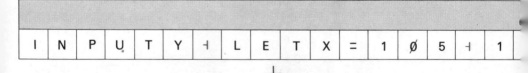

Do you remember the advice we gave as to how to write a program of machine instructions? The first stage is to scan your flow chart and allocate storage space for all the constants and variables in the program. By analogy, the first stage in compiling a program is to identify the data used. This involves setting up a table which lists all constants, variables and labels used in the program. Also, an important feature of the input string is that some of the characters have meanings by themselves, for example X and = in the above diagram, but other characters are part of substrings of two, three or more characters and have no meaning except as part of these substrings. For example, the substring

INPUT

is five characters long, but has meaning only as a single entity.

Since variable length data is so difficult to handle an efficient approach to compiling is to reduce each substring to fixed length as soon as possible. Thus the compiler starts with a routine to identify all the data in the program and to replace the input string by a string of symbols, each of which has a meaning as an entity. This process is called lexical analysis. A variable length item can be any one of the following.

LET
IF
GOTO
INPUT·
PRINT
END
THEN

⟨constant⟩ when it is more than one digit,

⟨variable⟩ when it is ⟨letter⟩⟨digit⟩,

⟨label⟩ when it is more than one digit.

Lexical analysis combines this replacement with a second task, that of deciding how the constants and variables will be laid out in store in the machine code or target program. Since the linkage editor accepts a semi-compiled program in which both instructions and data are based on location Ø, we shall assume that the target program uses the organization of store illustrated in Figure 14–4.

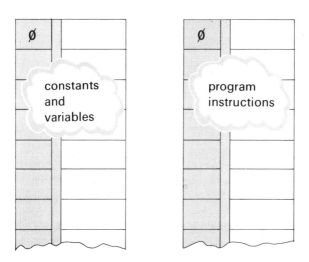

Figure 14–4   Storage layout used by the compiler

335

The compiler needs a method of allocating to each variable and each constant a number from $\emptyset$ onwards which will be its relative address in store. It also needs a method of describing each substring by a unique element. Both aims can be achieved by using a symbol table. This table is fundamental to lexical analysis and will be used again in the code generation routine of the compiler. An empty symbol table is given in Figure 14–5.

As each ACE statement is analysed the constants and the variable names are entered in the SYMBOL column of the table. At the same time the address in store where they will eventually be held is recorded in the PROPERTY column. Labels that appear in the program are also recorded in the SYMBOL column and the PROPERTY column is used to detect two kinds of error that can occur with labels. First, if a label occurs on the left of a statement it must never appear on the left again. For example, it is not permissible to have the following

```
10 LET X = 105
10 IF X < 1 THEN 20
```

since the subsequent instruction

```
GOTO 10
```

would be ambiguous. Second, a label may appear on the right of many statements, but each right label must appear exactly once as a left label. To check for these two errors, the computer places a flag in the PROPERTY column for each label by recording

$\emptyset$—if the label has occurred on the right of a statement, but not on the left of any statement yet processed;

1—if the label has occurred on the left of a statement.

In our compiler, the first seven locations of the symbol table will be used to record the reserved or keywords of ACE. These are LET, IF, GOTO, INPUT, PRINT, END and THEN.

The index in the symbol table is used to replace the keyword, constant, variable or label in the input string by a single element in the lexical string. Thus, for instance, when the constant 105 is first met in a program, the value 105 is entered in the first vacant row of the constants section of the table (in the SYMBOL column). The address of a location in store is recorded in the PROPERTY part of this row. The INDEX for this row is used to refer to this row, thus representing the constant 105 by a single element. Since it is very important in what follows that you understand how the symbol table is used, Figure 14–6 gives an example of how to fill it in. To see how the symbol table is used to generate the output from the lexical analysis stage of the compiler, the program from page 334 is expressed in its lexical form in Figure 14–7.

INDEX   SYMBOL   PROPERTY

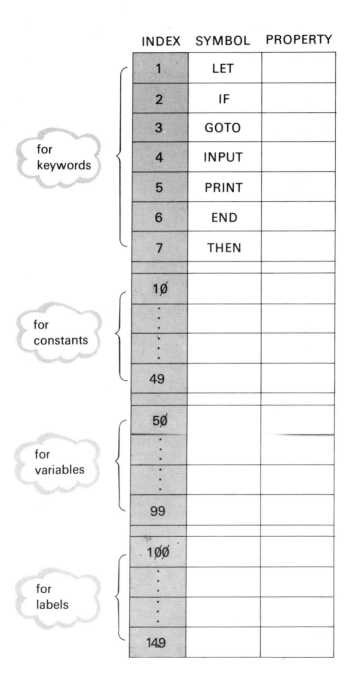

INDEX	SYMBOL	PROPERTY
1	LET	
2	IF	
3	GOTO	
4	INPUT	
5	PRINT	
6	END	
7	THEN	
10		
⋮		
⋮		
49		
50		
⋮		
⋮		
99		
100		
⋮		
⋮		
149		

for keywords

for constants

for variables

for labels

Figure 14–5   A symbol table

INDEX	SYMBOL	PROPERTY
1	LET	
2	IF	
3	GOTO	
4	INPUT	
5	PRINT	
6	END	
7	THEN	
1∅	1∅5	2
⋮	1	3
⋮		
49		
5∅	Y	∅
⋮	X	1
⋮		
99		
1∅∅	1∅	1
⋮	2∅	1
⋮		
149		

Figure 14–6   A symbol table for the sample program

Program Statements	Lexical Form

INPUT Y   4 5∅

LET X = 1∅5   1 51 = 1∅

1∅ IF X < 1 THEN 2∅   1∅∅ 2 51 < 11 7 1∅1

LET X = Y - X   1 51 = 5∅ — 51

GOTO 1∅   3 1∅∅

2∅ PRINT X   1∅1 5 51

END   6

Figure 14–7   An example of the output from lexical analysis

Parsing

On page 329 you saw that an arithmetic expression can be represented by a parse tree which breaks down the evaluation into basic steps. In a similar way any ACE statement can be represented by a tree. In fact all statements can be represented by variations of the following tree.

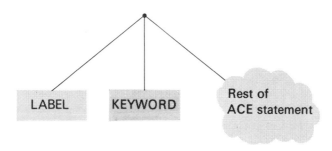

The keyword must be one of LET, IF, GOTO, INPUT, PRINT or END. The label is optional. Figure 14–8 gives some examples of parse trees for instructions from the sample program on page 334. You should notice that each entity in the instructions occurs somewhere on the tree. The parse trees can be stored as a collection of records.

Program Statement	Parse Tree

INPUT Y

LET X = Y - X

10 IF X < 1 THEN 20

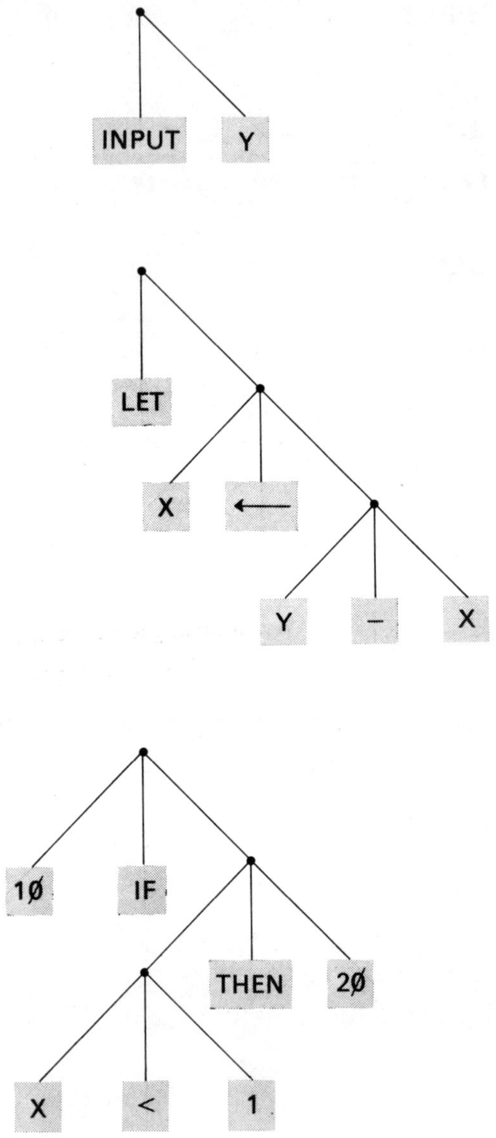

Figure 14–8   Examples of parse trees

(NB: The leaves of these trees would normally be single symbols taken from the lexical form of the program statements. However, for ease of reading, we have shown them in their program form.)

We will represent each parse record as an array with three columns and an unlimited number of rows.

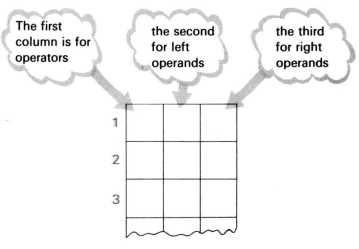

The first column is for operators

the second for left operands

the third for right operands

For example, the parse tree for the source statement

    LET X = A/B + C*D

is

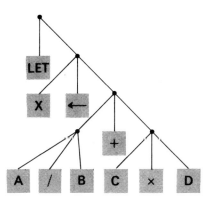

The tree shows that the statement is a valid one for the class ⟨LET statement⟩; it can be represented by the following matrix.

1	/	A	B
2	×	C	D
3	+	R_1	R_2
4	←	X	R_3

Note the entry R_1 in row 3 of the matrix. It refers to the value given by row 1. More generally, we shall use the notation

$$R_N$$

to refer to row N of a matrix. The order in which the rows occur in the matrix is important, since this order is the same as the sequence in which the corresponding machine instructions will be executed. Thus the notation R_N can be used only in a row which comes after the Nth row.

Our previous example of a parse matrix does not show what to do about labels nor how to parse decision expressions.

Labels

Consider a statement with a left label.

      10 LET A = B

To make a record that the original program statement was labelled we add a dummy row to the parse matrix for that statement. Thus the above statement gives the following matrix.

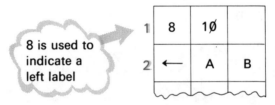

8 is used to indicate a left label

This dummy row does not correspond to a machine instruction. It is a signal to the code generation stage of the compiler to enter the address of the next machine instruction in the **PROPERTY** column of the symbol table row which refers to label 10.

Any other reference to the label 10 will be part of a statement which uses 10 as a right label. For example, an unconditional branch statement such as

      GOTO 10

is entered in the matrix as

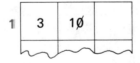

since 3 is the index for **GOTO**.

Decision Expressions

A conditional branch statement such as

      IF X = 1 THEN 10

is parsed as follows.

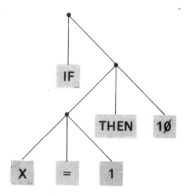

Since the code for **THEN** is 7, the parse matrix is as follows.

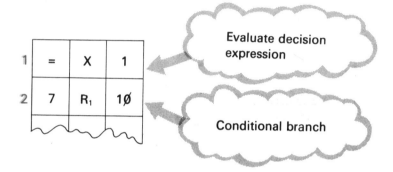

More complex decisions require that arithmetic expressions be evaluated before the test is made. For example, consider the following statement.

```
IF (X + Y) < (X * 2) THEN 20
```

To store this in the matrix we need the following.

1	+	X	Y
2	×	X	2
3	<	R_1	R_2
4	7	R_3	2∅

In general, the parse matrix from a decision expression takes the form given in Figure 14–9.

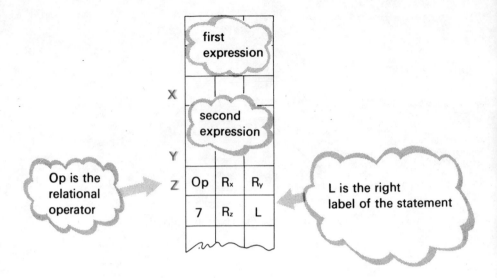

Figure 14–9   The parse matrix for a decision statement

Code Generation

The final stage of compiling is to generate machine instructions. This is reasonably straightforward because the lexical analysis has drawn up a table of all data used by the program and the parse routine has broken down the logic of the program into a sequence of small steps, each corresponding to a few machine instructions. The output from code generation is usually written to backing store and together with the header label forms the input to the linkage editor.

The major difficulty with code generation is to create machine instructions that are efficient. To give you a feeling for the problem, here is a program statement and its corresponding parse matrix.

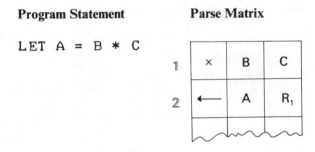

Suppose that for each row of the matrix we allow a temporary storage location to hold the outcome of execution. We could label these locations T_1, T_2, ... T_N, assigning one to each row of the matrix. This would allow us a very straightforward method of generating code.

```
R₁  LOAD      B
    MUL       C
    STORE     T₁


R₂  LOAD      T₁
    STORE     A
```

But it is easy to see that the two instructions

```
STORE          T₁
LOAD           T₁
```

are not needed. This much at least you would expect the code generation routine to spot. The situation is more complicated for a decision expression. For example, the statement

$$IF \; X \; + \; 3*Z \; > \; Y \; - \; 5 \; THEN \; 6\emptyset$$

has the following parse matrix.

1	×	3	Z
2	+	X	R₁
3	−	Y	5
4	<	R₂	R₃
5	7	R₄	6∅

If you were to start with the original statement, you would not find it difficult to generate the following machine instructions from it.

```
LOAD        "3"
MUL         Z
ADD         X
SUB         Y
ADD         "5"
BP          6∅
```

These represent a fairly efficient translation of the source statement.

The art of code generation is to turn this kind of efficient interpretation into a routine procedure that works for all possible source statements. It is an art that has been developed to the stage where, in many instances, a compiler will generate more efficient code than a low level programmer could reasonably expect to achieve.

Let us complete our discussion by putting the three stages together. Figure 14–10 is an outline flow chart for the complete compiler, showing the three principal stages in translating an ACE program into semi-compiled form. Each segment of the compiler scans an entire input string and generates a corresponding output string; this process is usually called a pass, and since the entire program is processed several times, the whole is referred to as a multipass compiler. We have described a three pass compiler. Others range from a single pass where each statement goes through all stages from input to generation of machine instructions before the next statement is read, to compilers used in minicomputers where the store is too small to hold a large program and the compiler is broken down into a large number of simple program segments. Whereas size is unlikely to be a problem for ACE, it can be an important consideration in, for instance, designing an ALGOL compiler to run on a small computer.

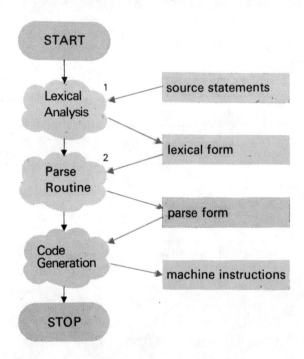

Figure 14–10   The ACE compiler

Error Detection

An important purpose of any compiler is to check for errors. For instance, there is no point in generating machine instructions for an ACE program which contains mistakes such as the following.

```
LET X = THEN 20
```

346

Errors can be trapped by either the lexical analysis or parse routines.

(i) Lexical Errors. These are errors caused by an input instruction having a substring of characters that is not allowed in the language, or an instruction not beginning with either a keyword, or a label followed by a keyword. Each of the following contains a lexical error.

$$X = X - Y$$

This does not begin with a label or a keyword

A statement which begins with keyword IF must contain the substring THEN

$$10 \ IF \ X < 1 \ THAN \ 40$$

(ii) Parse Errors. The parse routine attempts to create a parse tree for each source statement using the rules of the grammar. If it fails, the statement contains a syntax error. For example no parse tree can be created for either of the following statements

$$LET \ X + Y$$

An = symbol is needed after the first variable name

The IF statement requires a decision expression

$$IF \ X + 1 \ THEN \ 10$$

Each of these syntax errors arises from an error in a single statement. Other errors may not become apparent until all statements have been parsed. For example a program may have the statement

$$GOTO \ 10$$

but if the label 10 does not appear as a left label of any statement this is a meaningless instruction. Adding these checks to the outline gives the flow chart of Figure 14–11.

There is a further class of error that we cannot be expected to detect in the compiler. These are the semantic errors and can only be detected when the compiled program is executed. Of course, the program may even run, but contain a logical mistake so that it still gives the wrong results. Such is life.

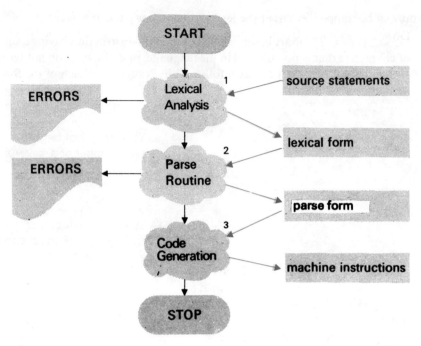

Figure 14—11   Error detection in the ACE compiler

Questions 14.2

1. Complete symbol tables for the following ACE programs.

i)
```
    LET I = 1
    INPUT C
30  INPUT B
    IF B > C THEN 70
50  LET I = I +1
    IF I < 100 THEN 30
    END
70  PRINT I, B
    GOTO 50
```

ii)
```
    INPUT N , A
30  LET L = A
40  LET N = N - 1
    IF N = 0 THEN 80
    INPUT A
    IF L < A THEN 30
    GOTO 40
80  PRINT L
    END
```

2. What check can be applied to the completed symbol table to ensure that every right label occurs once as a left label?

3. Give three examples, of source statements that contain lexical errors and give the syntax rule that they violate.

4. Write down the simple parse trees and matrix representations of the following source statements.

   (i)   LET X = Y * Z
   (ii) 10 LET Y = A + B*C + D
   (iii) IF X/2 > A + B*C + D THEN 70

5. Write down machine instructions for the source statements given in Question 4. Do you think the code generator would be able to write the same code as you have?

Appendix The Syntax of ACE

LEGEND

$::=$ "is defined as . . ."

| "or"

$\langle \; \rangle$ enclose an element of ACE

LANGUAGE RULES

1. A $\langle$label$\rangle$ must be between 1 and 999 inclusive.
2. A $\langle$program statement$\rangle$ must not exceed 72 characters.

$\langle$list$\rangle$	$::=$ $\langle$variable$\rangle$|$\langle$list$\rangle$, $\langle$variable$\rangle$
$\langle$variable$\rangle$	$::=$ $\langle$letter$\rangle$|$\langle$letter$\rangle$$\langle$digit$\rangle$
$\langle$letter$\rangle$	$::=$ A|B|C|D|E|F|G|H|I|J|K|L|M| N|O|P|Q|R|S|T|U|V|W|X|Y|Z
$\langle$constant$\rangle$	$::=$ $\langle$integer$\rangle$
$\langle$label$\rangle$	$::=$ $\langle$integer$\rangle$ (*SEE RULE 1*)
$\langle$integer$\rangle$	$::=$ $\langle$digit$\rangle$|$\langle$integer$\rangle$$\langle$digit$\rangle$
$\langle$digit$\rangle$	$::=$ Ø|1|2|3|4|5|6|7|8|9
$\langle$relational operator$\rangle$	$::=$ $<$ | $>$ | $=$ | $\#$
$\langle$decision expression$\rangle$	$::=$ $\langle$expression$\rangle$$\langle$relational operator$\rangle$$\langle$expression$\rangle$
$\langle$expression$\rangle$	$::=$ $\langle$term$\rangle$|$\langle$expression$\rangle$ $+$ $\langle$term$\rangle$|$\langle$expression$\rangle$ $-$ $\langle$term$\rangle$
$\langle$term$\rangle$	$::=$ $\langle$factor$\rangle$|$\langle$term$\rangle$ $\times$ $\langle$factor$\rangle$|$\langle$term$\rangle$ / $\langle$factor$\rangle$
$\langle$factor$\rangle$	$::=$ $\langle$primary$\rangle$|$\langle$factor$\rangle$ $\uparrow$ $\langle$primary$\rangle$
$\langle$primary$\rangle$	$::=$ $\langle$variable$\rangle$|$\langle$constant$\rangle$|($\langle$expression$\rangle$)
$\langle$program statement$\rangle$	$::=$ $\langle$label$\rangle$$\langle$ACE statement$\rangle$ ⊣ |$\langle$ACE statement$\rangle$ ⊣ (*SEE RULE 2*)
$\langle$ACE statement$\rangle$	$::=$ $\langle$LET statement$\rangle$|$\langle$IF statement$\rangle$|$\langle$GOTO statement$\rangle$ |$\langle$INPUT statement$\rangle$|$\langle$PRINT statement$\rangle$|$\langle$END statement$\rangle$
$\langle$LET statement$\rangle$	$::=$ LET $\langle$variable$\rangle$ $=$ $\langle$expression$\rangle$
$\langle$IF statement$\rangle$	$::=$ IF $\langle$decision expression$\rangle$ THEN $\langle$label$\rangle$
$\langle$GOTO statement$\rangle$	$::=$ GOTO $\langle$label$\rangle$
$\langle$INPUT statement$\rangle$	$::=$ INPUT $\langle$list$\rangle$
$\langle$PRINT statement$\rangle$	$::=$ PRINT $\langle$list$\rangle$
$\langle$END statement$\rangle$	$::=$ END

INDEX